W9-COJ-545

Fashion Patternmaking Techniques

HAUTE COUTURE

[VOL. 2]

Fashion Patternmaking Techniques

HAUTE COUTURE
[VOL. 2]

Creative Darts, Draping,
Frills and Flounces, Collars,
Necklines and Sleeves,
Trousers and Skirts

Antonio Donnanno

PROMOPRESS 11

Hoaki Books, S.L.
C/ Ausiàs March, 128
08013 Barcelona, Spain
T. 0034 935 952 283
F. 0034 932 654 883
info@hoaki.com
www.hoaki.com

hoaki_books

Fashion Patternmaking Techniques Haute Couture [Vol. 2]
Creative Darts, Draping, Frills and Flounces, Collars, Necklines and
Sleeves, Trousers and Skirts

ISBN: 978-84-17412-38-8

Copyright © 2021 Promopress, Hoaki Books, S.L.
Copyright © 2019 Ikon Editrice srl
Original title: *La tecnica dei modelli alta moda vol. 2*

Translation: Katherine Kirby
For the illustrations: Nadie Bonzi
Pattern assistance: Marisa Cassera, Cinzia Trovesi
For the graphics: Emanuela Donnanno
Runway images: Indigitalitalia srl Milano
Cover design: spread

All rights reserved. The total or partial reproduction of this book, its
transmission in any form or by any means or procedure, whether
electronic or mechanical, including photocopying, recording or
incorporation into an electronic storage and retrieval system, and the
distribution of copies of the work through rental or public lending are
not permitted without prior authorization from the publisher.

D.L.: B 26756-2019
Printed in Turkey

TABLE OF CONTENTS

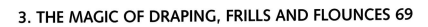

1. HAUTE COUTURE: PAST AND PRESENT

THE NINETEENTH CENTURY AND HAUTE COUTURE

Among all clothing categories, haute couture is surely the one most people associate with luxury and exclusivity. The creation of a made-to-measure garment is the oldest form of tailoring: before the industrial revolution and mass production, people went to the expert hands of tailors and dressmakers for their clothing, requesting the in-style fashions of the time. High fashion thus arose in contexts related to the French courts and the royal retinue of the nineteenth century, bringing Paris and France fame and primacy in this field for the centuries to come - and even still today.

The dresses sewn for upper middle class women were not just custom-made, but also unique and personalised according to the client's preferences. The magical aura that has always accompanied haute couture clothing is still relevant, now connected to the world's leading fashion brands.

The title of the first couturier in history is generally given to Charles Frederick Worth, an English-born stylist who moved to Paris as a young man, landing amid upper class society and the court of Napoleon III and his wife, Eugénie de Montijo, one of his most loyal customers.

Prized materials and textiles characterised the growth and development of exclusive fashions since the start, tied to appearances and social status. In short, there had to be a clear distinction between the upper classes and the common man, and this distinction was conveyed, first and foremost, through clothing. Passementerie, ribbons, embroidery, inserts and flounces embellished dresses, whose cuts varied depending on the time period and country. In general, from the mid-nineteenth century, London and Paris dictated the rules of Western fashion, the former for men (sober and elegant) and the latter for women second (composed and charming). Women from all corners of Europe flocked to the French capital at least twice a year to update their wardrobes with garments from the most famous dressmaking ateliers of the time. Worth was the first to introduce his signature to the garments he made, the precursor to a long series of designers that would use their own name as a distinctive signifier of exclusive, fashionable garments. It was in his atelier in 7 Rue de la Paix, that the first models in history walked down a runway in front of some of the most important noblewomen of the day, so that they could admire the couturier's creations and choose the styles that best suited their needs. High fashion - and the system connected to it - thus took shape among the shops of the City of Lights, with ladies eager to follow the latest trends, and tailors and seamstresses ready to make their dreams come true.

Social events were marked by specific items of clothing, in turn defined by etiquette that dictated the rules of banquets and daily strolls out in society. Ladies usually changed their clothes multiple times a day, going from daytime outfits to afternoon and evening dresses, which varied according to the context and occasion. Weekly attendances at the theatre and opera, and galas at exclusive salons were recurrent events suitable for showing off lace, ornamentation and sought-after textiles. Even accessories had an important role, completing and accenting an outfit: long gloves, jewellery (such as chokers and strands of pearls) and small bags with rhinestones and decorations in various colours accompanied the individual look of all ladies.

On the other hand, as Honoré de Balzac mentions in his 'Treatise on Elegant Living', published in sections in

Fashion plate, 1836.

Le Monde in 1830, 'clothing is an expression of society', and thus a reflection not only of social status, but also of morals and ideological choices. In the very same era, fashion journalism was born, with publications dedicated to the topic (such as the magazine titled *Mode Illustrée, Journal de la Famille*, 1860), which were meant to bear witness to the sudden changes in city fashions by documenting society. Fashion thus involved an ever-increasing number of people - men, but especially women who wanted to stay in step with the times. The target of reference was a cultured, educated audience, in that the topics covered in articles and columns were varied, not strictly limited to fashion. Articles written on fashion were often accompanied by fashion sketches and colour plates. At first, they were quite simple, simply illustrating a specific dress. Over time, the figures were placed in various contexts and settings, often linked to the social appearances and events of high society (theatres, cultural salons, gardens), demonstrating the latest trends in high fashion. Accessories were also quite important, including hats, gloves, shoes, jewellery and undergarments. The drawings were always accompanied by descriptions of varying lengths, which explained the garments to readers, providing style and fashion advice. Later on, the plates and figures were accompanied by paper patterns.

J. Doucet, afternoon dress, ca. 1903.

INNOVATION AND REVOLUTION

From 1760 to 1830, the industrial revolution had enormous impact on textile development and production, thanks largely to the invention of modern devices for spinning cotton and the mechanical loom. Mass production thus began, making fabric cheaper and more accessible even to the middle classes, which up until this point were excluded from fashion circuits. In addition, in 1851, I.M. Singer patented the changes to the sewing machine that would make him famous, improving the workflow for tailors and the burgeoning clothing industry forever. Around this time, the very first packaged, ready-to-wear garments began to appear, starting with knickers. Another important contribution to the creation of pre-made garments was the development of the paper pattern by Ebenezer Butterick in 1863, an invention entirely relevant to this book. Paper patterns were available in catalogues, encouraging production at home, with the obvious associated savings.

Even innovations in chemistry notably contributed to the industry, especially the discovery of aniline, ushering in the era of artificial dyes for fabric and leather. These weren't just the main innovations that emerged in the textile/tailoring field, but also the base of what would become prêt-à-porter in the mid twentieth century. The democratisation of fashion thus began from mechanical, chemical and technological innovations and inventions that defined and shaped the history of clothing forever.

Paris was still the haute couture world capital in the burgeoning century, with new dressmaker shop signs hanging amid its alleyways and boulevards: Jacques Doucet, Boué Soeurs (two sisters names Sylvie and Jeanne), and Jeanne Paquin. These ateliers became meeting places for the wealthiest ladies of high society - not just for the French, but for an international crowd. These ateliers gave rise to a new style of empire waist dress that offered a more natural silhouette, with softer, less voluminous lines, at least compared to the fashions of the nineteenth century. Paris was the centre of the fashion world, and fashion itself was gaining importance in the city, right before the entire world: during the 1900 Paris Exhibition, the Pavillon de l'Élegance was set up, meaning France's haute couture creations could be presented at the event.

The democratisation of fashion solidified in this century, with the expansion of department stores. Le Bon Marché was at the forefront of this trend, opening the doors to its revamped shop in around 1850 and reaching the height of its success in the early twentieth century. Within its walls, garments were displayed nicely on shelves, with their prices visible and attached to their tags. People had never seen such a wide array of goods in any other single store, and there were even sales clerks ready to satisfy customers' every demand, without, however, being too intrusive, leaving customers free to browse the departments on their own. The clothing available attracted an ever-increasing number of consumers, offering three categories of clothes: ready-to-wear, semi-finished and made-to-measure. It is precisely in shops like this that, for the first time in history, custom clothing and ready-to-wear garments were sold side-by-side.

Up until WWI broke out, high fashion was the only fashion there was, intrinsically linked to high society, its trends and its conventions. It was, undoubtedly, a luxurious world. The combination of landmark events, such as the industrial revolution (and the subsequent lowering of prices due to increased production) and the opening of department stores (and their wide selection of goods) made it possible for fashionable yet good-quality clothes to have a wider reach, with lower, fixed prices that were accessible to all.

NEW TRENDS AND FAMOUS LABELS

The early twentieth century ushered in a flourishing film industry linked to Hollywood and the resulting divas and their prima-donna behaviour. In it, high fashion found fertile ground for its creations: ceremonies, red carpets and premières became the perfect occasions to flaunt haute couture pieces. The dynamic spirit of the Roaring Twenties spread throughout Europe and America, bringing with it unscrupulous lifestyles that

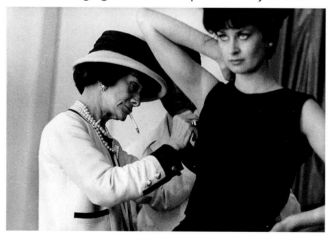

Chanel at work, early 1900s.

would influence everyday life and fashions. Hemlines on women's skirts shortened, shoulders were left exposed, necklines deepened, and the foxtrot, Charleston and dance fever spread like wildfire.

These were years ripe with important stylists, whose names are inextricably linked to haute couture: Chanel, Patou, Vionnet and Lanvin to name just a few. Their styles were seen around the world thanks to specialised print media and the sketches created by talented illustrators, guaranteeing their success.

In 1926, Coco Chanel launched *le petit noire*, the little black dress destined to become an emblem of elegance and refinement, especially when paired with long strands of pearls or choker.

Madeleine Vionnet, on the other hand, was a master of draped dresses. The brilliant idea of designing dresses with the fabric cut on the bias was a true fashion revolution, making it possible to take advantage of the material's natural elasticity and thereby infusing clothes with movement.

The Thirties, however, were defined by a global economic depression, following the Wall Street Crash in October 1929. People educed their expenses to a bare minimum and fashion was one of the worst-hit industries. The recession led to a return to sobriety even in clothing styles, quite distant from the Twenties. Fashion trends began to reverse: hemlines lengthened to below the knee for day wear and extended to the ankles for evening wear. Silhouettes become form-fitting again, highlighting the bust, waist and hips.

In this economic/social context, French designer Lucien Lelong stood out, one of the first to be inspired by mass-produced garments, creating his 'Les robes d'edition' collection, a small step towards the official arrival of prêt-à-porter. Unlike some of his contemporaries (such as Chanel, who continued to create her linear styles, selling them at high price points), Lelong found a midway point between high fashion and ready to wear. With the arrival of mass-production, the imitation of finely-tailored haute couture garments by large clothing manufacturers began. This still happens today, and it's quite easy to find garments in large clothing retailers inspired by the looks sent down the runway by important designers, aimed at consumers who are unwilling or unable to pay designer prices.

The Thirties ended with the breakout of WWII, and with the subsequent rationing of goods, especially fabric. Clothing was considered superfluous and people began 'recycling' the garments they already owned, simply modifying or altering them to bring them up to date and refreshing their look. Most new clothing being manufactured was for men in the war effort - especially nylon garments that, thanks to the material's durability, were used for the uniforms of the armed forces. Items that previously were easy to find, such as nylon stockings, thus became rare and often could only be bought on the black market at extremely high prices. Images of women with legs dyed various colours with tea or other spices are quite famous, often with a line drawn up the back to imitate the seam.

After the Germans invaded France, Paris and its haute couture empire struggled to survive. Many couturiers decided to close their shops or move abroad. Racial

Christian Dior.

persecution and the outbreak of WWII contributed to this exodus, as the story of Charles James, an English tailor who fled to the United states to start anew, reminds us.

The possibility of transferring French fashion houses to Berlin was warded off by the patience and mediation of Lucien Lelong, president of the Chambre Syndicale del la Couture Parisienne. The Nazi regime, like the Fascists in Italy, forced women to wear clothing representing their obligatory, idealised role as good, patriotic citizens and responsible mothers and wives. High fashion dames and ladies became the wives and lovers of German officials, refusing, in this dark time in world history, to give up the display of luxury in all its forms. Between light and darkness, the Forties did however bring us examples of rare genius in the ability to dress and enhance the female form. The master of haute couture was Christian Dior, a rising star in the global post-war era. His New Look, as it was christened by Carmel Snow, editor-in-chief of the American edition of *Harper's Bazaar*, was a true style revolution. The Dior woman accentuated her bust and had soft shoulders, and a thin waist that plunged into a wide circle skirt. Everything was complemented by small bags, gloves, high heels and hats: all that's necessary for a refined, feminine woman. His most famous lines, destined to forever define the history of fashion, were

inspired by letters of the alphabet (H, Y, I, A), but Dior was also a master of creating and structuring corolla and tulip shapes, veritable icons of the Fifties and beyond.

THE FIFTIES AND SIXTIES

The following decade was an important moment in fashion: Italian high fashion took off, becoming French fashion's biggest rival from that point on.

The runway event that marked the rise of Italian tailoring was organised and directed by Gian Battista Giorgini, who gathered talented people, sure, but more importantly those who had developed their own style, quite distinct from their French competitors.

One-hundred seventy garments were sent down the runway in front of America's most important buyers, showcasing not just evening gowns and cocktail dresses, but also looks that spanned from morning to afternoon. Italian craftsmanship highlighted the prized materials and noble fibres used, such as rhinestones, coral and mother-of-pearl applied with skilful mastery. The press enthusiastically welcomed this Italian runway show, the first of many. From that point on, the event was held annually in the beautiful Sala Bianca in the Pitti Palace in Florence.

Italian creativity can be credited with making garments 'wearable', suitable for daily life but still new and

Nude look, Yves Saint Laurent, 1968.

Haute couture was concentrated in the heart of Paris, where the display windows of Balenciaga, Lanvin, Chanel, Balmain and other cardinal designers stood side by side, creating the image of Paris as an elegant, sophisticated, chic and always on-trend city. With prized textiles and exclusive materials, these designers dressed the richest women on the planet, willing spend a fortune to wear clothes bearing prestigious labels. The image of a modern, refined, self-confident woman was perfectly embodied in the styles created by Coco Chanel, who began working again after WWII. She designed her own version of the suit: bouclé yarn fabric dyed in pastel tones or in black & white, with a boxy jacket and a barely-flared skirt, enriched by precious buttons and trimmings, and a blouse. Bouclé yarn became a distinguishing symbol of the fashion house, still today used in many new Chanel collections and styles, always accompanied by strands of pearls.

The technical and technological innovations that arose in the Fifties were perfected in the following decade, bringing big changes to the fashion world. Society had evolved, as did its way of seeing the body and sexuality. Designers from around the globe tried to keep up with the times, following trends and counter-trends arising from both high society and everyday citizens, especially the looks seen at youth protests.

imaginative, in a decade when sumptuous, ceremonial attire still dominated, much too deeply rooted in the French idea of style and haute couture. Italian designers sought to make everyday clothing elegant, a goal that would be reached with the arrival of prêt-à-porter, which would start its undisputed rise at this time thanks in part to the long-term vision of Italian stylists. Throughout the western hemisphere, the Fifties were a time of major social and economic change. First among them was the arrival of television, which took its place in the living rooms of every family that could afford one. The small screen immediately changed people's lives, now consumers of an enormous quantity of information and images. From the start, the media has always shaped fashion. Actors and actresses in particular have inspired men and women to dream thanks to clothes made by the world's leading designers - often recreated in more affordable versions made for everyday customers.

Within this context, accompanied by a new economic boom, advertising, technological advances and discoveries, and social protests, fashion became the principal symbol of change, transformation and current events, involving all social classes in different ways.

The privileges of the rich now seemed more accessible: all women dreamed of wearing a mink coat or feeling seductive in bright red lipstick.

Rita Hayworth in a dress by Jean Louis for Gilda, *1946.*

According to some fashion historians, the Fifties and Sixties marked the definitive collapse of high fashion, understood as the handmade production of clothing, in favour of prêt-à-porter. One thing is certain: thousands of fashion houses were forced to shutter their windows and close shop starting in the mid-Forties due to a sharp decline in demand. By comparison, the ready-to-wear clothing industry was able to produce in one day what a dressmaker would take months to sew. In addition, garment manufacturing was given a notable nudge by the invention of synthetic and artificial fabrics, which were embraced by high fashion designers.

In reality, the expansion of ready-made clothing didn't replace haute couture, but rather created a fortuitous union. Pino Lancetti is an excellent example of this trend: in 1961 he opened his atelier with a high fashion line, which he bolstered via prêt-à-porter collections. Many other designers soon followed suit.

Jean Louis for Marilyn Monroe, 1962.

In the meantime, Valentino became one of the most well-established names in international fashion, opening his first boutique in Paris in 1968. His garments were the first choice of celebrities like Jacqueline Kennedy, who wore one of his dresses when she married Aristotle Onassis that same year.

The Sixties were also notable for printed fabric, a look particularly embraced by designers like Roberta di Camerino and Ken Schott. The former used trompe-l'oeil motifs to create three-dimensional prints mainly seen on shirt dresses, collars, cuffs and belts. Scott, on the other hand, gained fame for his floral prints, used not just on dresses, but also for swimsuits, stockings and silk scarves.

It was a decade filled with youth movements, mini-skirts, the Beatles and pop art. In this new cultural climate, clothing seemed to undermine preconceived notions about age, gender and social class.

Some designers were inspired by the changes happening in society, which was particularly notable in England, leading them to create increasingly provoc-

ative, disruptive looks. The nude look came about in the Sixties too. For the AW 1968 collection, Yves Saint Laurent sent a long black evening gown down the runway, made of sheer muslin and embellished by ostrich feathers around the hips. Around the same time, the creations of Federico Forquet captured the attention of the *Times*, especially the 'dress' composed of a single red skirt, leaving the bust nude, decorated by a necklace. Even accessories were caught up in this 'nude' wave, made in new materials like polyvinyl and persplex.

YSL was a key player even in the following decade, characterised by hippie fashion and casual looks. After having opened a boutique of ready-to-wear clothing sold at lower in 1966, Rive Gauche prices, Saint Laurent updated women's fashion, adapting it to menswear, blending the two and launching the women's dinner suit, trench and pant-suit.

BETWEEN HIGH FASHION AND PRÊT-À-PORTER

In the Seventies, Paris opened its doors to a new generation of creatives that would come to rule the scene straight through the Eighties: Claude Montana, Jean-Charles de Castelbajac and, in particular, Jean Paul Gaultier. The latter's talent was quite admired by Pierre Cardin, who hired him as an assistant in 1970. His haute couture collections were eccentric and irreverent, yet also formal. Their success made him a mainstay in entertainment, creating looks for films, singers and actors.

Around the same time, Paris baptised new international talent, especially Japanese designers such as Issey Miyake and Yohji Yamamoto, who would influence Western runways during the Eighties.

In the field of fashion, a clear difference also developed between high fashion (thus handmade and ultra luxurious) and refined prêt-à-porter. Many designers had to adapt to the times, or risk going out of business. Of all the old guard, Valentino was the most adept at joining the two sides of the coin, able to transfer the elegance and sophistication of haute couture to his pre-made collections. He also was one of the best examples of Italian flair that, combined with entrepreneurial abilities, helped give Italian fashion a new image, synonymous with quality and refinement.

Towards the end of the century, especially during the Eighties, the figure of the designer himself became the focal point around which the label's entire image revolved: garments are rendered magnificent by their creator, the first-person embodiment of the message conveyed on the runway, even before the clothes are presented. Dresses were no longer seen simply as an item of clothing, but came to represent the exclusivity that the media's image of the designer embodied. By this time, fashion was intrinsically connected to life-style, and increasingly highlighted by mass marketing and advertising.

The changes that took place in society in the 1980s, taking on the form of hedonism, individualism and total sexual emancipation, were reflected in the way people dressed for their day-to-day activities, especially womenswear. The 'female manager' was perfectly represented by Armani and his neutral-colour jackets. But if, on the one hand, Italian designers were making perfectly-cut garments, on the other was the new phenomenon of Japanese designers, whose style was deeply influenced by Eastern culture. Their creations were often inspired by the kimono, a garment composed of multiple overlapping layers, and by oversize looks. Issey Miyake played with synthetic fibres to create infinite plissès and playful draping, while Kenzo found a new, exciting way to combine colours, silhouettes, and Japanese, Mexican and Northern European elements.

The decade that closed out the century was one of evolution and a fragmentation of trends and tastes: runways around the globe became stages for veritable performances intended to go beyond simply showing a new collection to audiences. Instead, they aimed to become true media events with difficult-to-wear, often shocking creations sent down the catwalk.

Meanwhile, despite having still maintained its excellent reputation in the world of high fashion, Paris suffered a setback that can be attributed to the drop in consumption of luxury goods and the explosion of ready-to-wear fashion. To face the crisis, leading fashion houses decided to recruit new, young talent, placed in the role of artistic director, to try to renew their image: John Galliano for Dior, Alexander McQueen for Givenchy, and Stella McCartney who worked for Chloé.

Even the Italian fashion industry showed some signs of crisis at this time, linked in particular to the competition coming from the numerous international designers that had, in the meantime, gained experience and a foothold in the world of fashion.

The twenty-first century started out with a more-or-less clear-cut division of clothing categories. Haute couture, sold at exorbitant prices by historical fashion houses, continued to be a French prerogative, while Italian designers offered intermediary creations manufactured with semi-industrial methods. Lastly, mass-produced affordable luxury was presented by a wide range of international brands, who offered garments with an advantageous price/quality ratio. These subdivisions are still around today, even if the lines between them are increasingly blurred, as the needs of the end consumer are constantly being studied and pinpointed. A label alone is no longer enough; today

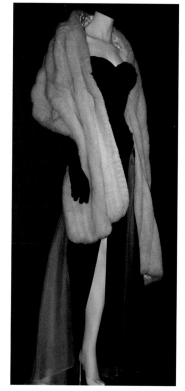

Piero Gherardi, costume for La dolce vita, 1960.

brands have to satisfy an emotional need, telling a story that can convince customers to prefer one label over another.

HIGH FASHION AND ENTERTAINMENT

Theatre, film and television have always been interconnected with fashion. First and foremost, the world's most important designers have created costumes for countless films, while large fashion houses have made and continue to make the clothes that stars wear to important social events, connected in varying degrees to film and television.

The first costume makers of the early twentieth century were Paul Poiret and Mariano Fortuny. Both began their career in the theatre: Poiret created the costumes for Sarah Bernhardt in *L'Aiglon*, while Fortuny created the sketches for the costumes of Gabriele D'Annun-

Grace Kelly, Princess of Monaco carrying the Kelly bag by Hermès.

zio's tragedy, *Francesca da Rimini*. Poiret then moved on to cinema, creating the costumes for *L'Inhumaine* (1924), directed by Marcel L'Herbier. During the 1920s, the influence of Hollywood and its stars grew exponentially.

Rudolph Valentino, Marlene Dietrich, Clark Gable and Clara Bow became new beauty icons, and people strove to imitate their everyday style. At this time, the role of costume designer began to be recognized, even if it was added as a category at the Academy Awards only in 1948.

The entertainment industry was a vehicle for numerous innovations in fashion, often linked to the evolution of costumes. This is true of trousers for women, which weren't immediately accepted by society, but worn in the early 1930s by divas such as Carol Lombard, Katharine Hepburn and Marlene Dietrich, often styled with a menswear-inspired jacket. Dietrich made this garment her signature look, creating an image as an androgynous, bold woman, yet one who was also quite sensual. Thanks to the aforementioned icons, trousers were embraced and worn with nonchalance by an increasing number of women, especially young women, during their free time.

Gilbert Adrian was one of Hollywood's most famous costume designers. He was more than a fashion designer who was simply passionate about on-stage costumes. Rather, he was a true industry professional who dedicated his entire career to dressing actors on some of history's most important sets. The close friend of countless divas, he created many costumes that have become film icons in their own right: the evening dress worn by Joan Crawford in *Letty Lynton* was even reproduced and sold at Macy's (a large American department store) while the film was in cinemas.

Another prolific costume designer was Walter Plunkett, famous mainly for his period-piece costumes. He worked on over 150 films, including *Gone with the Wind* (for which he designed the dresses of Scarlett O'Hara played by Vivien Leigh), *Little Women* and *An American in Paris*, the latter earning him the Oscar for Best Costume Design in 1952.

Jean Louis, a native Parisian who naturalised as an American citizen, dressed many Hollywood divas during his career, both on and off set. In particular, the black satin dress worn by Rita Hayworth in *Gilda* is worth mentioning, with its high side slit, and the iconic flesh-toned column dress a provocative Marilyn Monroe flaunted in 1962 at Madison Square Garden during the 45th birthday festivities held for President Kennedy. The white pleated dress with a halter neckline designed by William Travilla is equally iconic, worn

Audrey Hepburn in Breakfast at Tiffany's; *dress by Hubert de Givenchy, 1961.*

by the actress in *The Seven Year Itch* (1955).
Around the mid-1950s, Rome's Cinecittà was at the height of its fame, welcoming America's most acclaimed divas, including Linda Christian, Elisabeth Taylor, Ava Gardner. Travelling to Italy to promote their films, they often frequented local boutiques to be dressed by Italian designers. These were years in which Valentino, Mila Schon and Roberto Capucci opened their fashion ateliers in Rome.

La Dolce Vita surely best embodies that era, as well as the most famous and iconic: it won the Palme d'Or at Cannes, and Piero Gherardi received the Academy Award for the costumes. He had a close relationship with Federico Fellini, and the two worked together on many films. However, the scene depicting Anita Ekberg in the Trevi Fountain wearing a long, sensual black dress will forever be a defining moment of film history. Halfway between cinema and nobility is Grace Kelly, the blond actress (and later princess) often cast by Alfred Hitchcock. Here the connection to high fashion is even closer: Hermès created the Kelly bag just for her, an iconic leather purse with a metal clasp closure that became a cult accessory, today sold with a sky-high price tag.

The early Sixties were marked by the release of *Breakfast at Tiffany's* (1961), starring British actress Audrey

Audrey Hepburn in Two for the Road; *dress by A. Courrèges, 1967.*

Hepburn. She was the muse of designer Hubert de Givenchy, who created the ultra-famous little black dress made of Italian satin, featuring an ankle-length skirt with a side slit. The partnership between Hepburn and Givenchy was long (it began when Givenchy was the costume designer for *Sabrina*), and the stylist dressed the actress on many occasions, both for the big screen and in her private life.

Even the influential designer André Courrèges, inventor of 'space design', created a number of looks for Hepburn, though with styles and lines that were entirely different than those of Givenchy.

In *Two for the Road*, the 1967 film directed by Stanley Donen, the bon-ton queen worn PVC outfits inspired by sports and metallic accessories.

Even music has had a historically close relationship with fashion. In particular, the extraordinary Tina Turner, with her exuberant style, often chose to wear the creations of Azzedine Alaïa. For her, the designer created very short, form-fitting dresses frequently in jersey, a very popular fabric during the Eighties.

In line with this style, and during the same decade, newcomer Madonna flaunted eccentric, bold looks with leggings, ankle boots, chains, very short skirts, lace and plenty of make-up. She would become the idol of young women everywhere, wearing prestigious labels during her successive tours: Gucci, Moschino,

Madonna with the corset by Jean Paul Gaultier, 1990.

Prada and Alexander Wang.

Jean Paul Gaultier also designed an iconic look for the American signer: the now-famous silk corset with cone-shaped cups that Madonna wore during her Blond Ambition Tour in 1990. The garment was sold at auction in 2012, with a starting price of 12,000 pounds. Gaultier also dressed other musicians, such as Kylie Minogue and Mylène Farmer. In addition, he designed many garments for films such as *Kika* (1993) by Almodòvar, *The Fifth Element* (1997) by Luc Besson and *The City of Lost Children* (1995) by Jean-Pierre Jeunet.

Clothing worn in films or on the stage of the theatre has the power to taken on its own meaning, having far-reaching impact on the collective imagination as it is conveyed through a story and a character.

Today, high fashion is mainly focused on dressing celebrities on the red carpet for events like the Academy Awards and other festivals that take place through out the year, or in seeking out famous faces for advertising campaigns. On the red carpet, dresses are the true protagonists, and each star seeks to impress audiences and the press with gowns and accessories from prestigious fashion houses around the world. Try-ons for red-carpet looks begin months before, and each designer puts its best employees to work designing and crafting dresses that live up to the standards of their customers. Haute couture creations let us dream, even more so when they head down the red carpet, an important 'catwalk' for cinema celebs.

RUNWAY SHOWS

Runway shows are the main communication tool that fashion houses use to present their collections. Today, these events mark the seasons of the fashion industry, determining the success of a brand by attracting customers. However, they haven't always existed.

For centuries, tailors and dressmakers (especially in France, considering that all changes in fashion once came from France) used to display dolls of varying sizes dressed in their latest creations in their shop windows. Fashionable ladies could then stay up to date on the latest trends, simply by observing these small mannequins, or via specialised publications and the use of fashion figurines. The golden age of these 'models' was the eighteenth century, a time of important technological innovation in which getting around became easier. Not only did upper class women from all over Europe head to Paris to update their wardrobe, but the dolls were also shipped to dressmaking shops outside France, spreading new fashions far and wide.

The decline of these dolls began in the early nineteenth century, with the transition from handmade tailoring (with a small number of workers for a select elite) to more organised, grandiose manufacturing that set its sights on aristocrats and the upper and middle class. French designer Charles Worth was the first to think of having real models wear his creations, and thus his workshop at 7 Rue de la Paix was the site of the first runway shows in history, reserved for a select group of noblewomen. Worth dressed upper-class European and American women, and brought his aesthetics and taste when creating the by-then semi-standardised collections to appease his numerous clientèle.

In the early twentieth century, even Paul Poiret turned to splendid French models to present his creations. However, unlike Worth, he decided to promote his work in an itinerant way, organising 'tours' around Europe, thereby ushering in a long-lasting custom of presenting fashion collections on the catwalk. For the first time, models left the atelier to stride down the runways of the largest cities in the world (in 1913, Poiret repeated the experiment in the United States), launching the variety of professions that still today make runway events happen.

In Italy, runway shows began in 1951 when designer Giovanni Battista Giorgini organised the first one to draw international attention in the halls of Villa Torrigiani in Florence. Numerous journalists and buyers

Chanel FW 2018.

Christian Dior FW 2018.

from big American department stores were in attendance and, enthusiastic about the collection, they bought everything. Italian fashion and its high quality and creativity standards thus became part of the international fashion system.

Today, almost all runway shows take place during the 'Fashion Week' of various cities: Paris, Milan, London and New York are the most important official events, where the best stylists from around the globe present new collections twice a year. In particular, Paris fashion week is usually dedicated to Haute Couture, being its homeland after all.

Fashion week includes the exhibition of garments that will then be sold the following year, presenting new trends well in advance. This tradition was turned on its head in autumn of 2016 by American Designer Tommy Hilfiger who, during New York Fashion week, presented 'Tommy Now', a rather innovative runway show. Thanks to the 'see now, buy now' concept, Hilfiger implemented a new, democratising fashion strategy in which the audience that watches a runway show can buy the garments immediately. So, his 2016 fashion show brought the autumn collection's pieces for that year to the stage, making it possible to 'shop the runway' while watching the live stream of the presentation online. The experiment proved to be a success, so much so that the designer repeated the event in a number of capital cities.

From the start of the twenty-first century, other cities around the world have started their own Fashion Weeks: Shanghai, Rio de Janeiro, Hong Kong, Abu Dhabi, Tokyo, Tehran, Moscow and Singapore. Some of them are geared towards the presentation of specific products, such as swimsuits in Miami and 'green' fashion in Portland, Oregon. Today, the trend is to make runway shows true events where everything is perfect, something that people will talk about, from the setting to the guest list. The first rows are always reserved for the press and guests of honour such as actors and actresses, musicians, it girls and influencers. In addition, the models are essential to a show's success: some of them have become famous in their own right, in addition to the muses that inspire the designers to launch their capsule collections.

The setting, on the other hand, also plays a fundamental role in making runway shows not just simple presentations, but veritable events with performances that are edging closer and closer to theatrical productions. Music, lights, displays, choreography and spectacular runways combine to make these fashion shows truly unforgettable. Even the web has brought about benefits to the fashion industry. In particular, social media are an enormous resource for all companies that, through these young, real-time channels, are able to offer a broader range of services to their customers. Live streams broadcast on various platforms are used by brands to showcase their live runway presentations, making them more accessible to just about everyone.

As time goes on, fashion has continued to break down barriers, not just in terms of style, but perhaps most importantly through experimentation with channels that can achieve true democratisation.

2. CREATIVE DARTS IN HAUTE COUTURE

THE PRINCIPLES OF DARTS

Essential to successful patterns, darts are small, triangular, recessed folds used for both tailored and mass-produced garments. They are necessary to give shape to a garment, ensuring it properly contours the curves of the body. Darts are created by folding the fabric inward, then shaping by sewing. Darts are of fundamental importance, ensuring the perfect fit of a garment.

FORM AND FUNCTION

The dart is a triangle whose base is drawn onto the outer cut line of the pattern, while its apex (the point) is placed at the most protruding part of the body, thereby making use of the abundance of the fabric. There are seven main curves on the female body that require darts: 1) the bust; 2) the tip of the shoulder; 3) the waist; 4) the shoulder blade; 5) the elbow; 6) the buttocks; 7) the hips. However, for technical reasons, they may be placed in many other positions, both on the front and back; for the upper and lower parts of the body. This is true for all types of garments.

Bust darts (front bodice) can originate from any part of the six segments that make up the outer cut lines, and they are given names based on their origin, that is: shoulder, neckline, armscye and waist darts.

There are only two darts used on the back: waist and neckline darts. The latter can be shifted to the shoulder or eliminated in the centre back.

Their width (the intake) is proportionate to the protuberance to be covered: the greater the distance between the protruding element and the rest of the body, the larger the section to be regulated with darts will be. Here's what you need to consider when working with darts.

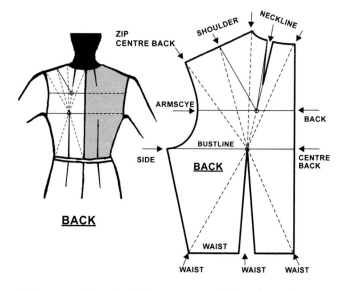

BACK

1) You need to study the purpose of the darts, how they work, their placement and how they are rotated (pivoted) on flat patterns in detail and in-depth, because their proper placement and application is essential to quickly making useful high-fashion patterns.

2) On the pattern, darts are marked by notches on the edges and circles at their point. The circumference of the circle is placed 2-3 cm (0.79-1.81") from the apex, enough to be enveloped in the seam and serve as a reference point during garment construction.

3) Dart lines can be straight or curved. Curved darts allow the garment to fit the body better, and can be curved inward (concave) if you want to add ease, or outwards (convex) if you want to remove it, making the garment fit closer to the body.

Concave darts are mainly used on skirts so that they smoothly adapt to the belly in the front and the buttocks at the rear. At times they are also used for neckline (or shoulder) darts. Convex darts are curved outwards and are generally used for the waist, or for the front of the bodice if the bust is large and the lower part of the torso is smaller by comparison. Any unnecessary ease is then taken up under the bust line.

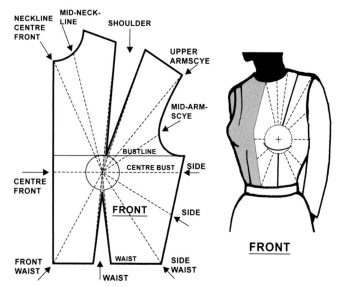

FRONT

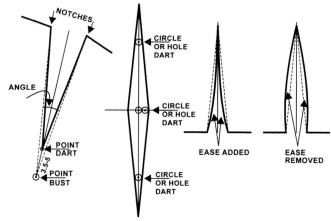

CONTOUR DARTS AND HOW TO SHIFT THEM

Contour darts are necessary and cannot be eliminated. However, they can be shifted and repositioned around the same protruding element, always in consideration of the client's build and proportions, the best possible dart direction and the type of fabric used. For example, on plain colour fabric, the addition of new darts (even diagonal ones) is not a problem aesthetically speaking. However, for striped, check or tartan prints, diagonal darts will result in an unattractive final product.

There are different ways to shift darts:
1) The pivot method, rotating the pattern around a fulcrum placed at the protruding part of the body (for

example, the bust point).
2) The slash and spread method, when you cut a straight line from one dart point to another edge of the pattern, then pivoted around the apex to shift the dart to a new position.
3) The combined method, used a) when both the base darts (shoulder and waist) are combined in a new position (e.g. a diagonal dart on the side, called a French dart); b) when a base dart on the front is combined with the other; c) when a dart is divided into one or more darts located in a single position; or d) when two or more front darts are pivoted to shift them to other positions.

SHOULDER DART SHIFTED TO THE SIDE (FRENCH DART)

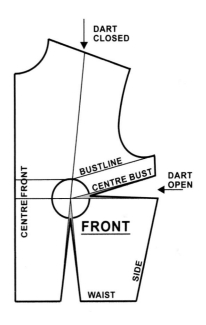

WAIST DART MERGED INTO THE SHOULDER AND SHIFTED TO THE ARMSCYE

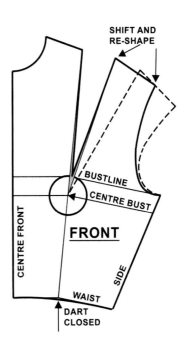

Waist dart merged into the shoulder and divided into three parts

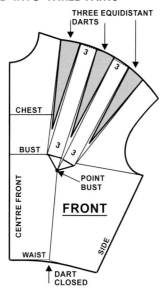

THREE EQUIDISTANT DARTS

CHEST

BUST

3

3

3

3

3

POINT BUST

CENTRE FRONT

FRONT

SIDE

WAIST

DART CLOSED

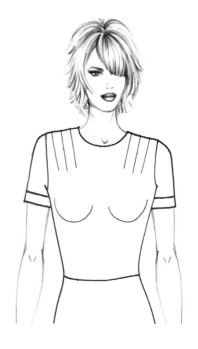

Shoulder dart merged into the waist

DART CLOSED

CENTRE FRONT

FRONT

BUSTLINE

CENTRE BUST

SIDE

WAIST

DART OPEN

Shoulder dart merged into the waist and divided into three parts

DART CLOSED

CENTRE FRONT

FRONT

BUSTLINE

CENTRE BUST

3

3

3

3

SIDE

WAIST

THREE EQUIDISTANT DARTS

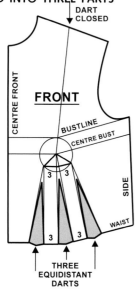

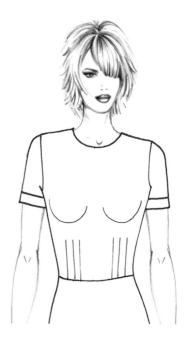

Bust dart shifted to the mid-armscye

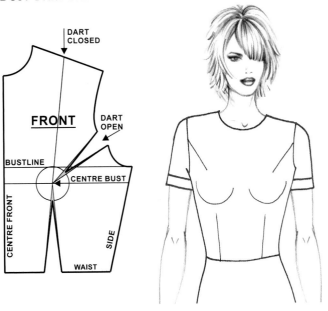

Bust and waist darts shifted to the centre front

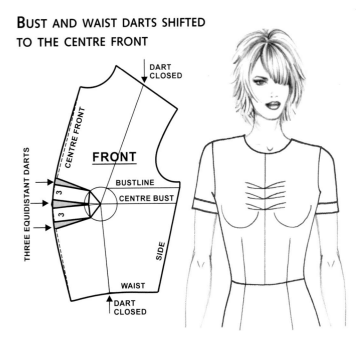

Bust and waist dart merged into the neckline and divided into three parts

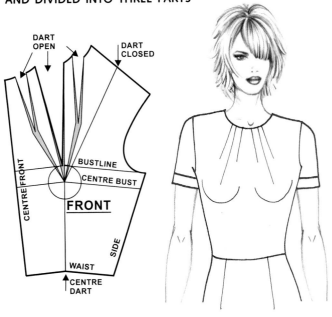

Neck dart shifted to the rear shoulder

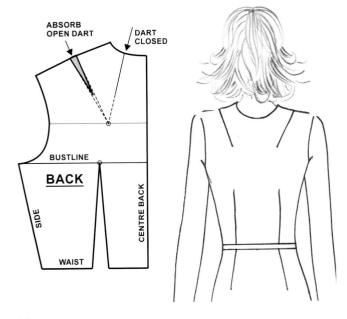

Neck dart shifted to the shoulder and discarded in the back armscye

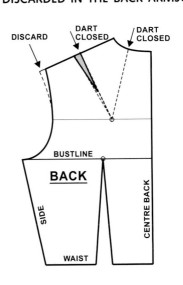

Neck dart discarded on the centre back

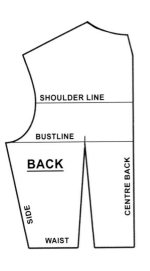

DARTS FOR DRESSES

WAIST DARTS

When creating a base pattern for a tight or fitted dress, as we've seen in previous books, the darts on the bodice and the skirt are combined at the waist, becoming diamond darts (fisheye or double darts). These are completed by drawing a parallel guideline at the centre front and centre back in the position of the original waist darts. They must be lined up with each pivot point on the bodice.

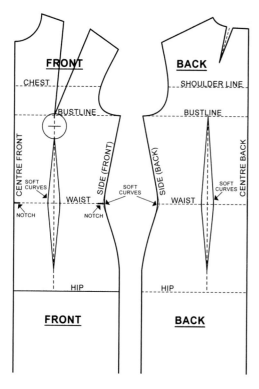

The waist darts of a full dress offer many possibilities in terms of the pattern. They can be partially or completely removed and side seams can be partially or completely straightened to create a soft, not-too-tight garment or even a loose garment.

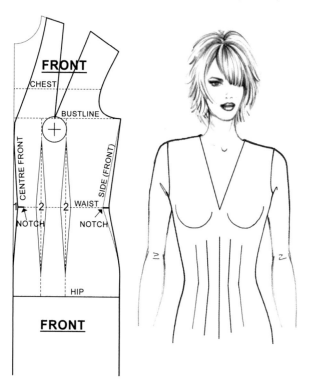

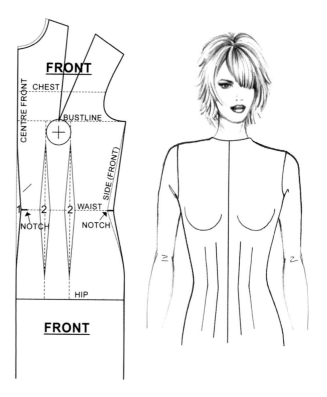

DIVISION OF WAIST DARTS

If the pattern requires it, the front can be shaped by constructing a dart on the centre front, even if there is no seam. The centre dart should be created by reducing the dart intake (the space between the dart legs) at the waist.

If there is a seam on the centre front, the shape of the dart should be incorporated into the seam.

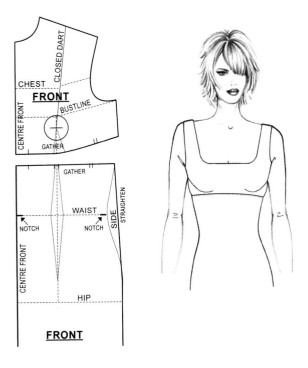

LONG FRENCH DARTS

In a full dress, you can create a French dart by combining the shoulder dart with the waist dart. The shoulder dart should be closed and shifted to the side cut line at 3-5 cm (1.18-1.97") from the pelvis or in another position. Cut and open the French dart and leave the seam allowance.

For a pattern with a waist that's been raised to just below the bust (empire waist), the shoulder dart should be merged into the waist dart.

After having positioned the notches, cut the pattern at the cut outline at 8-9 cm (3.15-3.54") below the bust. Shape as necessary.

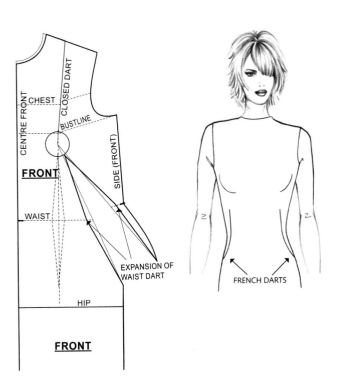

Darts for asymmetric motifs

When creating contoured patterns and garments, it's important to know how to combine various techniques and motifs on the bodice, skirt and sleeves, including yokes, pleats, gatherings, collars, etc. The front and back can be different from each other or have quite similar lines, or they can combine the various parts in various ways, but it's never a good idea to combine too many elements in a single garment. The example shown here has an asymmetrical shape shifted to the left, obtained by shifting the darts to the right.

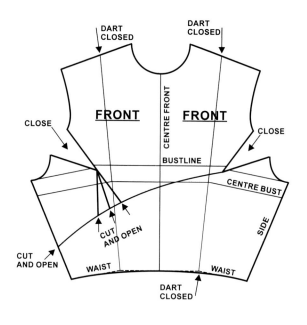

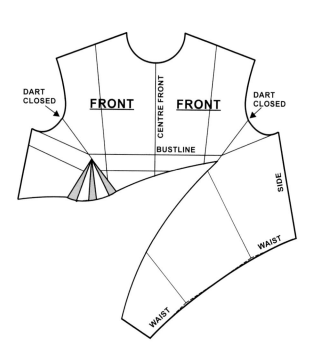

CURVED DARTS, DART INTAKE AND CUT LINES

In general, bodice blocks are geometric, made with straight lines, while in reality the body has more curved, harmonious outlines, with a flexible profile and well-smoothed roundness. To give the paper pattern the right amount of harmony, and properly contour the lines of the human body, you'll need to adjust the outline of the bodice block (the cut lines). Below are a few illustrations of these adjustments, which make it possible to make the lines of the pattern smoother and more graceful. The areas that require the most attention are generally the bust and shoulders, where darts are placed to shape the garment.

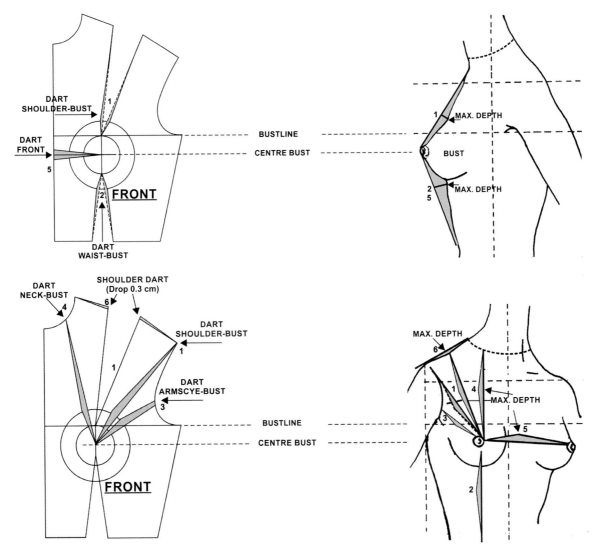

Front bodice:
- Drop the shoulder line by 0.3-0.5 cm (0.12-0.20").
- Armscye-bust darts are used mainly for garments with tight sleeves.
- Neckline-bust and shoulder-bust darts are used to make necklines fitted and avoid excess fabric gapping.
- Centre-front darts are used to account for the protrusion of the bust.
- Waist darts are used to balance out the connection with the centre bust.
Back bodice:

- Raise the shoulder line by 0.3-0.5 cm (0.12-0.20").
- The size and shape of the waist darts can be used to make deep back necklines adhere better to the body.

When studying the flat pattern method, shifting, darts and their transformation into gatherings, pleats, the ease or the cut line is essential to adapting the fabric to the curves of the body and to creating new shapes and new solutions.
In this chapter, we'll present a few transformations that will be useful bases, adaptable to perfectly suit the needs of each garment and client.

BODICE WITH BUST DARTS
BLENDED INTO THE SHOULDER DRAPING
AND SKIRT DARTS IN THE WAIST DRAPING

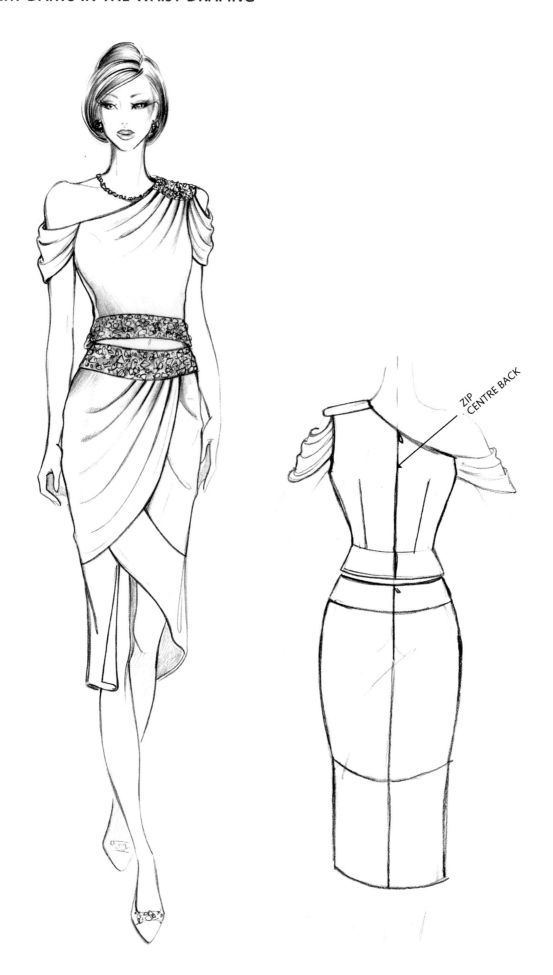

ZIP CENTRE BACK

ONE-SHOULDER TOP
DARTS DISCARDED IN THE SHOULDER GATHERING

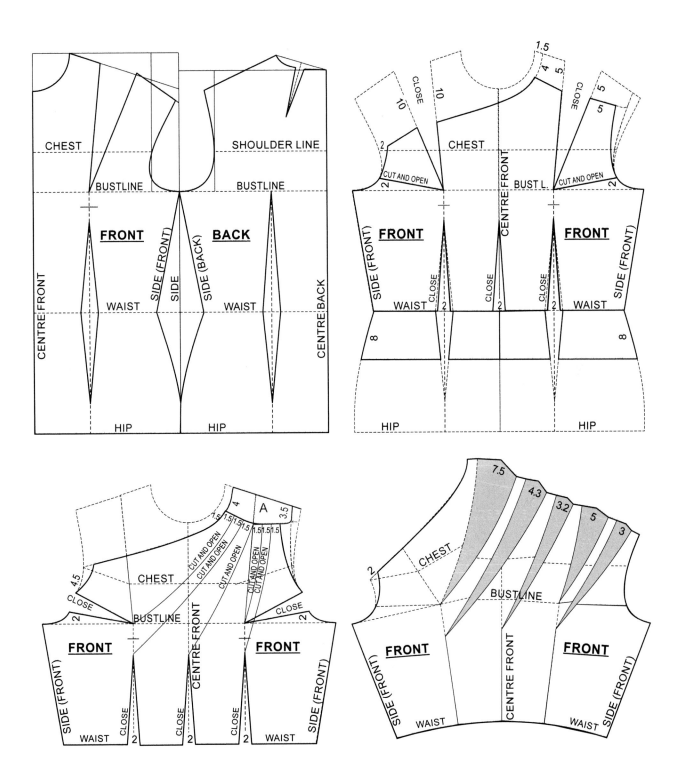

- Create a shirt bodice block with darts in the desired measurements and a fit suitable to the fabric to be used.
- Unite the right front with the left front and carry out the transformations as shown in the figure.
- Close the bust darts on the shoulder and open them in the armscye.
- Mark the transformation lines for the draping on the left shoulder.

- Take up the back, unite the back with the front and carry out the transformations as in the figure.
- Take up the front and back waistbands and close the darts.
- Draw the motif that creates the sleeves as illustrated.
- Create the left shoulder motif as illustrated.

SKIRT WITH DARTS AND WAISTBAND

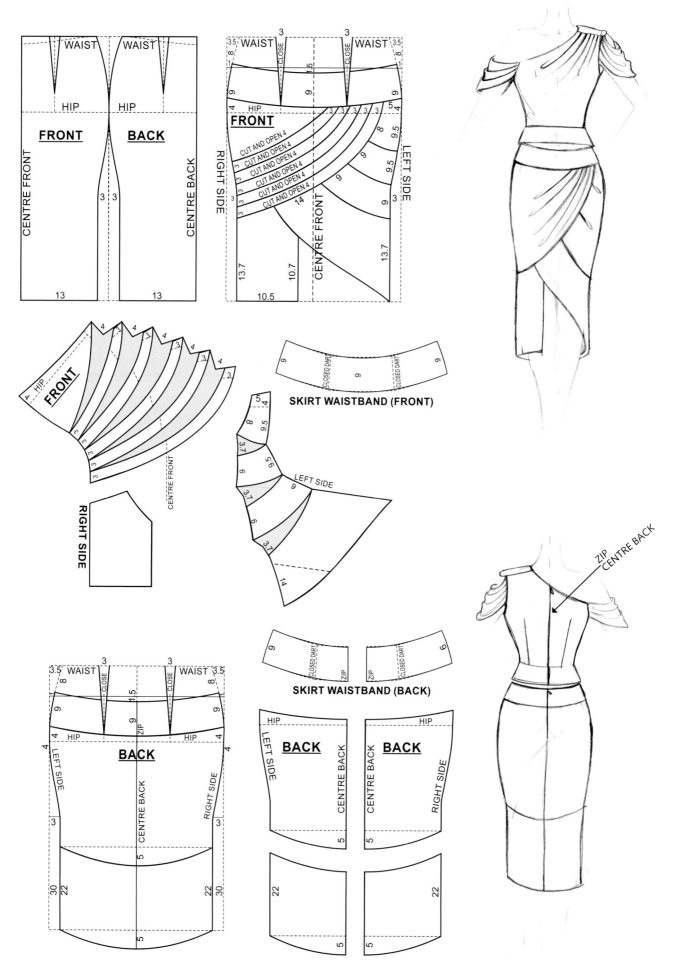

SKIRT WAISTBAND (FRONT)

SKIRT WAISTBAND (BACK)

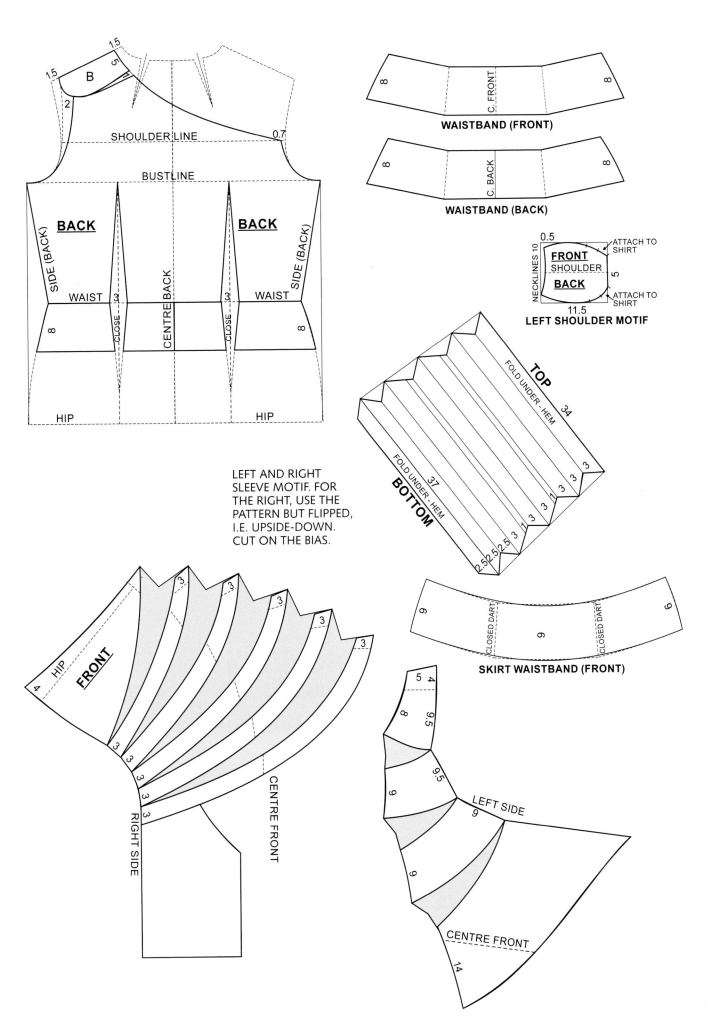

WAISTBAND (FRONT)

WAISTBAND (BACK)

SHOULDER LINE

BUSTLINE

BACK

BACK

SIDE (BACK)

SIDE (BACK)

CENTRE BACK

WAIST

WAIST

CLOSE

CLOSE

HIP

HIP

B

1.5

1.5

5

2

0.7

3

3

8

8

FRONT
SHOULDER
BACK

NECKLINES 10

0.5

5

11.5

ATTACH TO SHIRT

ATTACH TO SHIRT

LEFT SHOULDER MOTIF

TOP

BOTTOM

FOLD UNDER - HEM

FOLD UNDER - HEM

34

37

3

3

3

3

3

1

1

2.5 2.5 2.5

LEFT AND RIGHT
SLEEVE MOTIF. FOR
THE RIGHT, USE THE
PATTERN BUT FLIPPED,
I.E. UPSIDE-DOWN.
CUT ON THE BIAS.

SKIRT WAISTBAND (FRONT)

6

6

9

CLOSED DART

CLOSED DART

FRONT

HIP

RIGHT SIDE

CENTRE FRONT

4

3

3

3

3

3

3

3

3

3

3

3

3

LEFT SIDE

CENTRE FRONT

5

4

8

9.5

9.5

9

9

9

14

29

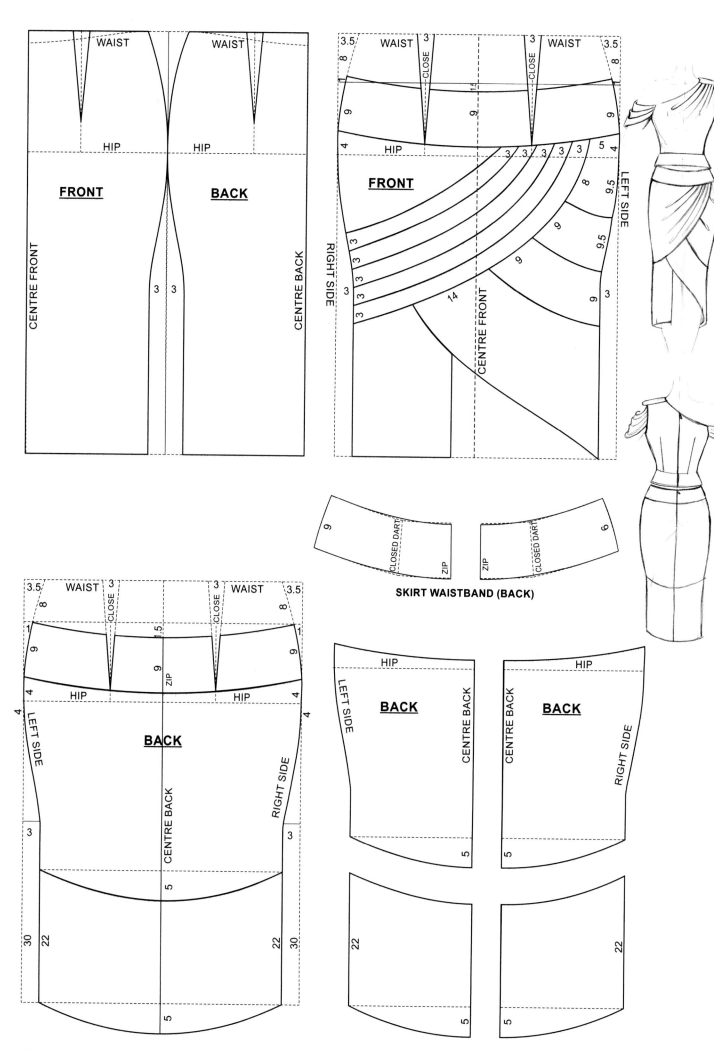

FRONT **BACK**

WAIST WAIST

HIP HIP

CENTRE FRONT CENTRE BACK

3 3

FRONT

3.5 WAIST 3 CLOSE 3 CLOSE WAIST 3 3.5

8 8

9 1.5 9 9

4 HIP 3 3 3 3 3 5 4

RIGHT SIDE LEFT SIDE

3 3 8 9.5

3 9

3 9.5

3 9

3 14 9 3

CENTRE FRONT

SKIRT WAISTBAND (BACK)

9 CLOSED DART ZIP ZIP CLOSED DART 6

BACK

3.5 WAIST 3 CLOSE 3 CLOSE WAIST 3.5

8 8

1 9 1.5 9 ZIP 9 9 1

4 HIP HIP 4

4 4

LEFT SIDE RIGHT SIDE

CENTRE BACK

3 3

5

30 22 22 30

5

BACK **BACK**

HIP HIP

LEFT SIDE CENTRE BACK CENTRE BACK RIGHT SIDE

5 5

22 22

5 5

30

DRESS WITH DARTS MERGED INTO THE SEAMS
FITTED BUST WITH AN AMPLE SKIRT.
RIBBON INSERT OR APPLIED TO THE BUST

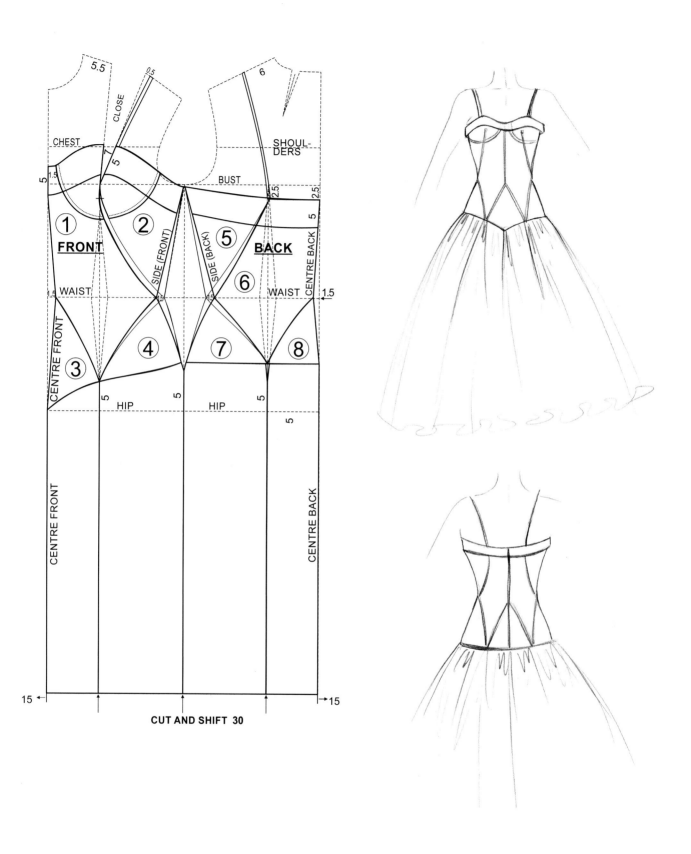

5.5

CLOSE

0.5

6

CHEST

SHOUL-
DERS

5

1.5

5

BUST

2.5

2.5

① FRONT

②

SIDE (FRONT)

SIDE (BACK)

⑤ BACK

⑥

CENTRE BACK

5

CENTRE FRONT

1.5 WAIST

15 15

WAIST 1.5

④

③

⑦

⑧

5 5 5

HIP

HIP

5

CENTRE FRONT

CENTRE BACK

15 ← →15

CUT AND SHIFT 30

32

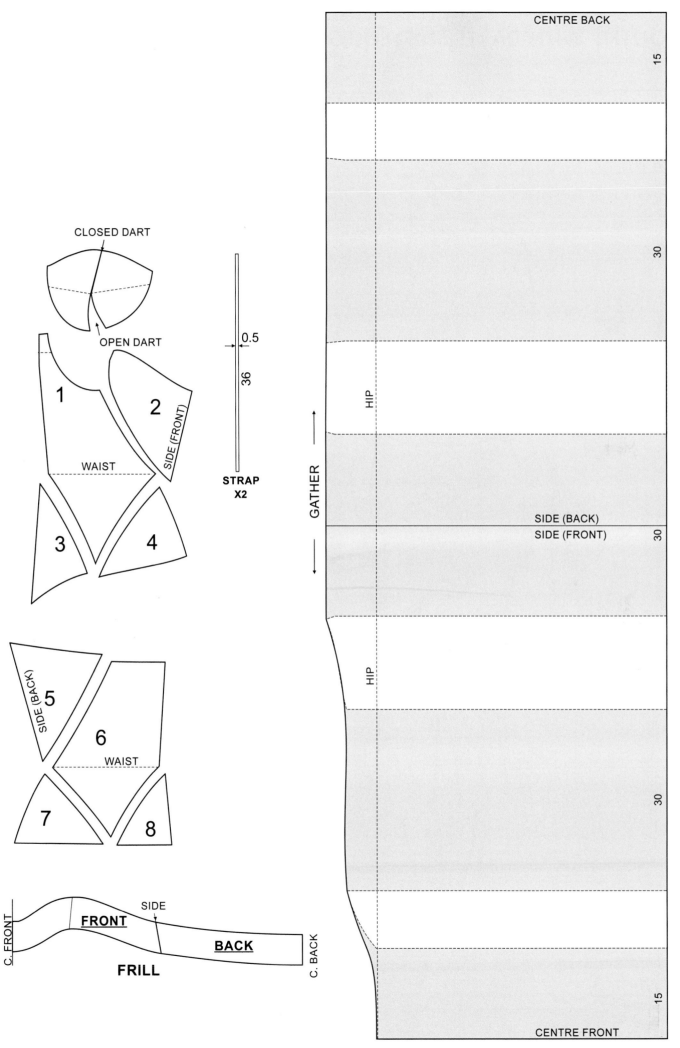

CLOSED DART

OPEN DART

0.5

36

STRAP
X2

1

2

SIDE (FRONT)

WAIST

3

4

SIDE (BACK)

5

6

WAIST

7

8

C. FRONT

FRONT

SIDE

BACK

C. BACK

FRILL

CENTRE BACK

15

30

HIP

GATHER

SIDE (BACK)

SIDE (FRONT)

30

HIP

30

15

CENTRE FRONT

33

OUTFIT WITH DARTS SHIFTED TO THE WAIST

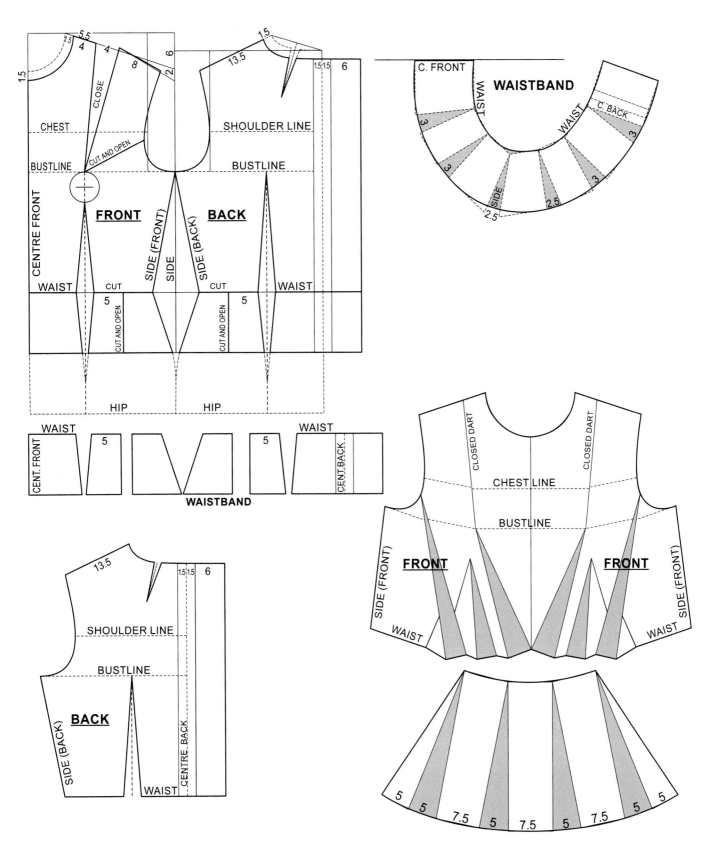

- Draw the shirt base block with darts in the appropriate measurements and the right fit, with a fastening
  at the back.
- Copy the front and back bodice and the waistband
- Close the bust dart on the shoulder and open it in
  the armscye.
- Draw the lines as in the figure.
- Close the darts and create openings on the waistline
  for the expansion, as illustrated.

- Copy the back.
- Copy the waistband and transform it, opening it at the
  bottom as illustrated, until you reach the desired size.
- Draw the sleeve in a suitable measurement in relation
  to the armscye of the bodice. The length of the sleeve
  should reach down to the wrist, plus the extension in
  the desire volume.
- Trace the sleeve extension and widen at the bottom as
  illustrated.

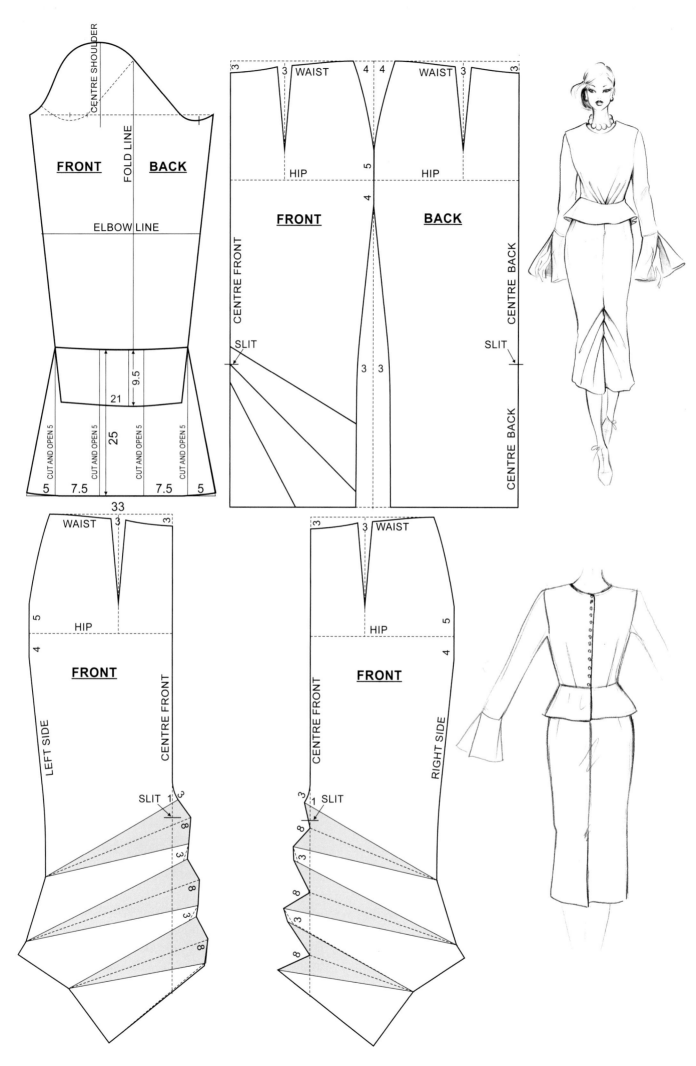

FRONT **BACK**

CENTRE SHOULDER

FOLD LINE

ELBOW LINE

9.5

21

25

CUT AND OPEN 5

5 7.5 7.5 5

33

3 3 WAIST 4 4 WAIST 3 3

HIP 5 HIP

FRONT **BACK**

CENTRE FRONT

CENTRE BACK

CENTRE BACK

SLIT SLIT

4

3 3

WAIST 3 3

HIP

5

4

FRONT

LEFT SIDE

CENTRE FRONT

SLIT 1 3

8

3

8

3

8

3 3 WAIST

HIP

5

4

FRONT

CENTRE FRONT

RIGHT SIDE

3 1 SLIT

8

3

8

3

8

DRESS WITH BUST AND WAIST DARTS
MADE TO MERGE INTO THE SEAMS

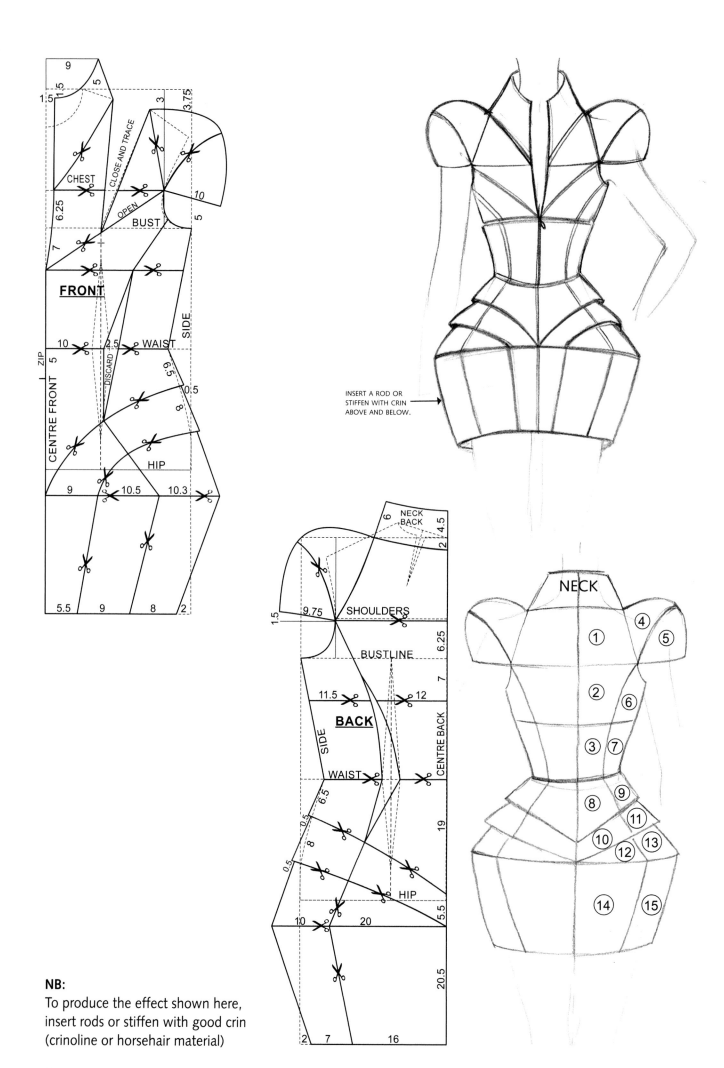

FRONT

CHEST

BUST

SIDE

CENTRE FRONT

ZIP

WAIST

DISCARD

HIP

CLOSE AND TRACE

OPEN

9
5
1.5
1.5
3
3.75
10
6.25
5
7
10
2.5
5
6.5
0.5
8
9
10.5
10.3
5.5
9
8
2

BACK

NECK BACK

SHOULDERS

BUSTLINE

SIDE

WAIST

CENTRE BACK

HIP

6
4.5
2
1.5
9.75
6.25
7
11.5
12
6.5
0.5
8
0.5
10
20
5.5
19
20.5
2
7
16

INSERT A ROD OR
STIFFEN WITH CRIN
ABOVE AND BELOW.

NECK

① ④ ⑤
② ⑥
③ ⑦
⑧ ⑨
⑪
⑩ ⑬
⑫
⑭ ⑮

NB:
To produce the effect shown here,
insert rods or stiffen with good crin
(crinoline or horsehair material)

38

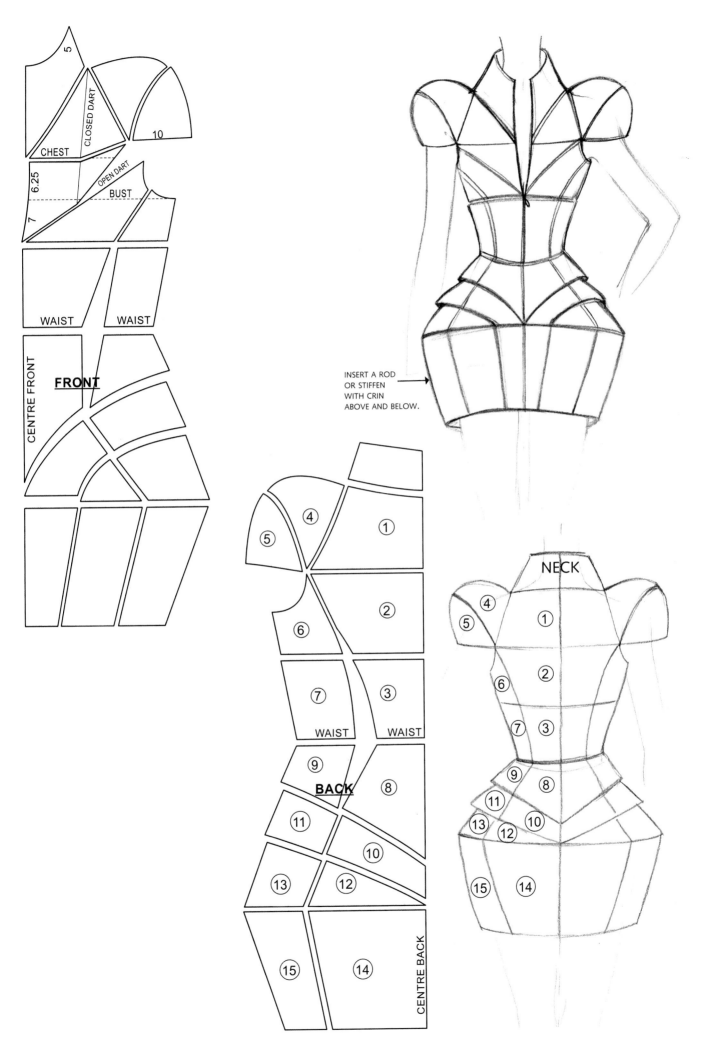

5

CLOSED DART

CHEST

10

6.25

OPEN DART

BUST

7

WAIST   WAIST

CENTRE FRONT

FRONT

INSERT A ROD
OR STIFFEN
WITH CRIN
ABOVE AND BELOW.

④
⑤
①
②
⑥
⑦   ③
WAIST   WAIST
⑨
BACK   ⑧
⑪
⑩
⑬   ⑫
⑮   ⑭

CENTRE BACK

NECK

④
⑤   ①
⑥   ②
⑦   ③
⑨   ⑧
⑪
⑬   ⑩
⑫
⑮   ⑭

TRUMPET GOWN WITH A SEAM MOTIF
AT THE FRONT AND SIDES
BUST AND WAIST DARTS MERGED INTO THE SEAMS

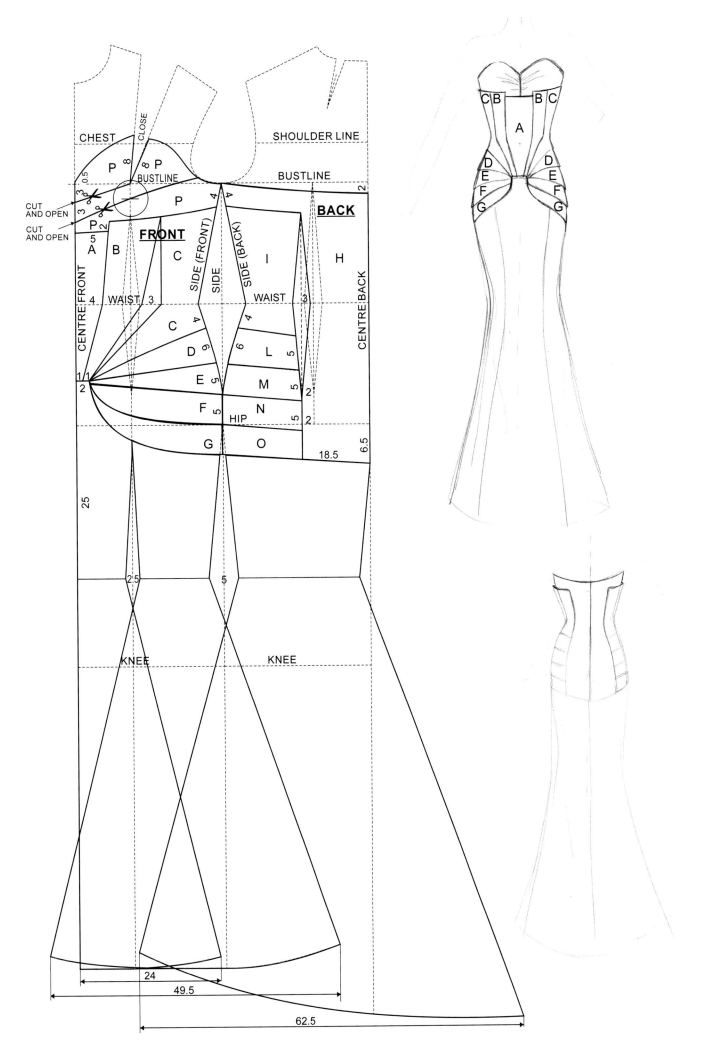

CHEST   CLOSE   SHOULDER LINE

P 8   P
0.5
P   BUSTLINE   BUSTLINE   2
3 3   P   4   A   BACK
CUT AND OPEN   3   P 2
CUT AND OPEN   5   FRONT
A   B   C   SIDE (FRONT)   SIDE   SIDE (BACK)   I   H

CENTRE FRONT
4   WAIST   3   WAIST   3   CENTRE BACK

C   4
D   6   6   L   5
E   5   M   5   2
F   5   N   5   2
HIP
G   O   18.5   6.5

25

2.5   5

KNEE   KNEE

24
49.5
62.5

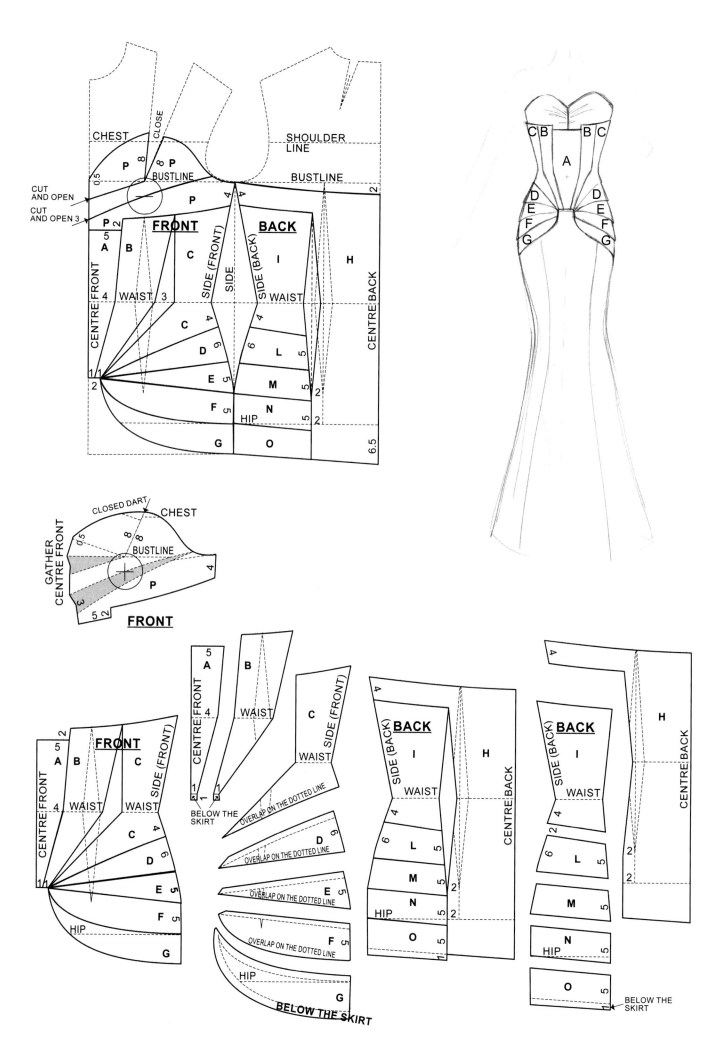

CHEST

CLOSE

SHOULDER LINE

BUSTLINE

BUSTLINE

P 8 P

0.5

P

CUT AND OPEN

CUT AND OPEN 3

P 2

5

FRONT

BACK

A B

C

SIDE (FRONT)

SIDE

SIDE (BACK)

I

H

CENTRE FRONT

4 WAIST 3

WAIST

CENTRE BACK

C 4

D 6

6 L 5

E 5

M 5

1 1

2

F 5

N 5 2

HIP 5 2

G

O

6.5

CLOSED DART

CHEST

GATHER CENTRE FRONT

0.5 8 8

BUSTLINE

P

4

3

5 2

FRONT

2

5

FRONT

A B

C

SIDE (FRONT)

CENTRE FRONT

4 WAIST

WAIST

C 4

D 6

1 1

E 5

F 5

HIP

G

5

A

B

CENTRE FRONT

4

WAIST

C

SIDE (FRONT)

WAIST

1 1

BELOW THE SKIRT

OVERLAP ON THE DOTTED LINE

D 9

OVERLAP ON THE DOTTED LINE

E 5

OVERLAP ON THE DOTTED LINE

F 5

HIP

G

BELOW THE SKIRT

4

BACK

SIDE (BACK)

I

H

WAIST

CENTRE BACK

4

6 L 5

M 5

N 5 2

HIP 5 2

O 5

1

4

BACK

SIDE (BACK)

I

H

WAIST

CENTRE BACK

4

6 L 5

2

M 5

2

N 5

HIP

O 5

1

BELOW THE SKIRT

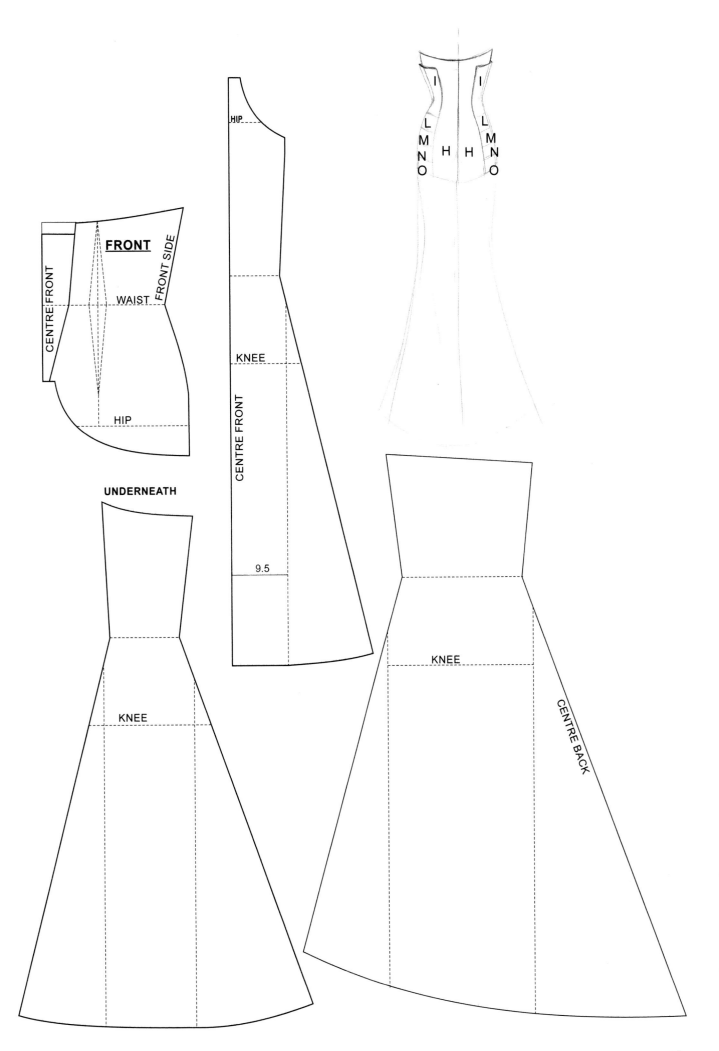

FRONT

CENTRE FRONT

FRONT SIDE

WAIST

HIP

UNDERNEATH

HIP

KNEE

CENTRE FRONT

9.5

KNEE

KNEE

KNEE

CENTRE BACK

I I
L L
M M
N H H N
O O

43

OFF-SHOULDER DRESS
DARTS MERGED INTO THE SEAMS, MOTIFS AND FOLDS

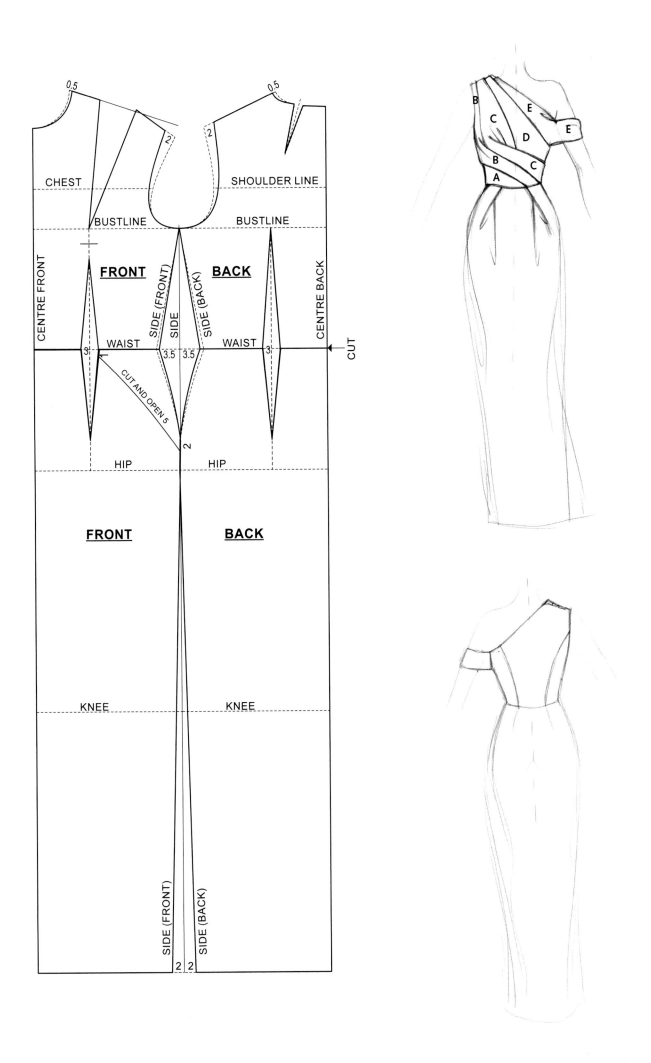

0.5

0.5

2

2

CHEST

SHOULDER LINE

BUSTLINE

BUSTLINE

CENTRE FRONT

FRONT

SIDE (FRONT)

SIDE

SIDE (BACK)

BACK

CENTRE BACK

CUT

3

WAIST

3.5

3.5

WAIST

3

CUT AND OPEN 5

2

HIP

HIP

FRONT

BACK

KNEE

KNEE

SIDE (FRONT)

SIDE (BACK)

2

2

B

E

C

E

D

B

C

A

45

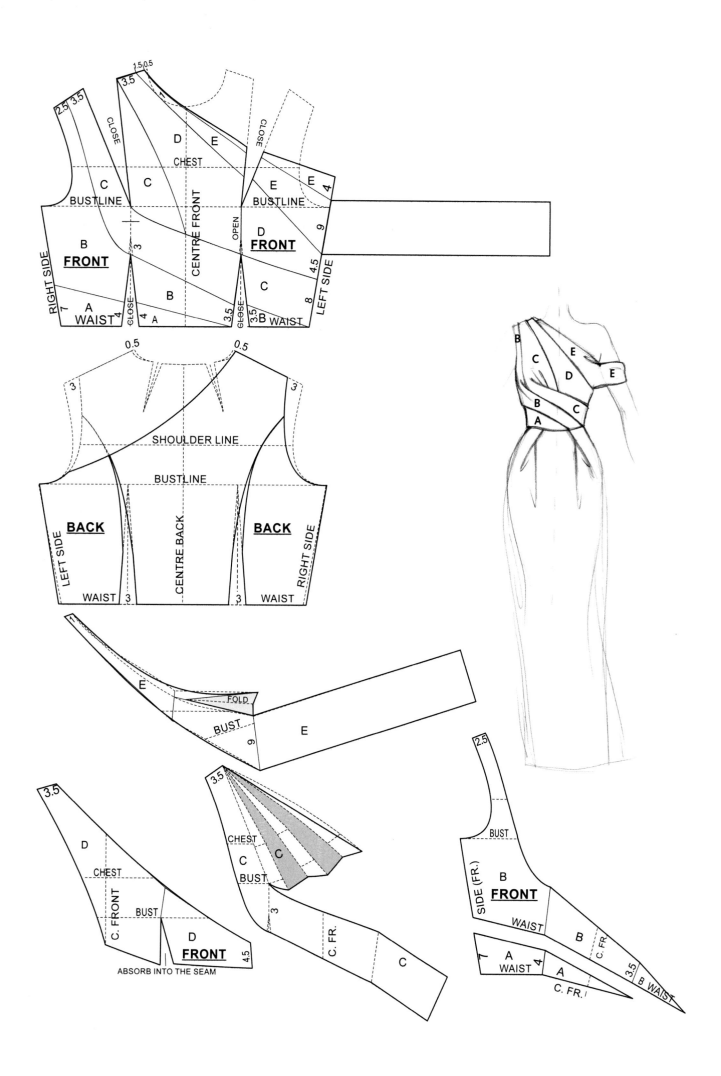

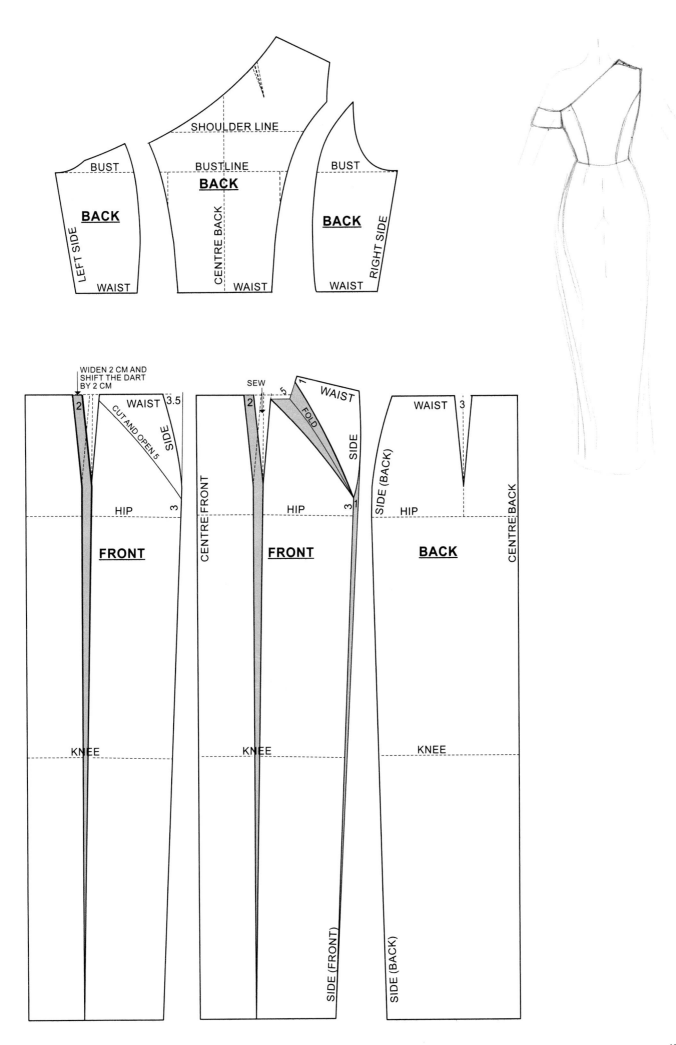

BACK

BUST

BACK

LEFT SIDE

WAIST

SHOULDER LINE

BUSTLINE

BACK

CENTRE BACK

WAIST

BUST

BACK

RIGHT SIDE

WAIST

WIDEN 2 CM AND
SHIFT THE DART
BY 2 CM

2

WAIST

3.5

CUT AND OPEN 5

SIDE

HIP

3

FRONT

KNEE

SEW

2

5

1

WAIST

FOLD

SIDE

CENTRE FRONT

HIP

3

1

FRONT

KNEE

SIDE (FRONT)

WAIST

3

SIDE (BACK)

HIP

BACK

CENTRE BACK

KNEE

SIDE (BACK)

DRESS WITH AN AMPLE BOAT NECKLINE
BUST AND WAIST DARTS SHIFTED TO THE SIDES AND MOTIFS

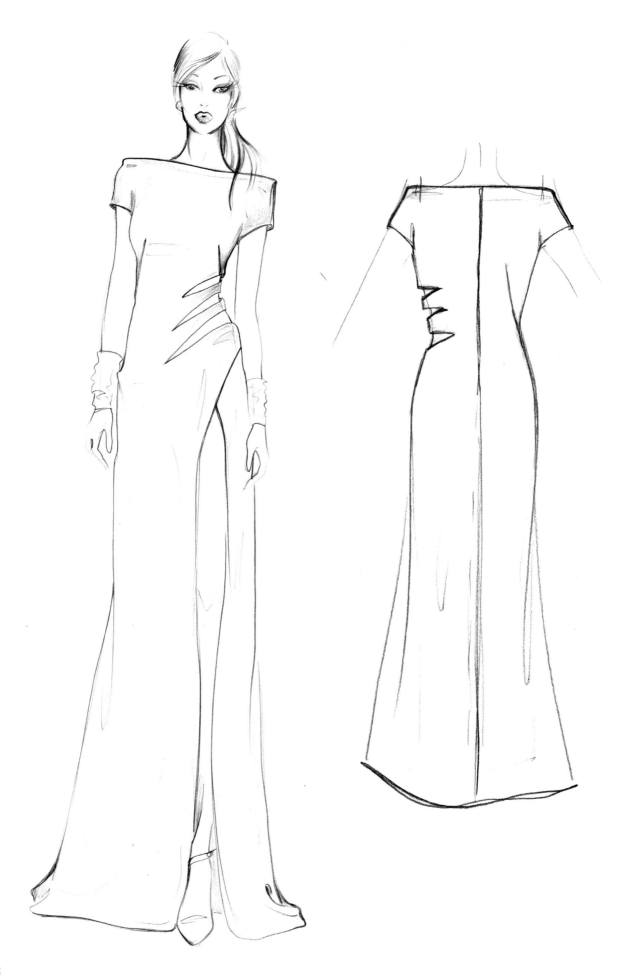

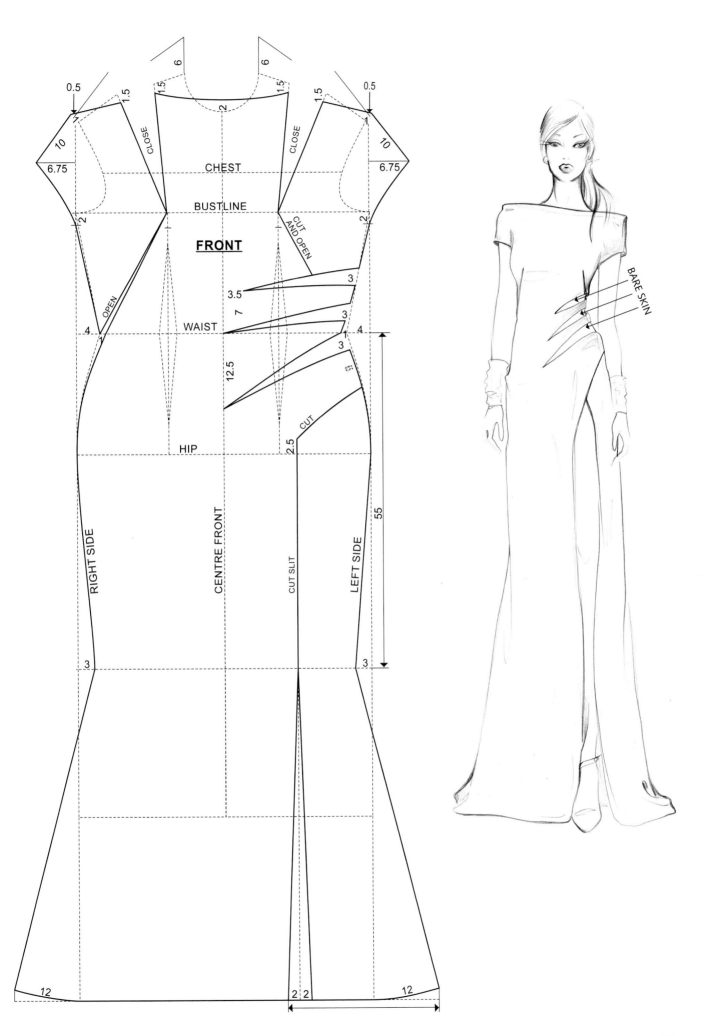

0.5
1.5
6
1.5
1.5
6
1.5
1.5
0.5

10
6.75

CLOSE

CHEST

CLOSE

10
6.75

2

BUSTLINE

CUT AND OPEN

2

FRONT

CUT AND OPEN

3

OPEN

3.5
7

3

WAIST

4

3

4

12.5

3

HIP

2.5

CUT

55

RIGHT SIDE

CENTRE FRONT

CUT SLIT

LEFT SIDE

3

3

12

2 2

12

49

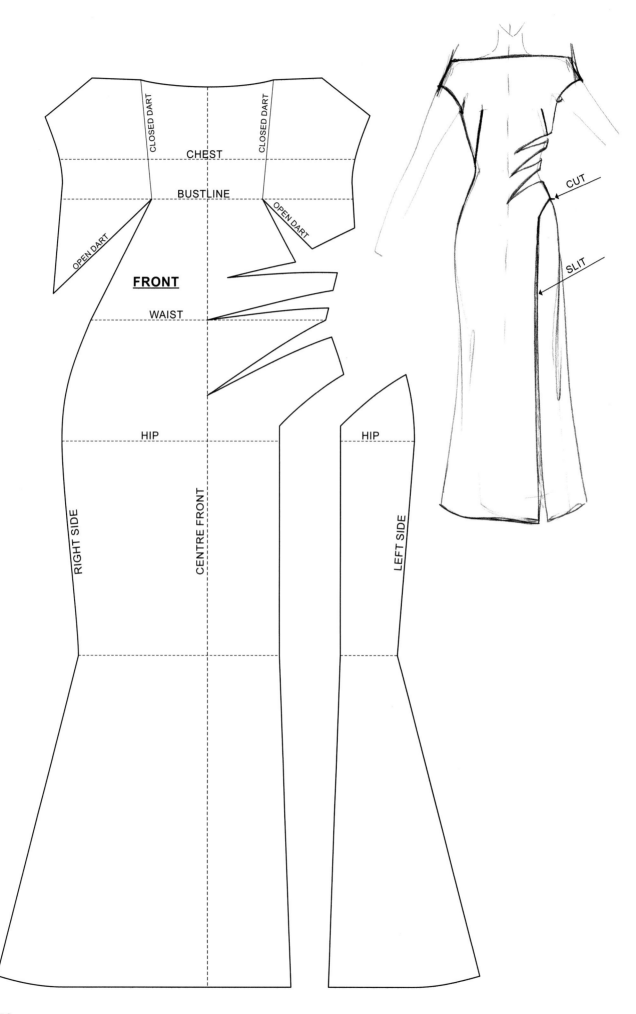

CLOSED DART

CLOSED DART

CHEST

BUSTLINE

OPEN DART

OPEN DART

FRONT

WAIST

HIP

HIP

RIGHT SIDE

CENTRE FRONT

LEFT SIDE

CUT

SLIT

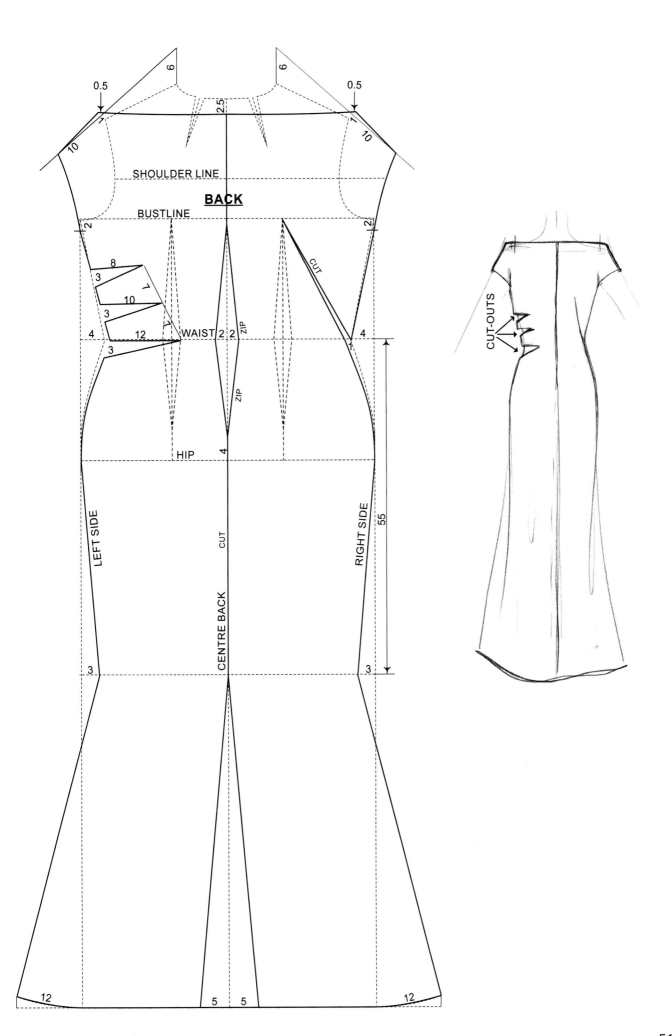

SHOULDER LINE

BACK

BUSTLINE

WAIST

HIP

LEFT SIDE

RIGHT SIDE

CENTRE BACK

ZIP

CUT

CUT-OUTS

0.5

6

2.5

6

0.5

1

10

10

1

2

2

8

3

7

10

3

12

4

2

2

4

3

3

55

4

3

3

12

5

5

12

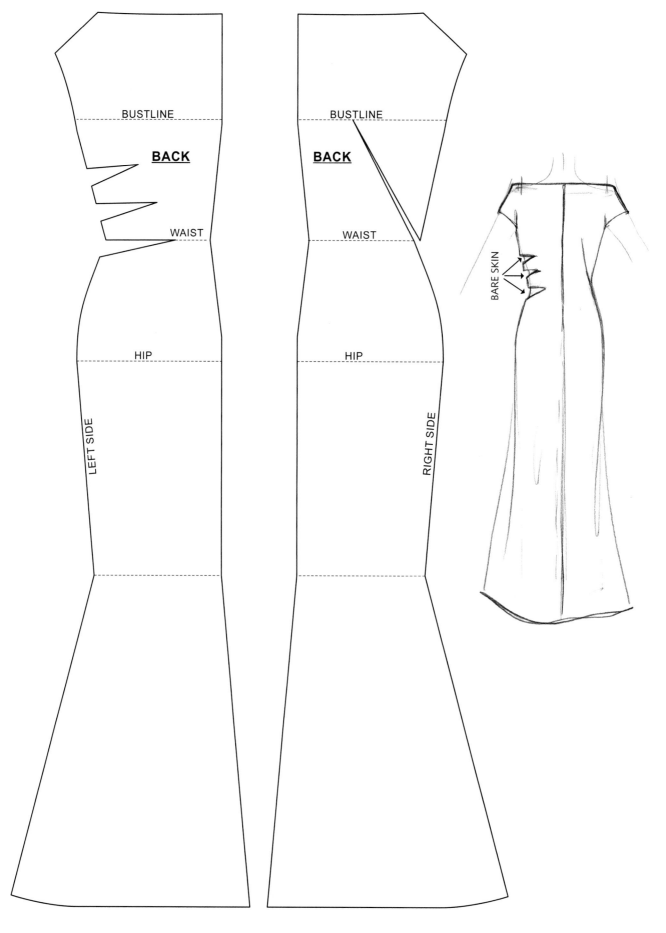

BUSTLINE

BACK

WAIST

HIP

LEFT SIDE

BUSTLINE

BACK

WAIST

HIP

RIGHT SIDE

BARE SKIN

DRESS WITH A YOKE AND FLOUNCE BISHOP SLEEVES
BUST DART MERGED INTO THE SIDES
WAIST DART IN THE MOTIF AND SEAMS

CHEST

BUST LINE

CENTRE FRONT

FRONT

SIDE (FRONT)

6

5

12

6

5

3.5 2 3.5 3.5

3.5 3.5

3.5

5.7

WAIST

8.5

HIP

5 5 6 6 6 6

CUT

CUT

CUT

ELASTIC

5

8

5.5

5

5

CUT AND OPEN 5 CM BELOW

CENTRE FRONT

95

KNEE

CUT

CUT

CUT

7.5 7.5 10 10 10 10

CUT AND OPEN 10 CM AT TOP AND 15 CM BELOW

FLAT MICRO FOLDS

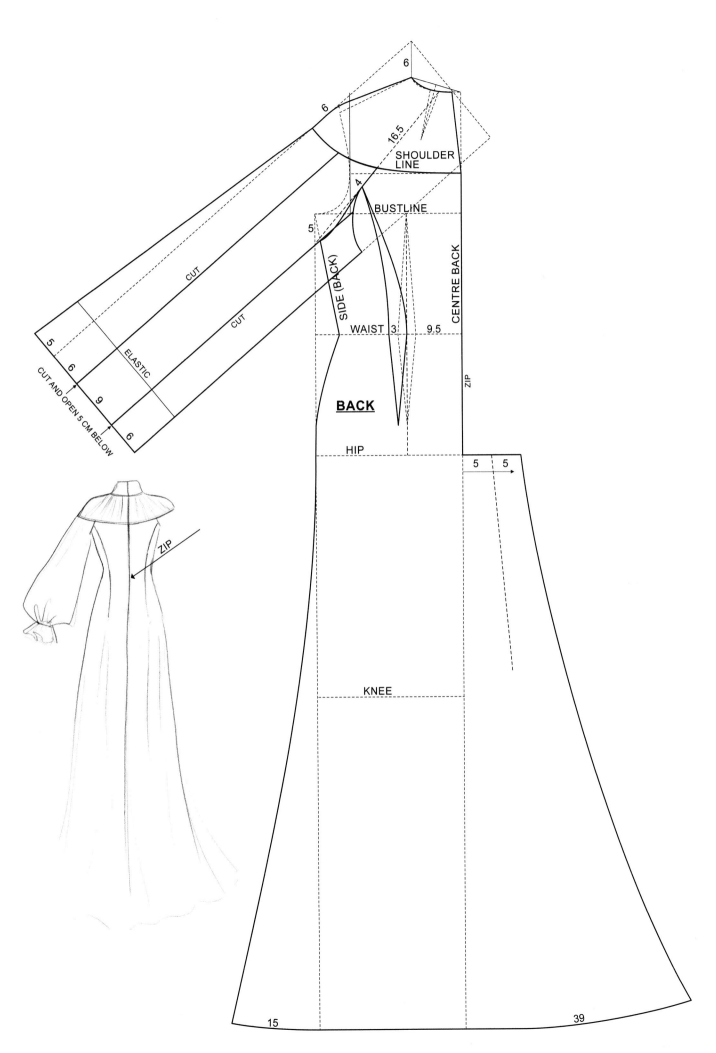

6

6

16.5

SHOULDER
LINE

BUSTLINE

CUT

CUT

4

5

SIDE (BACK)

CENTRE BACK

WAIST 3   9.5

ZIP

5

6

ELASTIC

9

CUT AND OPEN 5 CM BELOW

6

BACK

HIP

5   5

ZIP

KNEE

15

39

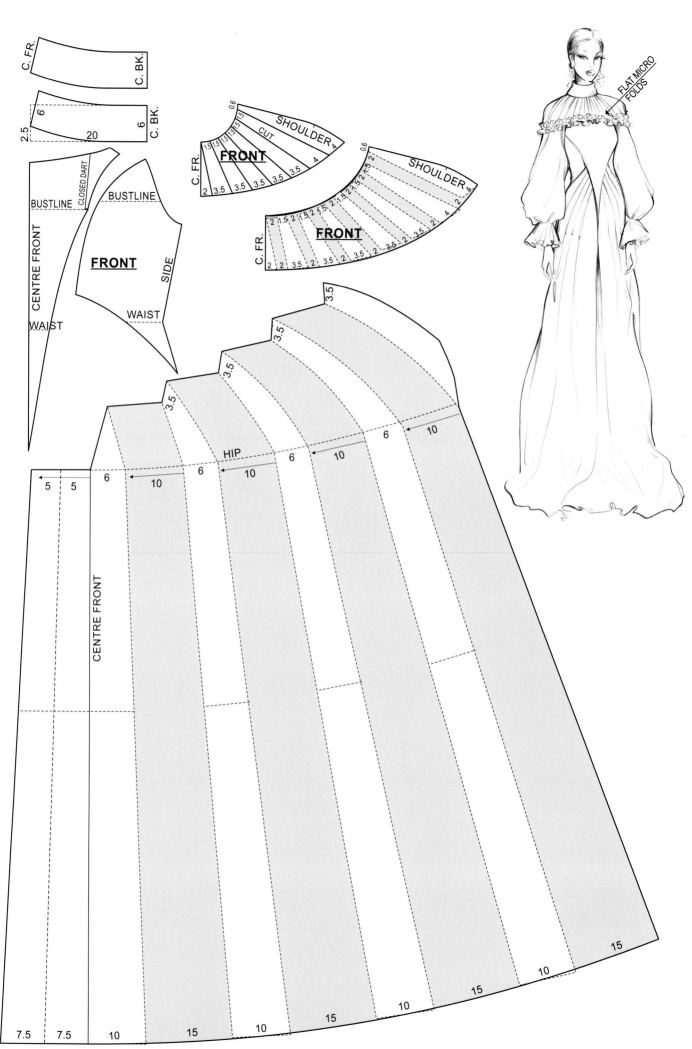

C. FR.

C. BK.

C. BK.

2.5 6 20 6

CLOSED DART

BUSTLINE

BUSTLINE

CENTRE FRONT

FRONT

SIDE

WAIST

WAIST

0.6

SHOULDER

CUT

FRONT

C. FR.

1.5 1.5 1.5 1.5 1.5

2 3.5 3.5 3.5 3.5 4 4

0.6

SHOULDER

FRONT

C. FR.

1.5 1.5 2 2 2 1.5 2 1.5 2

2 1.5 2 1.5 2 1.5 2 1.5 2 3.5 2 4

2 2 3.5 2 3.5 2 3.5 2 4

FLAT MICRO FOLDS

3.5

3.5

3.5

3.5

3.5

6 10

HIP

6 10

6 10

6 10

5 5

CENTRE FRONT

7.5 7.5 10 15 10 15 10 15 10 15

56

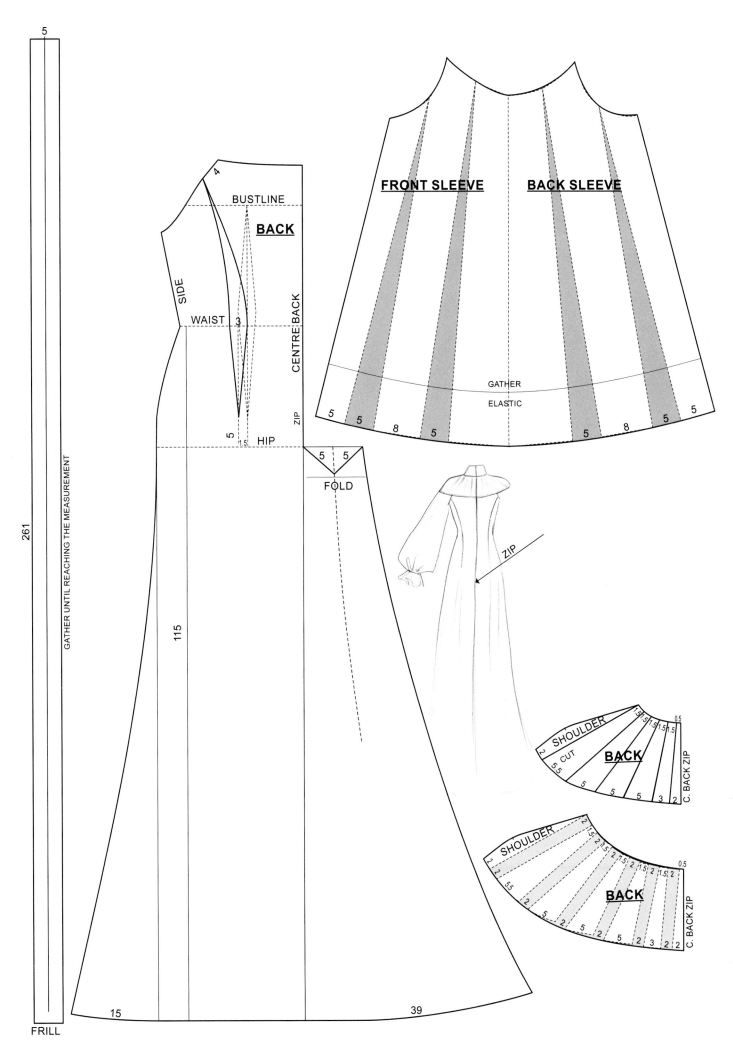

5

261

GATHER UNTIL REACHING THE MEASUREMENT

FRILL

15

115

WAIST 3

SIDE

BUSTLINE

BACK

CENTRE BACK

ZIP

5

1.5

HIP

4

5 5

FOLD

39

FRONT SLEEVE

BACK SLEEVE

GATHER

ELASTIC

5 5 8 5 5 8 5 5

ZIP

SHOULDER

CUT

BACK

C. BACK ZIP

2

5.5

5

5

3

2

1.5 1.5 1.5 1.5

0.5

SHOULDER

BACK

C. BACK ZIP

2

2

5.5

5

2

5

2

2

2.5

2

5

2

1.5 2 1.5

2 1.5 2

2 1.5

3 2 2

2.5

0.5

57

UNIQUE BODICE & TROUSERS SET
BUST DART DISCARDED IN THE MOTIF AND THE SEAMS; WAIST DART

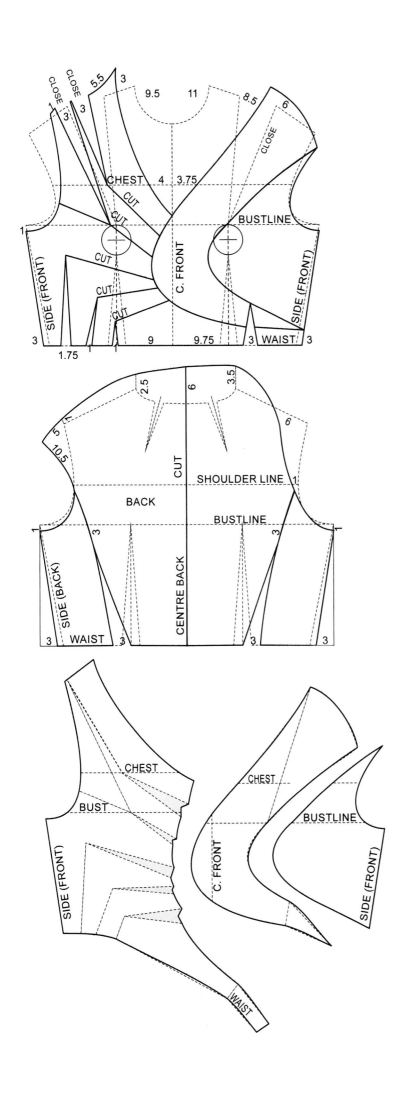

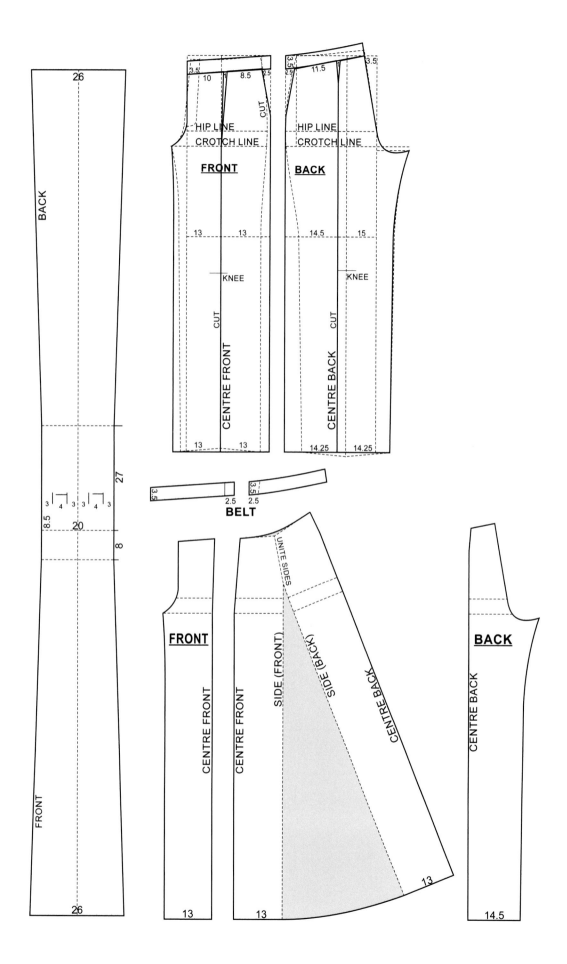

BACK

26

27

3 |4 3 3 |4 3

8.5 20 8

FRONT

26

3.5 10 8.5 2.5

HIP LINE
CROTCH LINE

FRONT

13 13

KNEE

CUT

CENTRE FRONT

13 13

3.5 2.5 11.5 3.5

HIP LINE
CROTCH LINE

BACK

14.5 15

KNEE

CUT

CENTRE BACK

14.25 14.25

3.5 2.5 2.5 3.5

BELT

FRONT

CENTRE FRONT

CENTRE FRONT

13

13

UNITE SIDES

SIDE (FRONT)

SIDE (BACK)

CENTRE BACK

13

BACK

CENTRE BACK

14.5

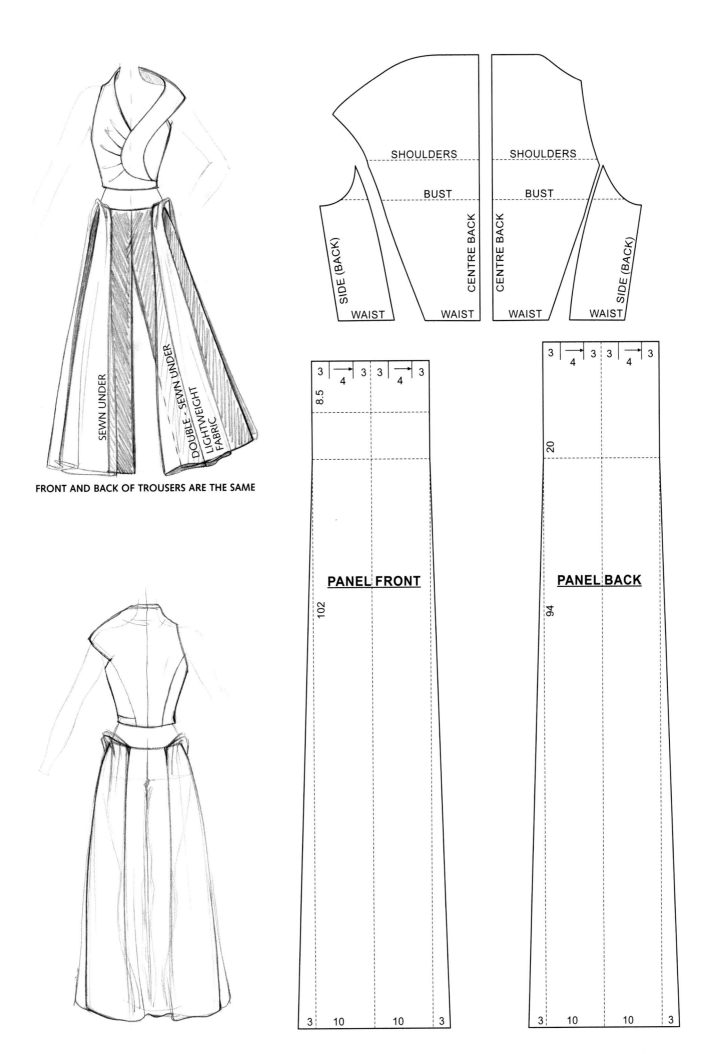

FRONT AND BACK OF TROUSERS ARE THE SAME

SEWN UNDER

DOUBLE - SEWN UNDER

LIGHTWEIGHT FABRIC

SHOULDERS

SHOULDERS

BUST

BUST

SIDE (BACK)

CENTRE BACK

CENTRE BACK

SIDE (BACK)

WAIST

WAIST

WAIST

WAIST

PANEL FRONT

PANEL BACK

3 | 4 | 3 | 3 | 4 | 3

8.5

102

3 | 10 | 10 | 3

3 | 4 | 3 | 3 | 4 | 3

20

94

3 | 10 | 10 | 3

HOODED DRESS WITH A WRAP SKIRT
BUST DARTS SHIFTED TO THE SIDE AND SPLIT IN TWO
WAIST DARTS MERGED INTO THE SEAMS

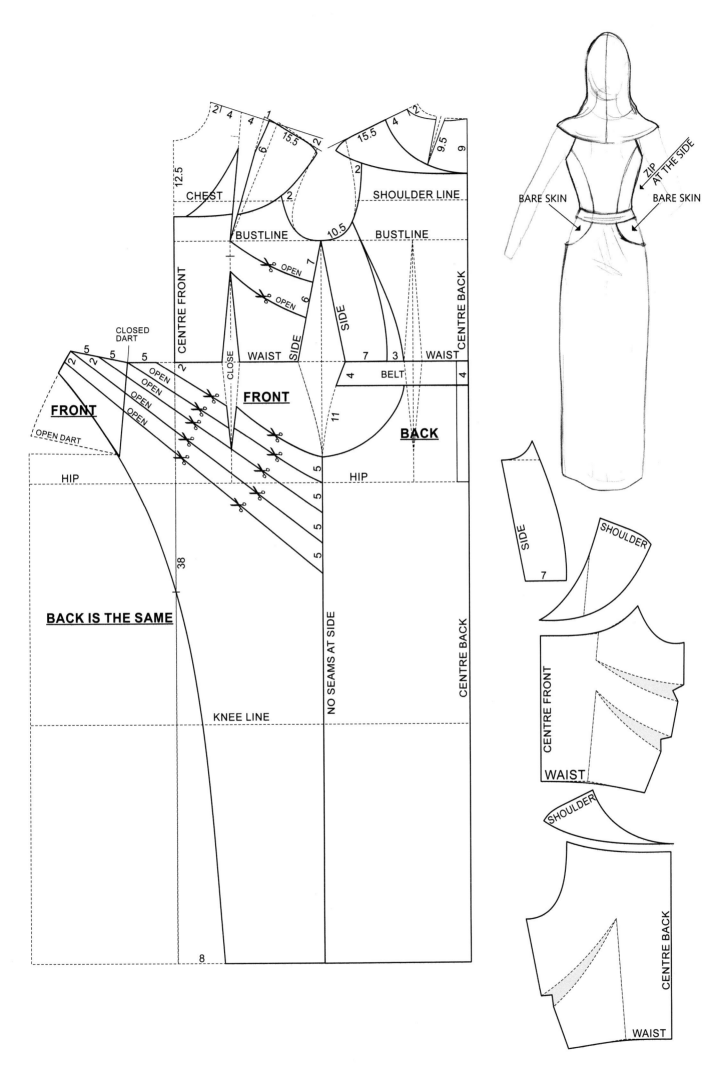

CHEST

SHOULDER LINE

BUSTLINE

BUSTLINE

CENTRE FRONT

CENTRE BACK

OPEN
OPEN

CLOSE

SIDE

SIDE

WAIST

SIDE

WAIST

FRONT

BACK

BELT

CLOSED
DART

FRONT

OPEN
OPEN
OPEN
OPEN

OPEN DART

HIP

HIP

BACK IS THE SAME

NO SEAMS AT SIDE

CENTRE BACK

KNEE LINE

SIDE

SHOULDER

CENTRE FRONT

WAIST

SHOULDER

CENTRE BACK

WAIST

BARE SKIN

BARE SKIN

ZIP AT THE SIDE

12.5

15.5

10.5

15.5

9.5

9

11

38

8

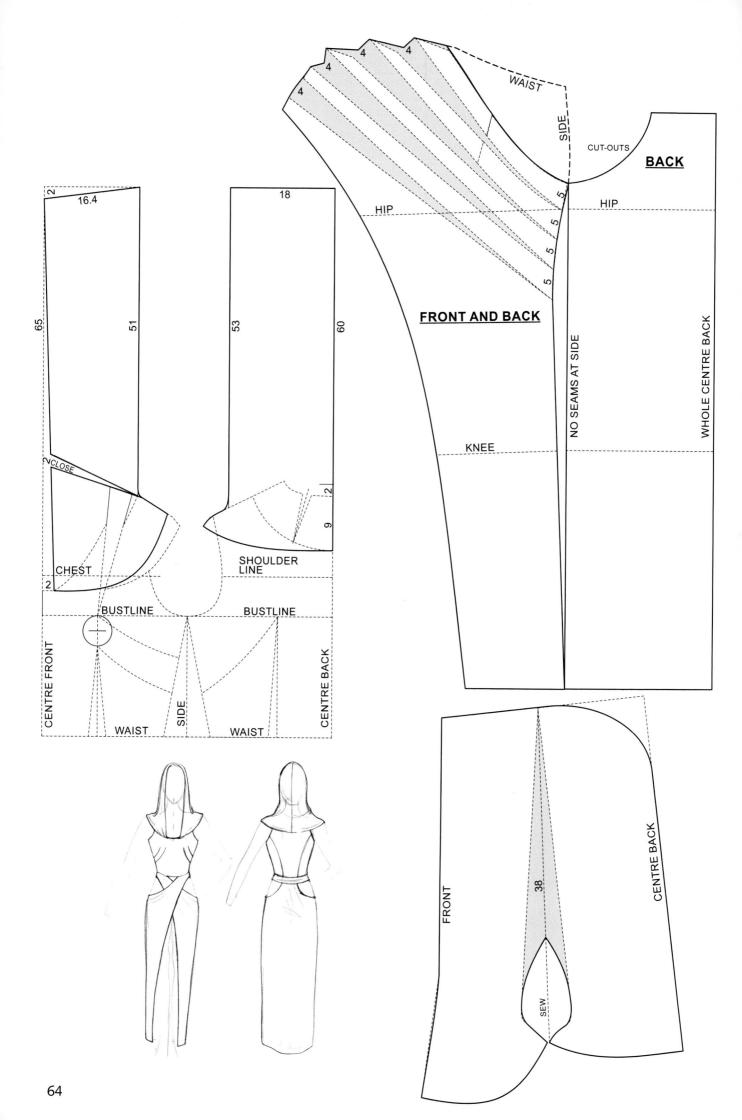

BACK

CUT-OUTS

WAIST

SIDE

FRONT AND BACK

HIP

HIP

4

4

4

5

5

5

5

5

NO SEAMS AT SIDE

WHOLE CENTRE BACK

KNEE

2

16.4

18

65

51

53

60

CLOSE

2

9

2

CHEST

SHOULDER LINE

2

BUSTLINE

BUSTLINE

CENTRE FRONT

CENTRE BACK

WAIST

SIDE

WAIST

FRONT

38

SEW

CENTRE BACK

64

DRESS WITH SLEEVES THAT FORM A CAPE IN THE BACK

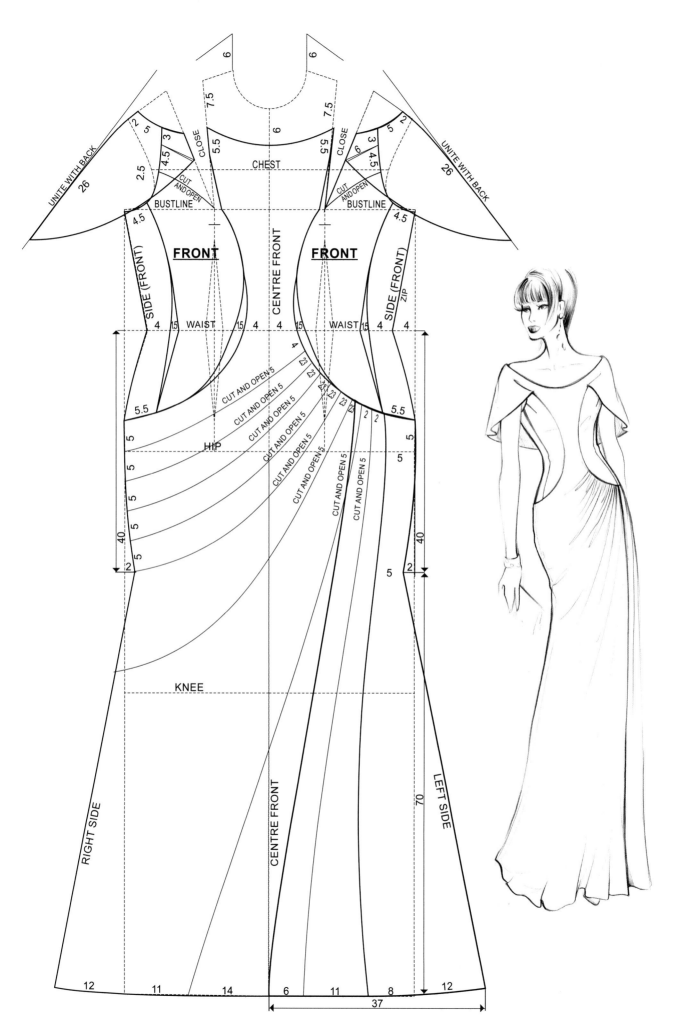

UNITE WITH BACK 26

UNITE WITH BACK 26

2 5 3
2.5
4.5
CLOSE
7.5
6
6
6
7.5
CLOSE
6
4.5
3 5 2

CUT AND OPEN

CUT AND OPEN

CHEST

5.5 5.5

BUSTLINE

BUSTLINE

4.5

4.5

SIDE (FRONT)

FRONT

CENTRE FRONT

FRONT

SIDE (FRONT)

ZIP

4 15 WAIST 15 4

4 15

WAIST 15 4

4

23 23
23 23
23

CUT AND OPEN 5

CUT AND OPEN 5

CUT AND OPEN 5

CUT AND OPEN 5

CUT AND OPEN 5

CUT AND OPEN 5

CUT AND OPEN 5

CUT AND OPEN 5

CUT AND OPEN 5

2 2

5.5

5.5

5

HIP

5

5

5

5

5

5

5

5

5

5

5

40

40

2

2

5

KNEE

RIGHT SIDE

CENTRE FRONT

LEFT SIDE

70

12
11
14
6
11
8
12

37

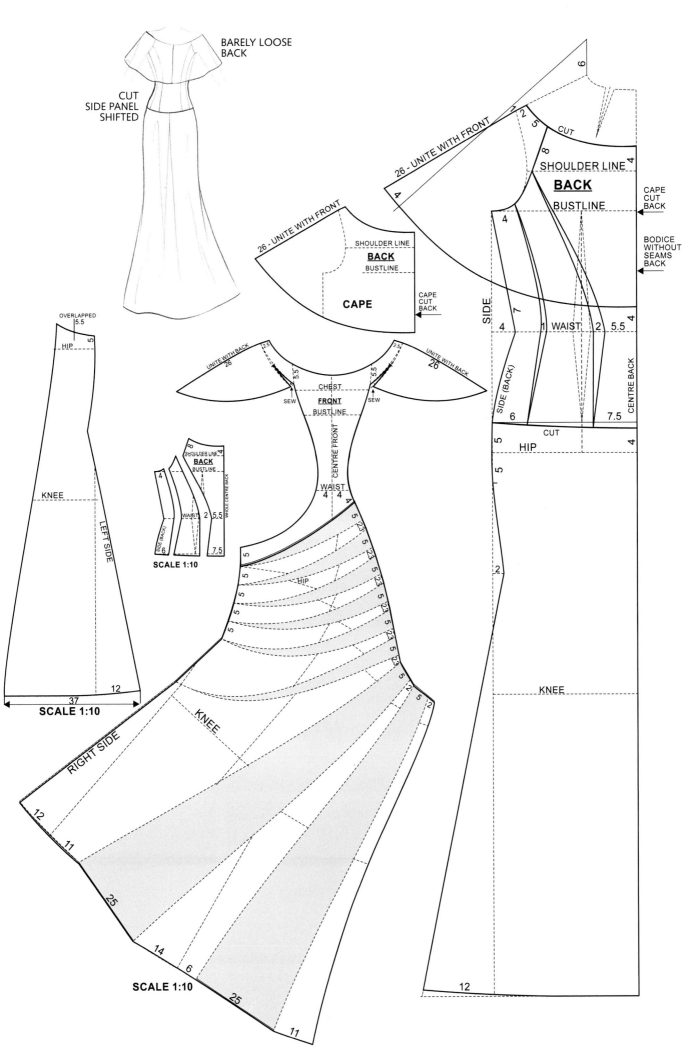

BARELY LOOSE
BACK

CUT
SIDE PANEL
SHIFTED

26 - UNITE WITH FRONT

6

2
5 CUT
8 4
SHOULDER LINE 4

BACK

BUSTLINE

CAPE
CUT
BACK

BODICE
WITHOUT
SEAMS
BACK

4

SIDE

4 7

4 1 WAIST 2 5.5 4

SIDE (BACK)

CENTRE BACK

6 7.5
CUT
5 HIP 4

KNEE

2

26 - UNITE WITH FRONT

4

SHOULDER LINE

BACK

BUSTLINE

CAPE

CAPE
CUT
BACK

OVERLAPPED
5.5
HIP 5

UNITE WITH BACK 26 2.5 2.5 UNITE WITH BACK 26
5.5 5.5
CHEST
SEW **FRONT** SEW
BUSTLINE

CENTRE FRONT

KNEE

8 4
SHOULDER LINE
BACK
BUSTLINE
4
WHOLE CENTRE BACK
WAIST 2 5.5
SIDE (BACK) 6 7.5

SCALE 1:10

WAIST
4 4
4
5
5 23
5
5 5 23
5
5 5 23
5 HIP
5 5 23
5
5 5 23
5
5 5 23
5 KNEE
5
5 23
5 5
5 23
5 12

LEFT SIDE

12
37
SCALE 1:10

RIGHT SIDE

KNEE

12

11

25

14

6

25

11

KNEE

12

SCALE 1:10

67

SEWING WITH JUST ONE THREAD

When sewing sheer fabric on a sewing machine, it's important not to ruin the appearance of the darts or any pleats. To do so, it's necessary to eliminate any knots and back-stitching, obtaining the desired results with just one piece of thread. This technique can be used for any sewing machine: it's always the same no matter the type of machine and the process is repeated for each of the folds or darts.

PROCEDURE

First, thread the machine's bobbin with just one thread. However, the thread has to be inserted backwards: first insert it in the needle, then in the thread-guide and then in the tension discs.
For small pleats:
1) Start by marking the seam lines with chalk, then fold the fabric wrong side to wrong side, making sure the lines match up. Thread the sewing machine and drop the needle in the fabric at the base of the fold.
2) Pull the thread up from the bobbin through the layers of fabric to remove the spool, thread the thread of the bobbin working backwards: needle, thread guides and then tension discs. Pull the thread past the discs

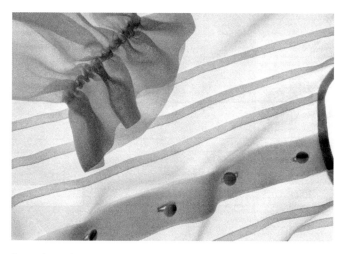

for a length greater than the finished fold: the tension of the machine will control it.
3) Sew the fold and iron it. Repeat the threading and sewing procedure for each small fold.
For darts, repeat the process above: pull the thread from the bobbin up and thread the machine. Sew the dart starting from the apex (fig. 4) and iron as desired.

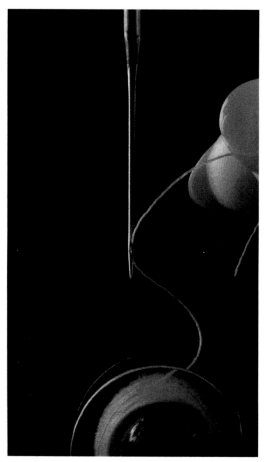

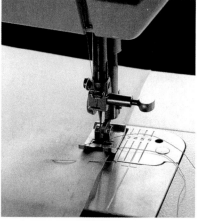

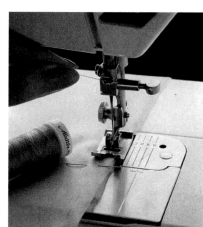

3. THE MAGIC OF DRAPING, FRILLS AND FLOUNCES

Throughout fashion history, trends are repeated though updated for the present, bringing an echo of resonance with the society of the day.
Starting with French fashion in the 1800s up to the 1950s with Dior (and even still today), ruffles, flounces and frills as well as draping cycled in and out of the looks presented by designers, especially in summer collections, becoming a recurrent theme in haute couture and everyday fashion. Women's fashion, starting with high fashion, has always been distinguished by its variety in terms of categories, forms and details.
In the 1950s, Christian Dior created what American journalist Carmel Show coined the 'New Look'.
In this chapter, we'll present styles inspired by French fashion in the late nineteenth century, given a modern twist, in which elegance and luxury are concentrated in unique garments. Draping, frills, flounces and ruffles decorate them to highlight the grace and opulence of the dresses and their femininity, accented by shapes and volumes designed to enhance the body. Though everything tends to return in fashion eventually, there isn't a woman alive who doesn't have at least one garment with these decorative details in her closet.

DRESS WITH A DIAGONAL BODICE FLOUNCE
AND A DOUBLE FLOUNCE ON THE SKIRT WITH A BACK FASTENING

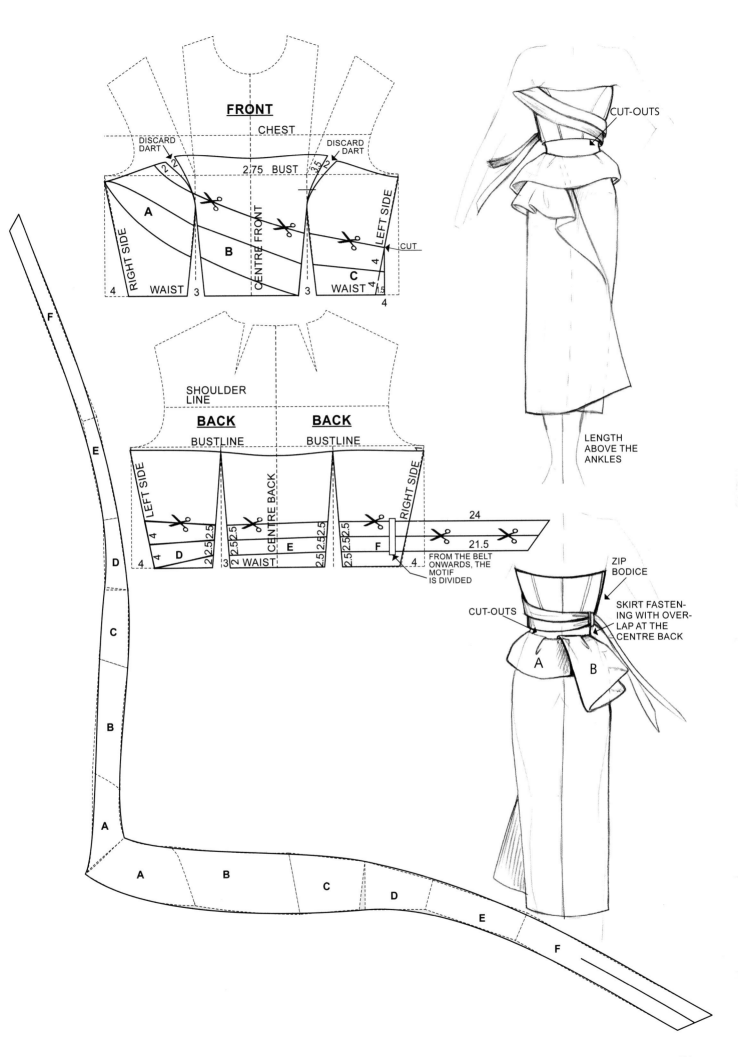

FRONT

CHEST

DISCARD DART

DISCARD DART

2 2   2.75 BUST   3.5 2

A

B

C

RIGHT SIDE

CENTRE FRONT

LEFT SIDE

CUT

4   WAIST   3   3   WAIST   4 1.5

4

SHOULDER LINE

BACK   **BACK**

BUSTLINE   BUSTLINE

LEFT SIDE

CENTRE BACK

RIGHT SIDE

1

D

E

F

4   4   2 2.5 2.5   2.5 2.5 2.5   2.5 2.5 2.5 2.5   24

4   3   2 WAIST   21.5

4

FROM THE BELT ONWARDS, THE MOTIF IS DIVIDED

F

E

D

C

B

A

A   B   C   D   E   F

CUT-OUTS

LENGTH ABOVE THE ANKLES

ZIP BODICE

SKIRT FASTENING WITH OVERLAP AT THE CENTRE BACK

CUT-OUTS

A   B

71

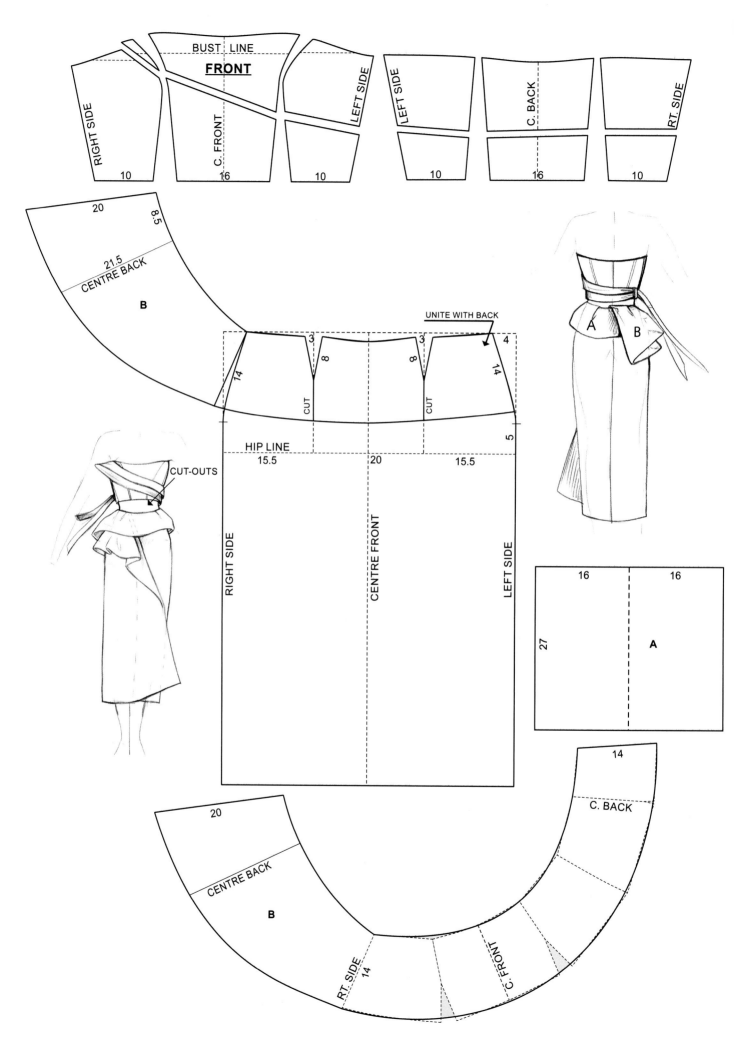

BUST LINE

FRONT

RIGHT SIDE
10

C. FRONT
16

10

LEFT SIDE

LEFT SIDE
10

C. BACK
16

RT. SIDE
10

20   8.5

21.5
CENTRE BACK

B

UNITE WITH BACK

3   3   4

14   8   8   14

CUT   CUT   5

HIP LINE
15.5   20   15.5

RIGHT SIDE   CENTRE FRONT   LEFT SIDE

CUT-OUTS

A   B

16   16

27   A

20
CENTRE BACK
B

14
C. BACK

RT. SIDE
14   C. FRONT

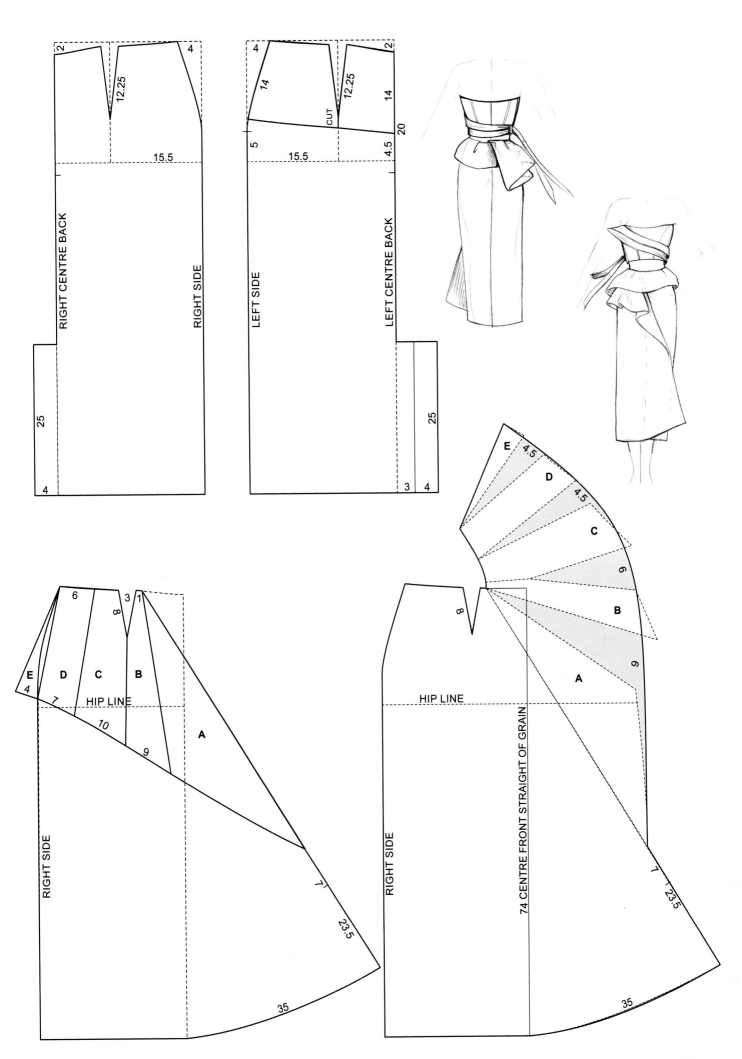

RIGHT CENTRE BACK

2
12.25
4

15.5

RIGHT SIDE

25
4

LEFT SIDE

4
14
14
12.25
2
CUT
5
15.5
4.5
20

LEFT CENTRE BACK

25
3 4

6 3 1
8
E D C B
4 7
HIP LINE
10
9
A

RIGHT SIDE

7
23.5
35

E 4.5
D 4.5
C
6
B
9
8
A
9

HIP LINE

RIGHT SIDE

74 CENTRE FRONT STRAIGHT OF GRAIN

7 23.5
35

DRESS WITH FLOUNCES AND SHEER FABRIC
ON THE BODICE AND SKIRT

SHEER FABRIC

SEAMS

SHEER FABRIC

SHEER FABRIC

LINING UNDER

LINING UNDER

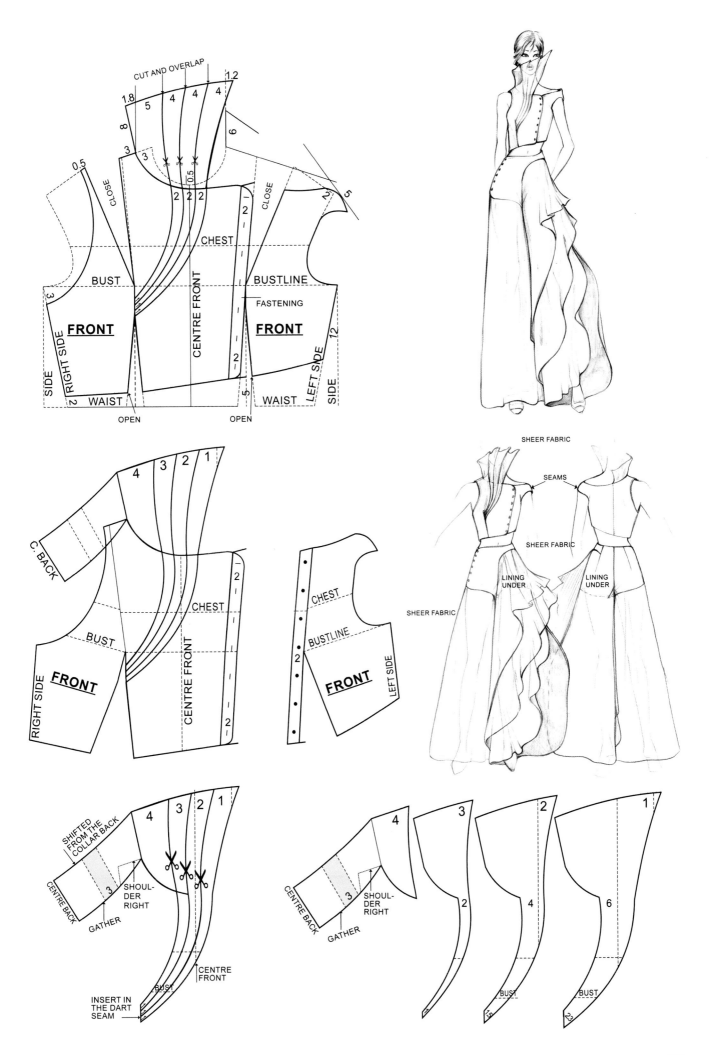

CUT AND OVERLAP

1.8   5   4   4   4   1.2

∞   6

3   3   0.5

0.5

CLOSE   CLOSE

2   2   2   2   5

CHEST

BUST   BUSTLINE

3   FASTENING

FRONT   CENTRE FRONT   **FRONT**

RIGHT SIDE   2   LEFT SIDE   12

SIDE   SIDE

2   WAIST   5   WAIST

OPEN   OPEN

4   3   2   1

C. BACK

CHEST   2

CHEST

BUST   BUSTLINE

RIGHT SIDE   **FRONT**   CENTRE FRONT   2   **FRONT**   LEFT SIDE

2

SHEER FABRIC

SEAMS

SHEER FABRIC

LINING UNDER   LINING UNDER

SHEER FABRIC

SHIFTED FROM THE COLLAR BACK   4   3   2   1

CENTRE BACK   3   SHOULDER RIGHT

GATHER   CENTRE FRONT

BUST

INSERT IN THE DART SEAM

4   3   2   1

CENTRE BACK   3   SHOULDER RIGHT

GATHER   2   4   6

BUST   BUST

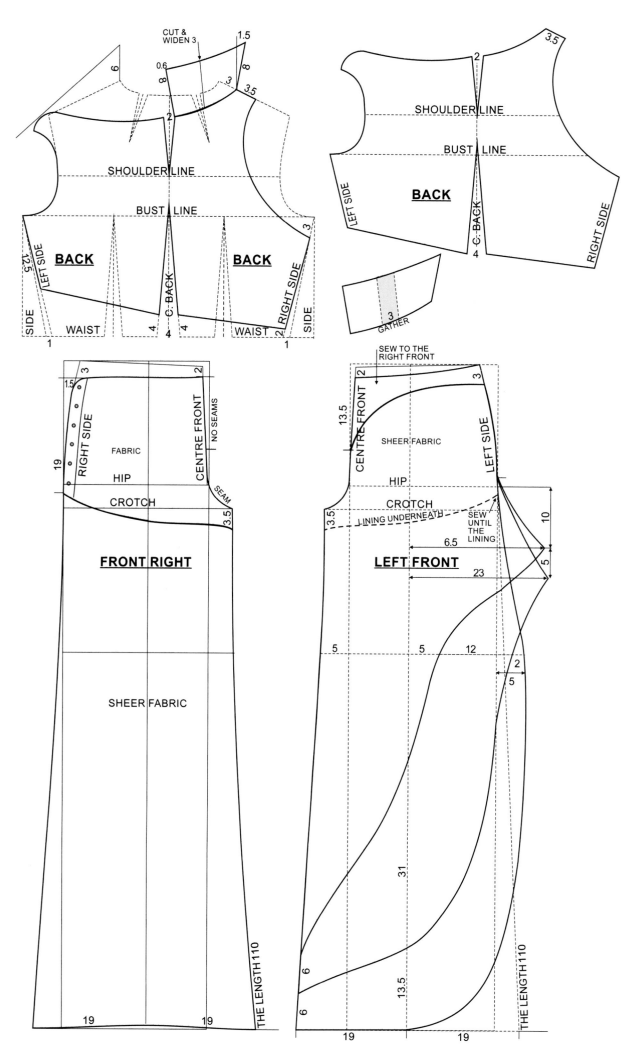

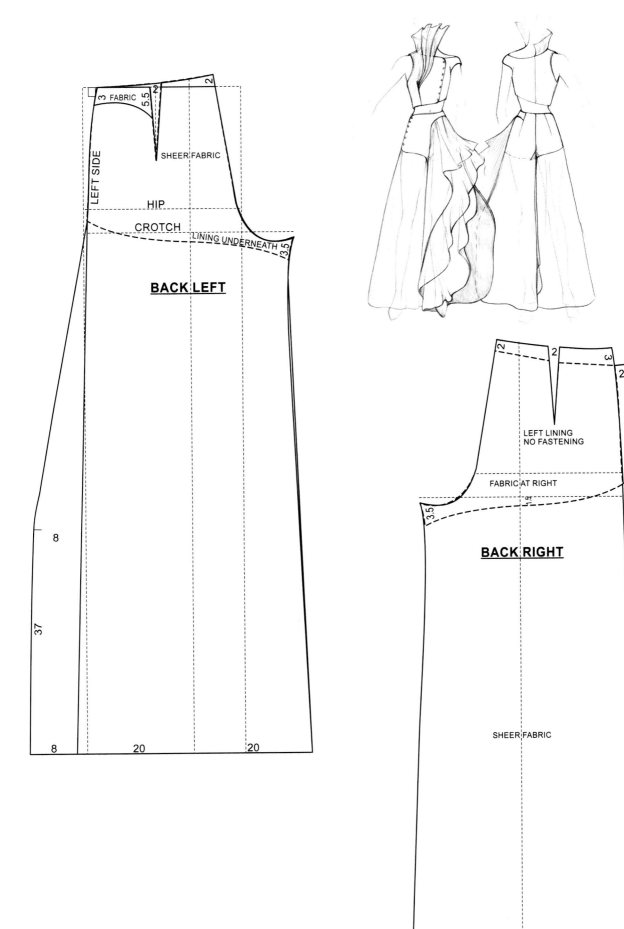

BACK LEFT

3 FABRIC

5.5

2

2

SHEER FABRIC

LEFT SIDE

HIP

CROTCH

LINING UNDERNEATH

3.5

8

37

8

20

20

BACK RIGHT

2

2

3

2

FASTENING

LEFT LINING
NO FASTENING

FABRIC AT RIGHT

2

3.5

SHEER FABRIC

40

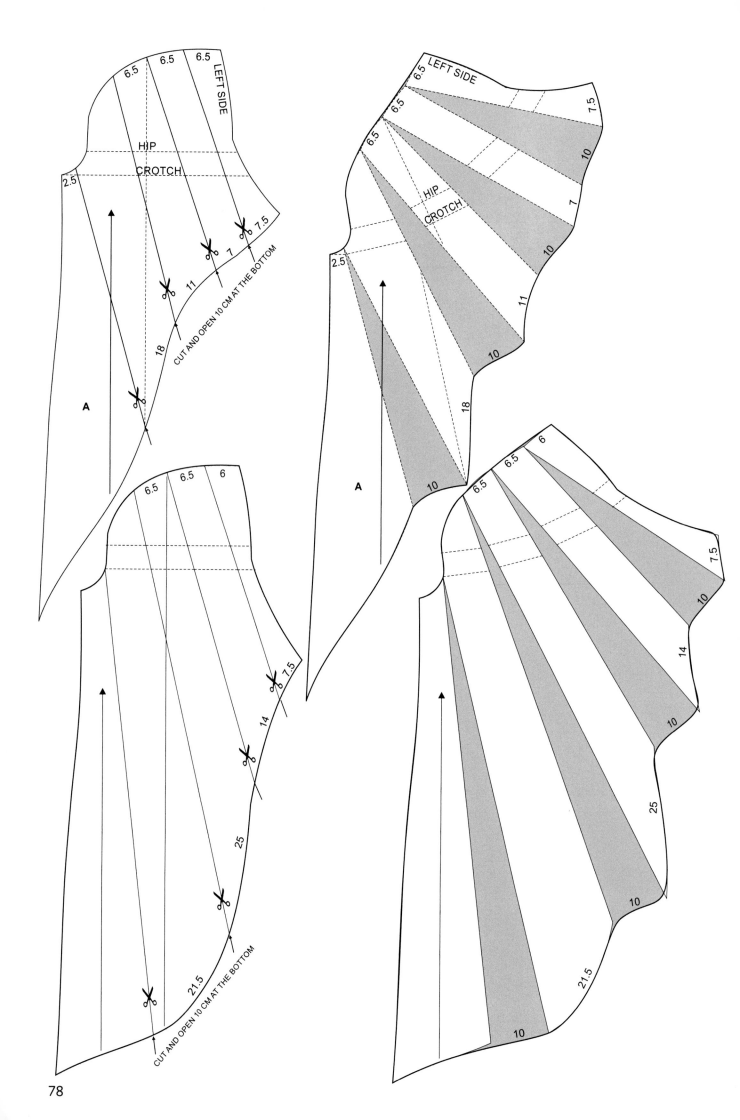

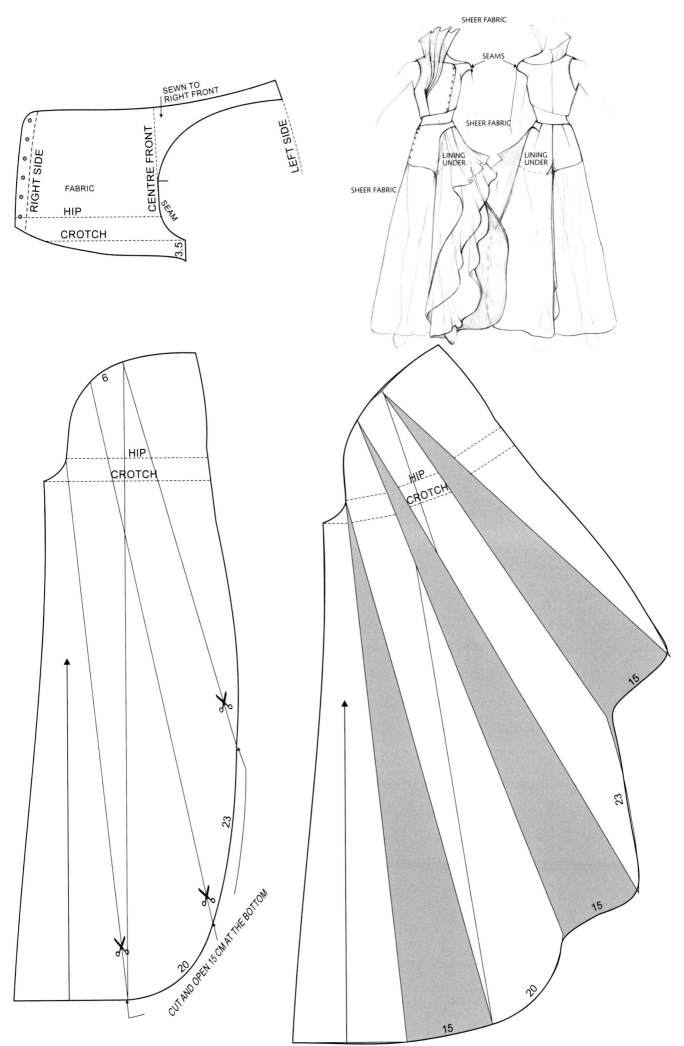

RIGHT SIDE

FABRIC

HIP

CROTCH

CENTRE FRONT

SEAM

SEWN TO
RIGHT FRONT

LEFT SIDE

3.5

SHEER FABRIC

SEAMS

SHEER FABRIC

LINING
UNDER

LINING
UNDER

SHEER FABRIC

6

HIP

CROTCH

23

20

CUT AND OPEN 15 CM AT THE BOTTOM

HIP

CROTCH

15

23

20

15

15

FLOWING DRESS WITH A WAIST FLOUNCE AND HEM INSERTS

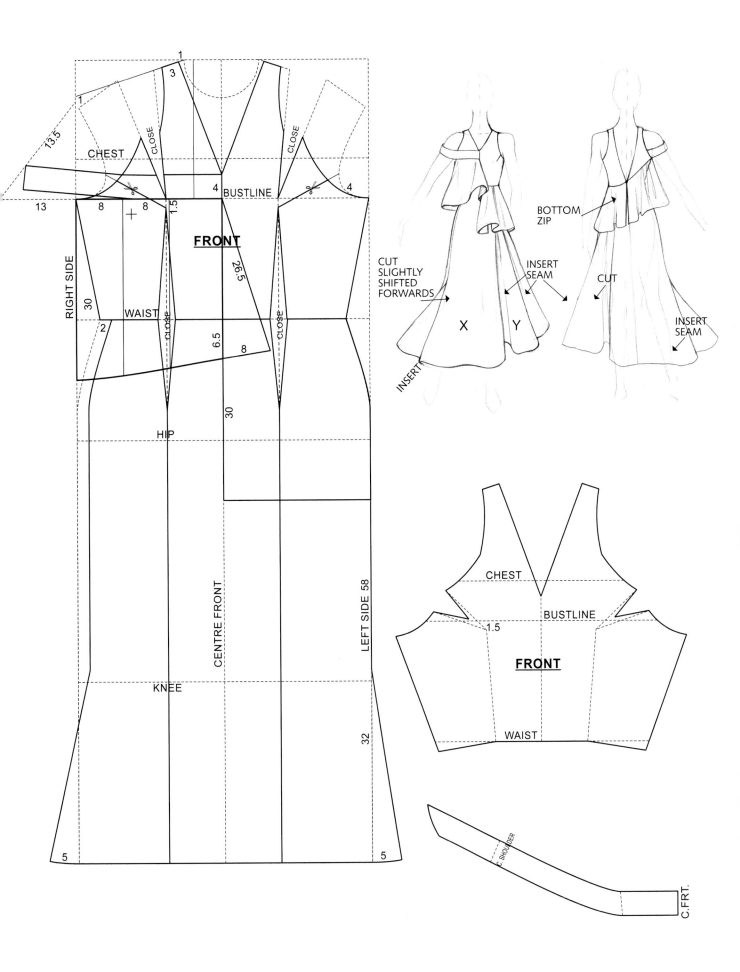

CHEST

13.5

CLOSE

CLOSE

13

CHEST

BUSTLINE

8

8

1.5

4

4

FRONT

RIGHT SIDE

30

26.5

2

WAIST

CLOSE

6.5

8

CLOSE

30

HIP

CENTRE FRONT

LEFT SIDE 58

KNEE

32

5

5

CUT
SLIGHTLY
SHIFTED
FORWARDS

BOTTOM
ZIP

INSERT
SEAM

CUT

X   Y

INSERT

INSERT
SEAM

CHEST

BUSTLINE

1.5

FRONT

WAIST

C. SHOULDER

C. FRT.

BACK

SHOULDER LINE

BUSTLINE

WAIST

HIP

ZIP

CENTRE BACK

LEFT SIDE 58

RIGHT SIDE

KNEE

32

SHOULDER LINE

BUSTLINE

WAIST

BUSTLINE

RIGHT SIDE

WAIST

CENTRE FRONT

CENTRE BACK

CENTRE BACK

CENTRE BACK

RIGHT SIDE

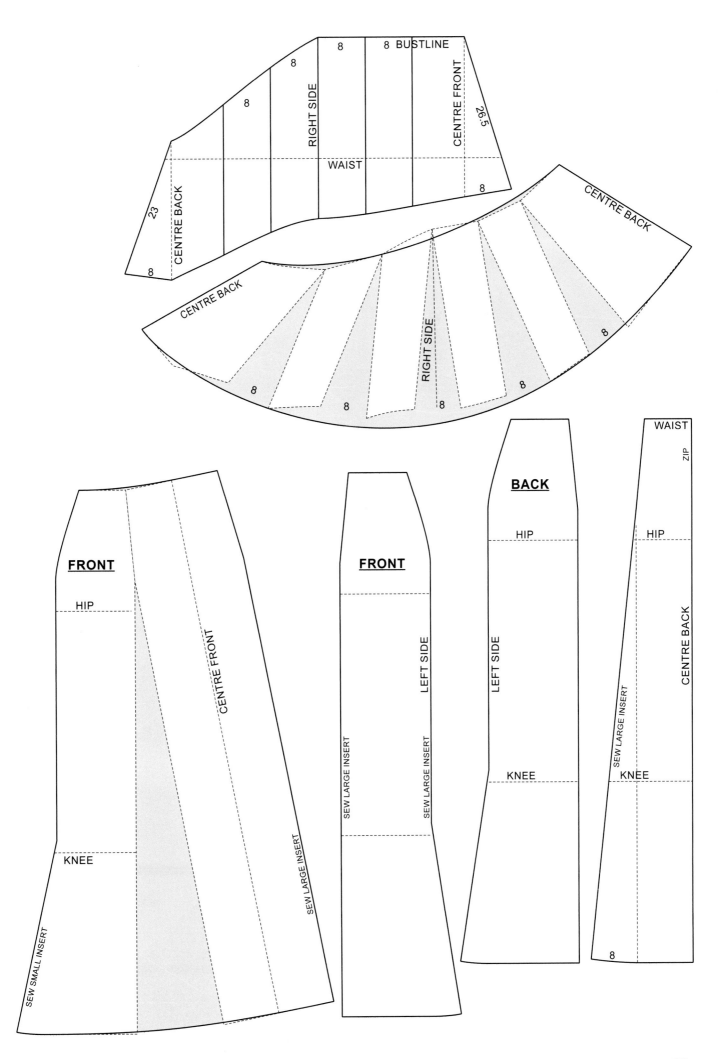

83

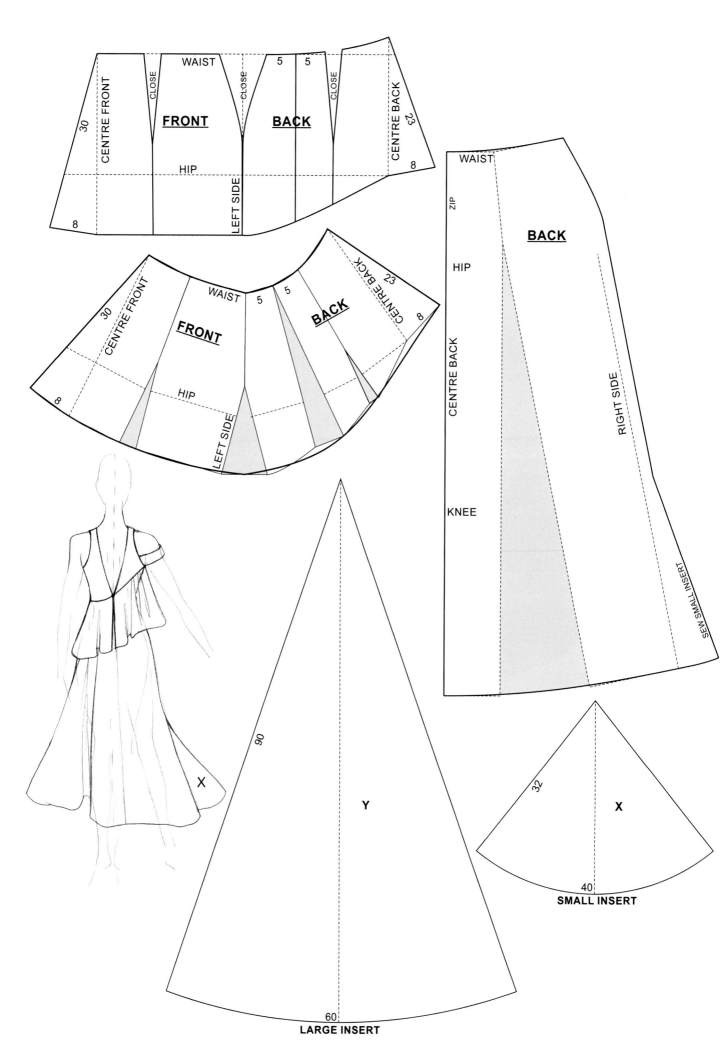

WAIST

CLOSE

30

CENTRE FRONT

FRONT

CLOSE

5 5

BACK

CLOSE

CENTRE BACK

23

HIP

LEFT SIDE

8

8

30

CENTRE FRONT

WAIST

FRONT

5 5

BACK

CENTRE BACK

23

8

8

HIP

LEFT SIDE

WAIST

ZIP

HIP

BACK

CENTRE BACK

RIGHT SIDE

KNEE

SEW SMALL INSERT

X

90

Y

60

LARGE INSERT

32

X

40

SMALL INSERT

DRESS WITH A FLOUNCE ON THE SHOULDER,
HIP AND HEM

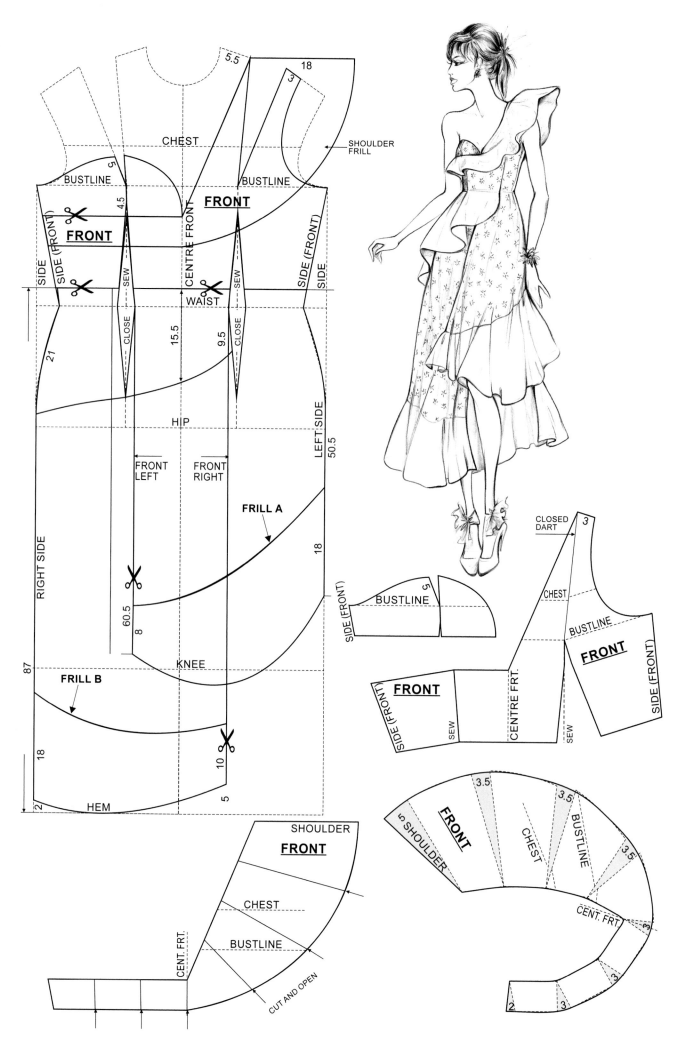

CHEST

5.5

18

3

SHOULDER
FRILL

BUSTLINE

FRONT

BUSTLINE

FRONT

SIDE

SIDE (FRONT)

FRONT

4.5

5

CENTRE FRONT

SEW

CLOSE

SEW

CLOSE

SIDE (FRONT)

SIDE

WAIST

SIDE

21

15.5

9.5

LEFT SIDE

50.5

HIP

FRONT
LEFT

FRONT
RIGHT

FRILL A

RIGHT SIDE

60.5

8

18

KNEE

87

FRILL B

BUSTLINE

5

SIDE (FRONT)

18

10

FRONT

FRONT

CLOSED
DART

3

CHEST

BUSTLINE

2

5

HEM

SIDE (FRONT)

SEW

CENTRE FRT.

SEW

FRONT

SIDE (FRONT)

SHOULDER

FRONT

CHEST

BUSTLINE

CENT. FRT.

CUT AND OPEN

3.5

3.5

FRONT

5 SHOULDER

CHEST

BUSTLINE

3.5

3.5

CENT. FRT

3

2

3

3

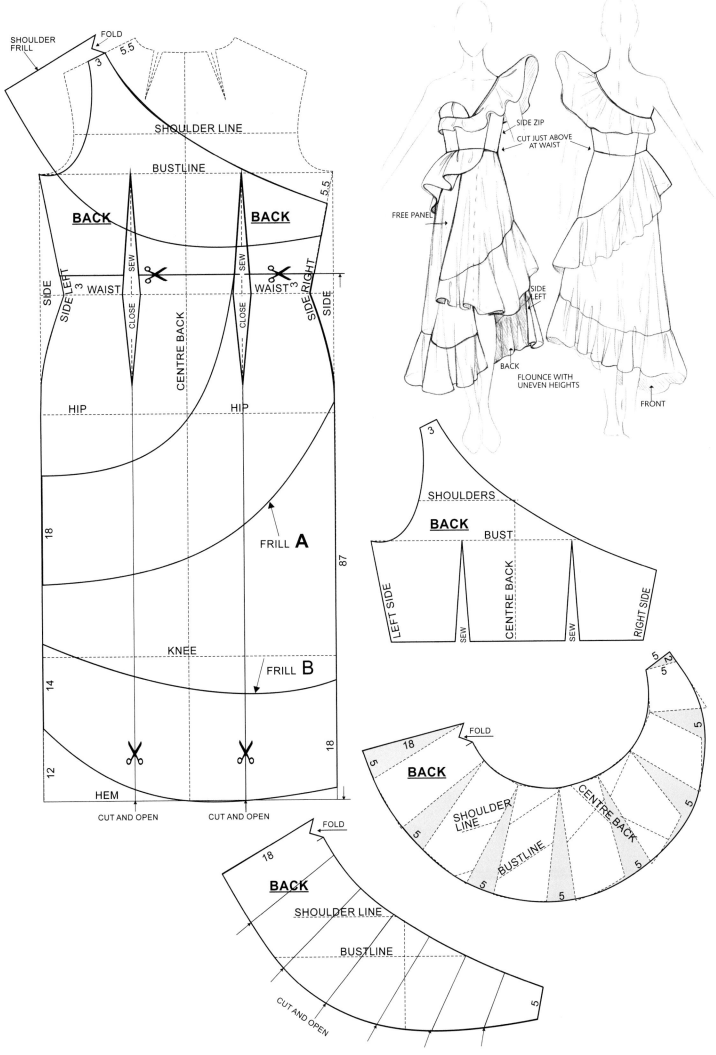

SHOULDER FRILL

FOLD

3   5.5

SHOULDER LINE

BUSTLINE

BACK   **BACK**

5.5

SIDE LEFT

SIDE

SEW   CLOSE

3   WAIST   WAIST   3

SEW   CLOSE

CENTRE BACK

SIDE RIGHT

SIDE

HIP   HIP

18

87

FRILL **A**

14

KNEE

FRILL **B**

18

12

HEM

CUT AND OPEN   CUT AND OPEN

SIDE ZIP

CUT JUST ABOVE AT WAIST

FREE PANEL

SIDE LEFT

BACK

FLOUNCE WITH UNEVEN HEIGHTS

FRONT

3

SHOULDERS

BACK

BUST

LEFT SIDE   SEW   CENTRE BACK   SEW   RIGHT SIDE

5   2
5

18

FOLD

5

BACK

5   SHOULDER LINE   CENTRE BACK

5   BUSTLINE   5

5   5

5

5

FOLD

18

BACK

SHOULDER LINE

BUSTLINE

CUT AND OPEN

5

SCALE 1:10

BACK

FRILL A

FRILL B

FRILL A

FRILL A

FRILL A

FRILL B

FREE PANEL

88

LARGE FLOUNCE-MOTIF ON THE FRONT
FROM THE SHOULDER TO THE CALF
FOR THIS GARMENT WITH A BALLOON SKIRT

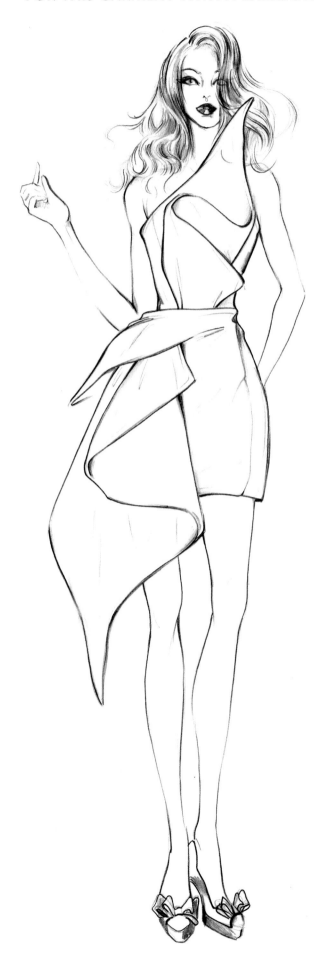

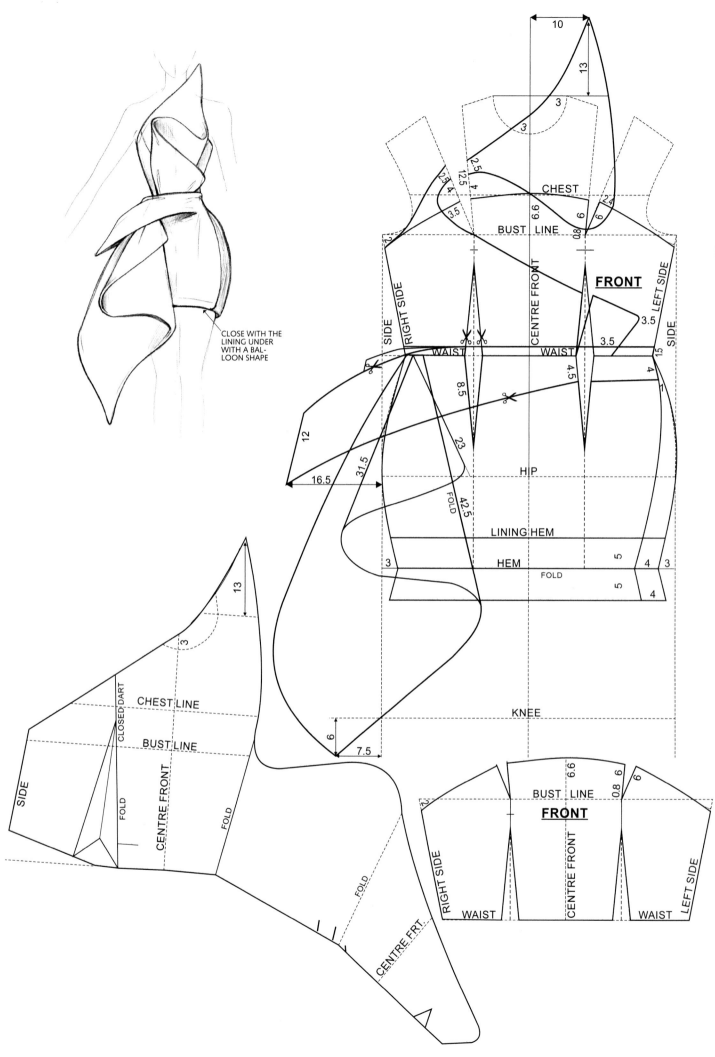

CLOSE WITH THE
LINING UNDER
WITH A BAL-
LOON SHAPE

10

13

3

3

2.5

12.5

4

CHEST

2.4

2.3

4

6.6

6

6

3.5

BUST LINE

0.8

2

CENTRE FRONT

FRONT

RIGHT SIDE

LEFT SIDE

SIDE

SIDE

3.5

3.5

WAIST

WAIST

1.5

8.5

4.5

4

12

23

1

16.5

31.5

HIP

FOLD

42.5

LINING HEM

3

HEM

5

4

3

FOLD

5

4

KNEE

6

7.5

13

3

CHEST LINE

BUST LINE

SIDE

CLOSED DART

CENTRE FRONT

FOLD

FOLD

FOLD

CENTRE FRT.

6.6

6

6

BUST LINE

0.8

2

FRONT

RIGHT SIDE

CENTRE FRONT

LEFT SIDE

WAIST

WAIST

90

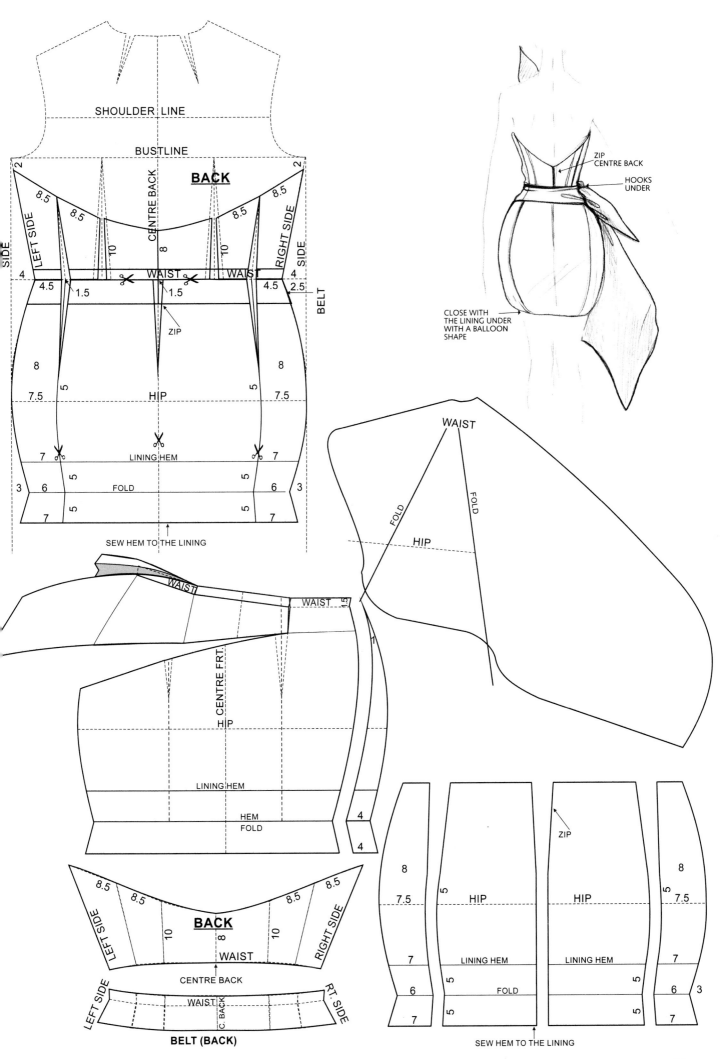

SHOULDER LINE

BUSTLINE

BACK

CENTRE BACK

LEFT SIDE

RIGHT SIDE

SIDE

SIDE

2

8.5

8.5

8.5

8.5

10

8

10

2

4

4.5

WAIST

WAIST

4

4.5

1.5

1.5

ZIP

BELT

2.5

8

5

5

8

7.5

HIP

7.5

7

LINING HEM

7

3   6

FOLD

6   3

7

5

5

7

SEW HEM TO THE LINING

ZIP
CENTRE BACK

HOOKS
UNDER

CLOSE WITH
THE LINING UNDER
WITH A BALLOON
SHAPE

WAIST

WAIST

CENTRE FRT.

HIP

FOLD

FOLD

WAIST

HIP

LINING HEM

HEM
FOLD

4

4

ZIP

8.5

8.5

8.5

8.5

BACK

LEFT SIDE

RIGHT SIDE

10

8

10

WAIST

CENTRE BACK

LEFT SIDE

RT. SIDE

WAIST

C. BACK

BELT (BACK)

8

5

HIP

HIP

5

8

7.5

7.5

7

LINING HEM

LINING HEM

7

6

5

FOLD

5

6   3

7

5

5

7

SEW HEM TO THE LINING

91

DRESS WITH A TRIPLE COLLAR AND PLEATED PANEL SKIRT

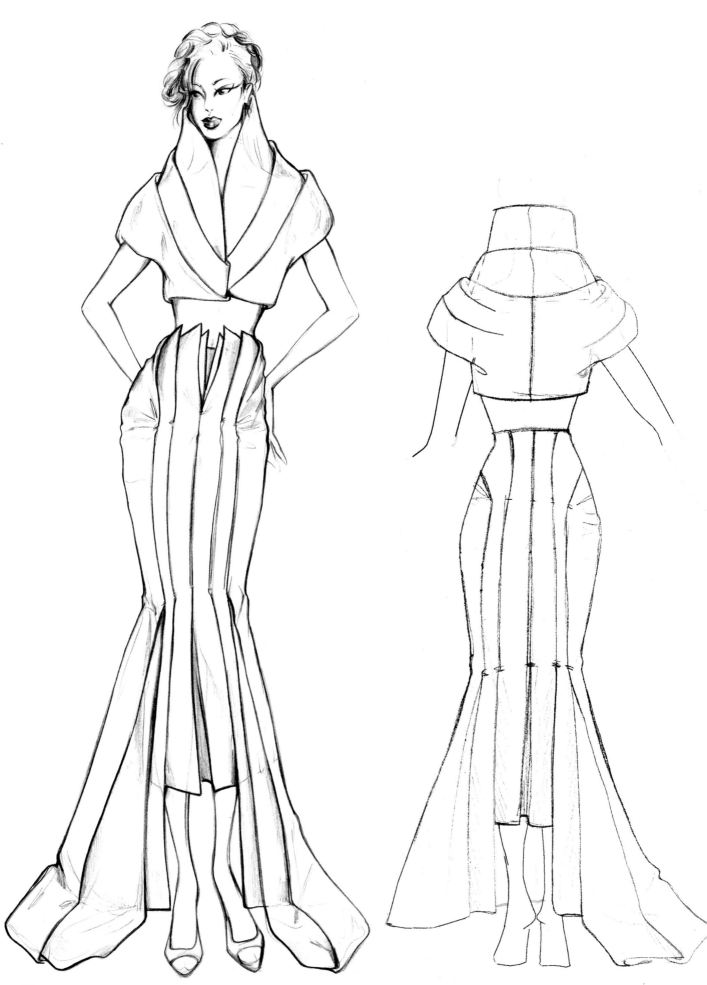

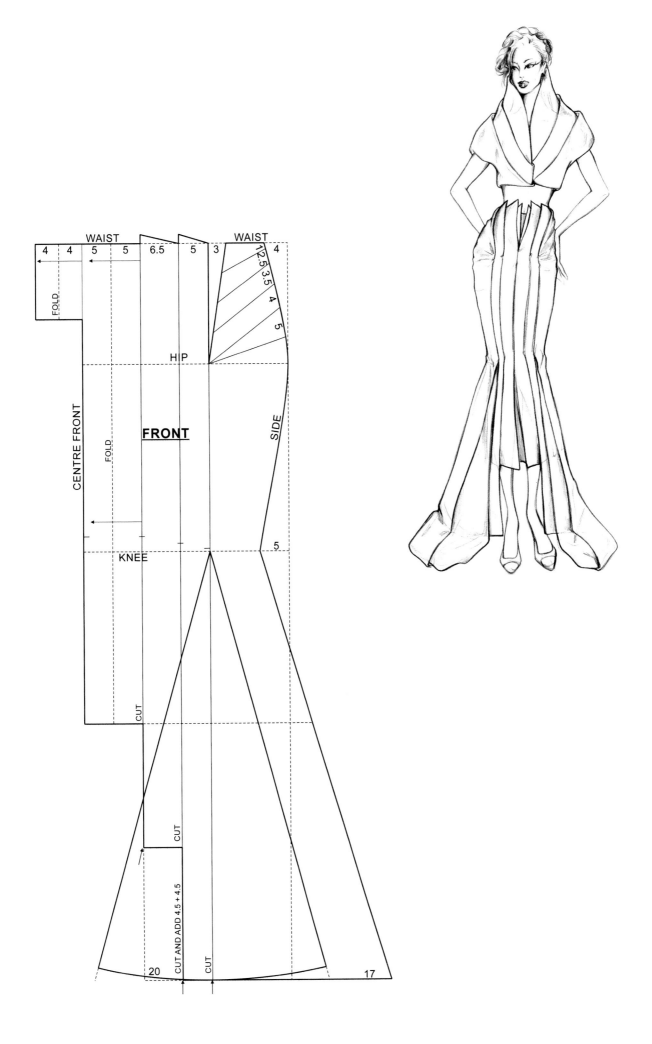

WAIST

4 | 4 | 5 | 5 | 6.5 | 5 | 3 | WAIST | 4

FOLD

CENTRE FRONT

FOLD

FRONT

HIP

12.5 | 3.5 | 4 | 5

SIDE

KNEE

5

CUT

CUT

CUT AND ADD 4.5 + 4.5

CUT

20

17

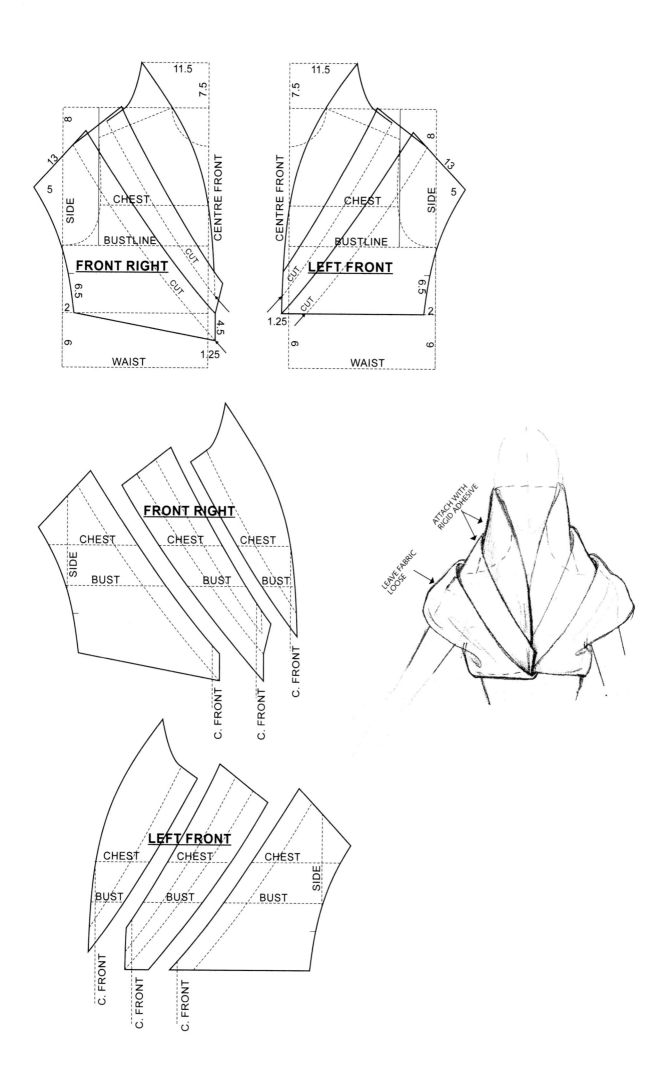

FRONT RIGHT

LEFT FRONT

FRONT RIGHT

LEFT FRONT

FRONT

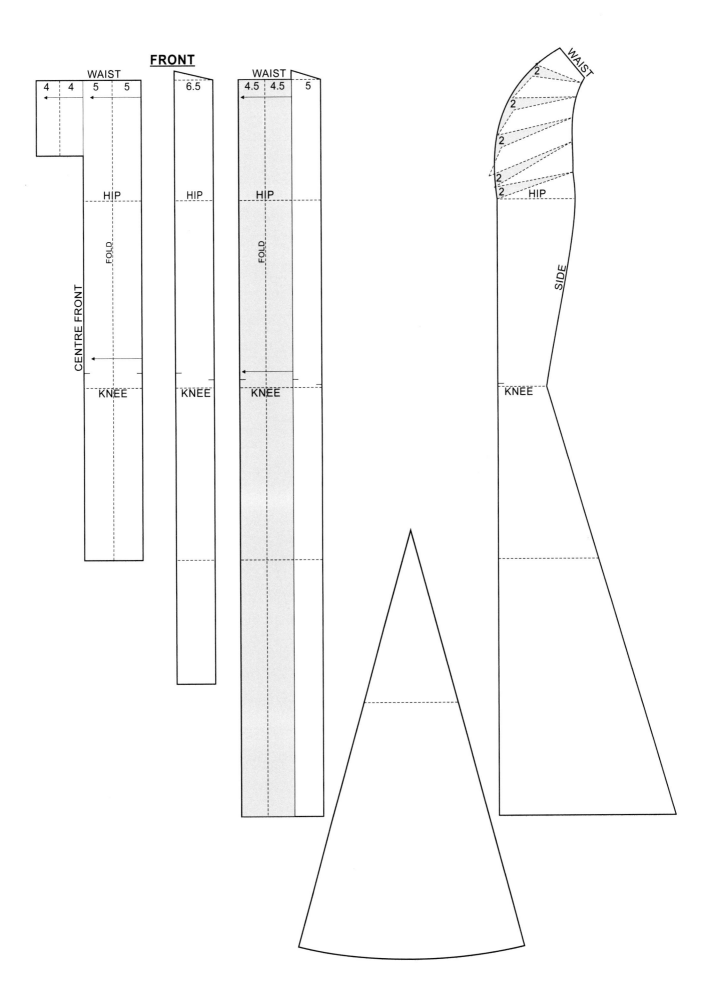

WAIST

4 | 4 | 5 | 5

CENTRE FRONT

HIP

FOLD

KNEE

6.5

HIP

FOLD

KNEE

WAIST

4.5 | 4.5 | 5

HIP

FOLD

KNEE

WAIST

2
2
2
2
2

HIP

SIDE

KNEE

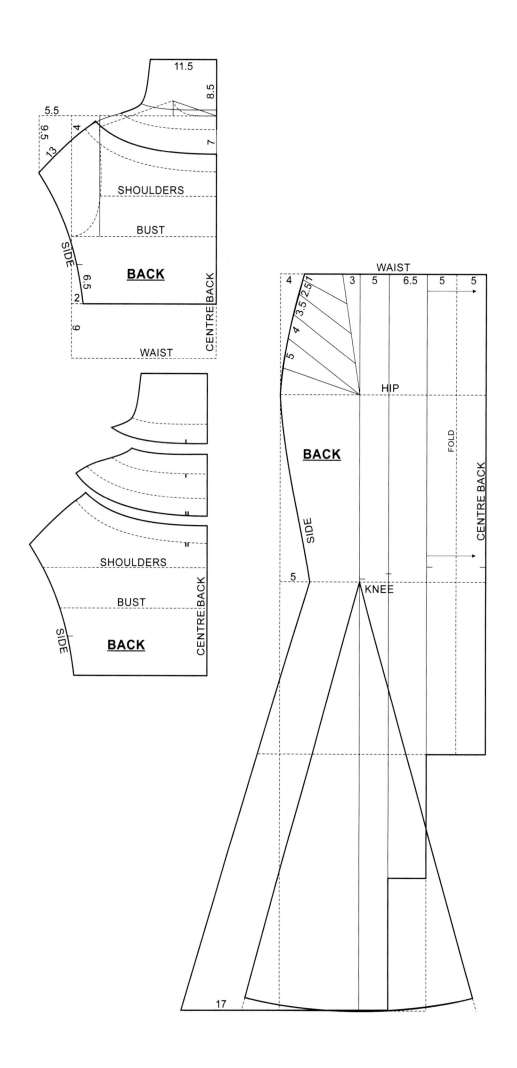

BACK

SHOULDERS

BUST

CENTRE BACK

SIDE

WAIST

11.5

8.5

5.5

9.5

13

4

7

6.5

2

9

BACK

SHOULDERS

BUST

CENTRE BACK

SIDE

SIDE

WAIST

BACK

SIDE

HIP

KNEE

FOLD

CENTRE BACK

4

2.5 1

3.5

4

5

3

5

6.5

5

5

5

17

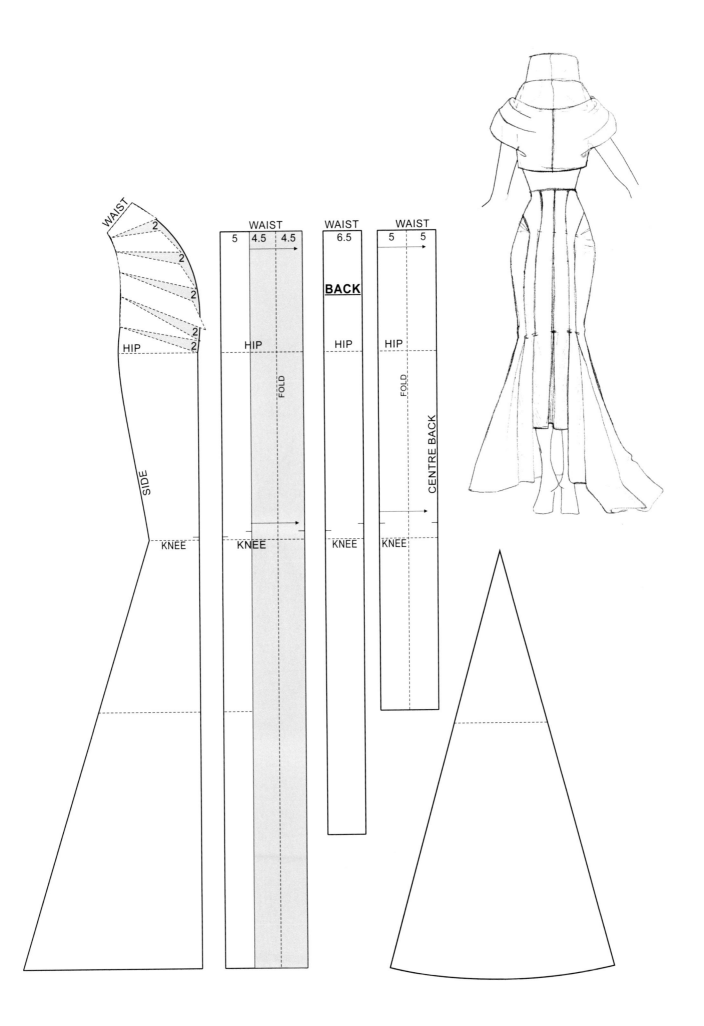

WAIST

2
2
2
2
2
2

HIP

SIDE

KNEE

WAIST

5 | 4.5 | 4.5

HIP

FOLD

KNEE

WAIST

6.5

BACK

HIP

KNEE

WAIST

5 | 5

HIP

FOLD

CENTRE BACK

KNEE

DRAPED DRESS WITH TWISTED PIECES

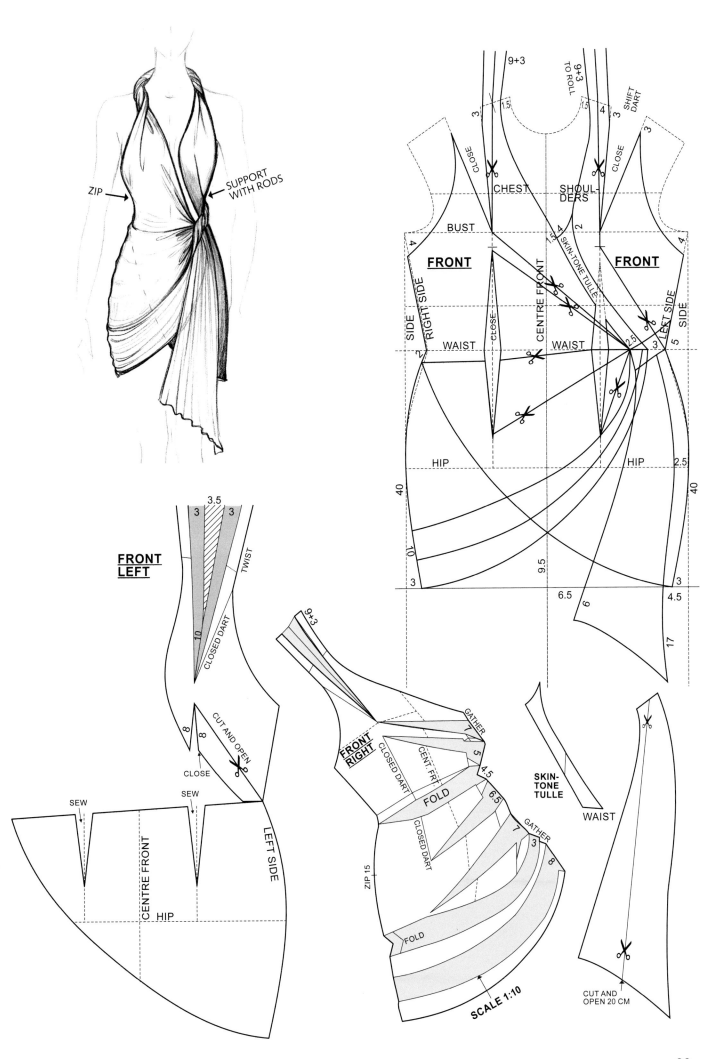

ZIP

SUPPORT WITH RODS

9+3

9+3
TO ROLL

3

1.5

1.5

4

SHIFT DART

3

CLOSE

CLOSE

CHEST

SHOUL-DERS

BUST

4

4

1.5

4

2

SKIN-TONE TULLE

FRONT

FRONT

SIDE

RIGHT SIDE

CLOSE

CENTRE FRONT

LEFT SIDE

SIDE

WAIST

WAIST

2

2.5

3

5

HIP

HIP

2.5

40

40

10

9.5

3

3

6.5

9

4.5

17

FRONT LEFT

3.5

3

3

10

TWIST

CLOSED DART

8

8

CUT AND OPEN

CLOSE

SEW

SEW

CENTRE FRONT

LEFT SIDE

HIP

9+3

FRONT RIGHT

CLOSED DART

CENT. FRT.

FOLD

CLOSED DART

GATHER

5

4.5

6.5

7

3

8

GATHER

ZIP 15

FOLD

SKIN-TONE TULLE

WAIST

CUT AND OPEN 20 CM

SCALE 1:10

99

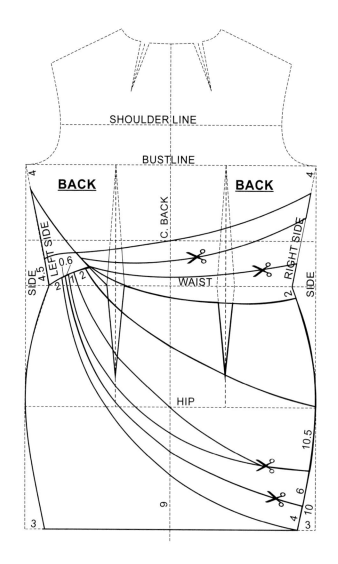

SHOULDER LINE

BUSTLINE

BACK C. BACK **BACK**

LEFT SIDE 0.6 RIGHT SIDE

SIDE 4.5 2 1 2

WAIST

SIDE

HIP

10.5

9 6

4 3 10

3 3

ZIP

BUSTLINE

BACK CENTRE BACK **BACK**

LEFT SIDE 0.6 RIGHT SIDE

SIDE 4.5 2 1 2

WAIST

SIDE

HIP

10.5

9 6

4 3 10

3 3

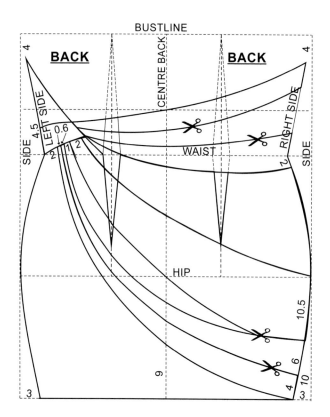

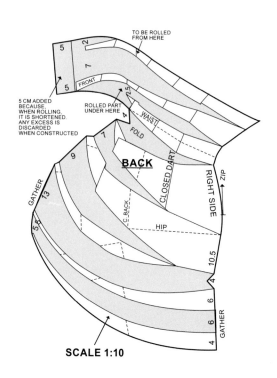

TO BE ROLLED FROM HERE

5 2

7

5 FRONT

5 CM ADDED BECAUSE, WHEN ROLLING, IT IS SHORTENED. ANY EXCESS IS DISCARDED WHEN CONSTRUCTED

ROLLED PART UNDER HERE

2.5 WAIST

4 FOLD

7

9

BACK CLOSED DART

GATHER

13

C. BACK RIGHT SIDE ZIP

5.5

HIP

10.5

4 6

6 GATHER

4

SCALE 1:10

100

DRESS WITH RADIAL FRONT DRAPING

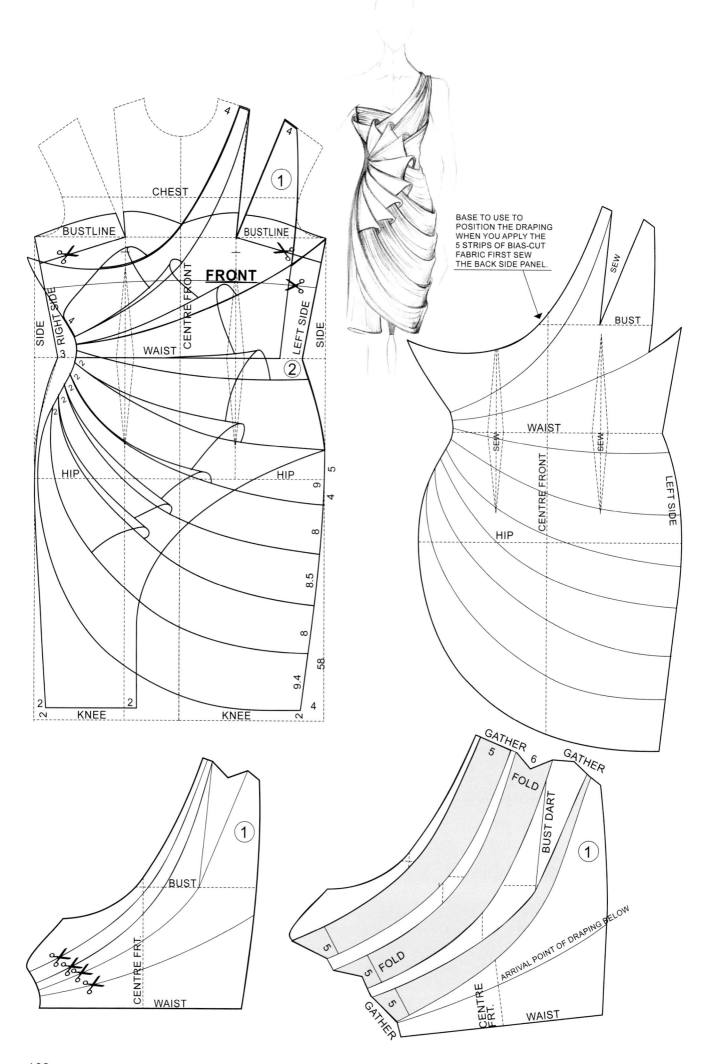

CHEST

BUSTLINE   BUSTLINE

①

FRONT

RIGHT SIDE   SIDE   CENTRE FRONT   LEFT SIDE   SIDE

4

3

②

2
2
2
2
2

WAIST

HIP   HIP   5

9

4

8

8.5

8

58

9.4

2   2
2   KNEE   KNEE   2
4

BASE TO USE TO
POSITION THE DRAPING
WHEN YOU APPLY THE
5 STRIPS OF BIAS-CUT
FABRIC FIRST SEW
THE BACK SIDE PANEL.

SEW

BUST

WAIST

SEW   SEW

CENTRE FRONT   LEFT SIDE

HIP

①

BUST

CENTRE FRT.

WAIST

GATHER   GATHER
5   6
FOLD

BUST DART

①

FOLD
5
5
5   ARRIVAL POINT OF DRAPING BELOW

GATHER   CENTRE FRT.   WAIST

102

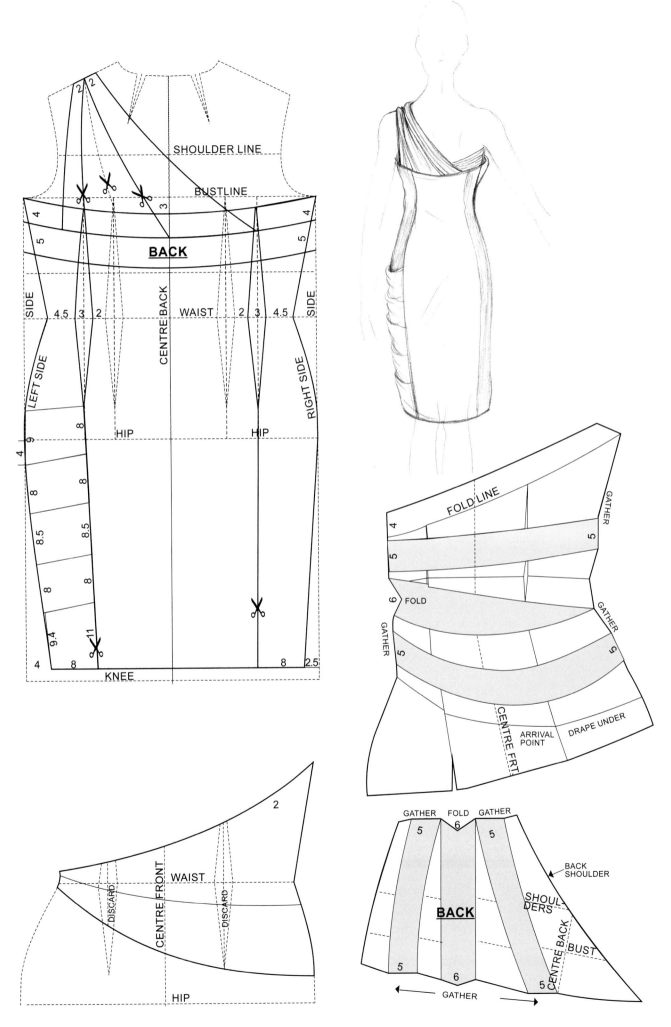

SHOULDER LINE

BUSTLINE

BACK

4

5

4

5

SIDE

LEFT SIDE

4.5 3 2

CENTRE BACK

WAIST

2 3 4.5

SIDE

RIGHT SIDE

9 8

HIP

HIP

4

8

8

8.5 8.5

8 8

9.4 11

4 8

8 2.5

KNEE

2

DISCARD

CENTRE FRONT

WAIST

DISCARD

HIP

FOLD LINE

4

5

GATHER

5

6 FOLD

GATHER

5

GATHER

5

CENTRE FRT

ARRIVAL POINT

DRAPE UNDER

GATHER FOLD GATHER

5 6 5

BACK SHOULDER

BACK

SHOULDERS

CENTRE BACK

BUST

5 6 5

← GATHER →

103

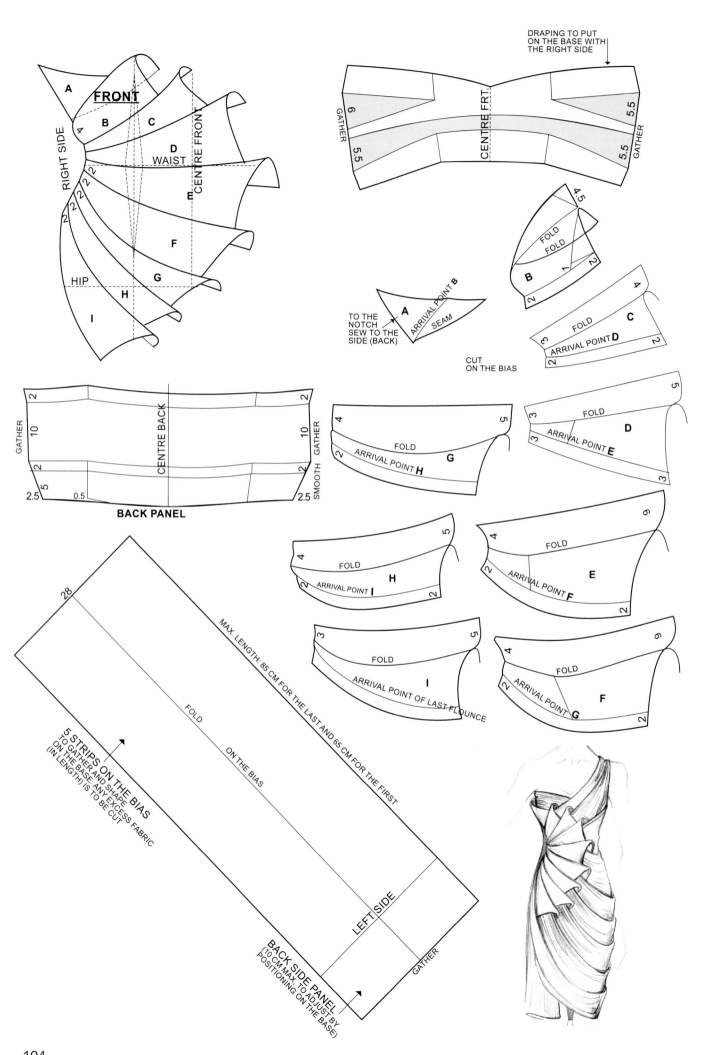

FRONT

RIGHT SIDE

A

B

C

D

WAIST

E

CENTRE FRONT

F

G

HIP

H

I

4

2
2
2
2
2

DRAPING TO PUT
ON THE BASE WITH
THE RIGHT SIDE

GATHER

6

5.5

CENTRE FRT.

5.5

5.5

GATHER

TO THE
NOTCH
SEW TO THE
SIDE (BACK)

ARRIVAL POINT B

A

SEAM

CUT
ON THE BIAS

B

FOLD
FOLD

4.5

2
1
2

2

FOLD

C

4

ARRIVAL POINT D

3
2
2

5

FOLD

D

3
3

ARRIVAL POINT E

3

BACK PANEL

GATHER

2
10
2
5
2.5

CENTRE BACK

0.5

SMOOTH GATHER

2
10
2
2.5

4

FOLD

ARRIVAL POINT H

G

5
2

4

FOLD

E

6

2

ARRIVAL POINT F

2

4

FOLD

ARRIVAL POINT

H

I

5
2
2

3

FOLD

ARRIVAL POINT OF LAST FLOUNCE

I

5

4

FOLD

ARRIVAL POINT

F

G

6

2
2

28

MAX LENGTH: 85 CM FOR THE LAST AND 65 CM FOR THE FIRST

FOLD

ON THE BIAS

5 STRIPS ON THE BIAS
TO GATHER AND SHAPE ANY EXCESS FABRIC
ON THE BASE
(IN LENGTH) IS TO BE CUT

LEFT SIDE

GATHER

BACK SIDE PANEL
(10 CM MAX. TO ADJUST BY
POSITIONING ON THE BASE)

SHIRT WITH KNOTTED FLOUNCES AND BOWS

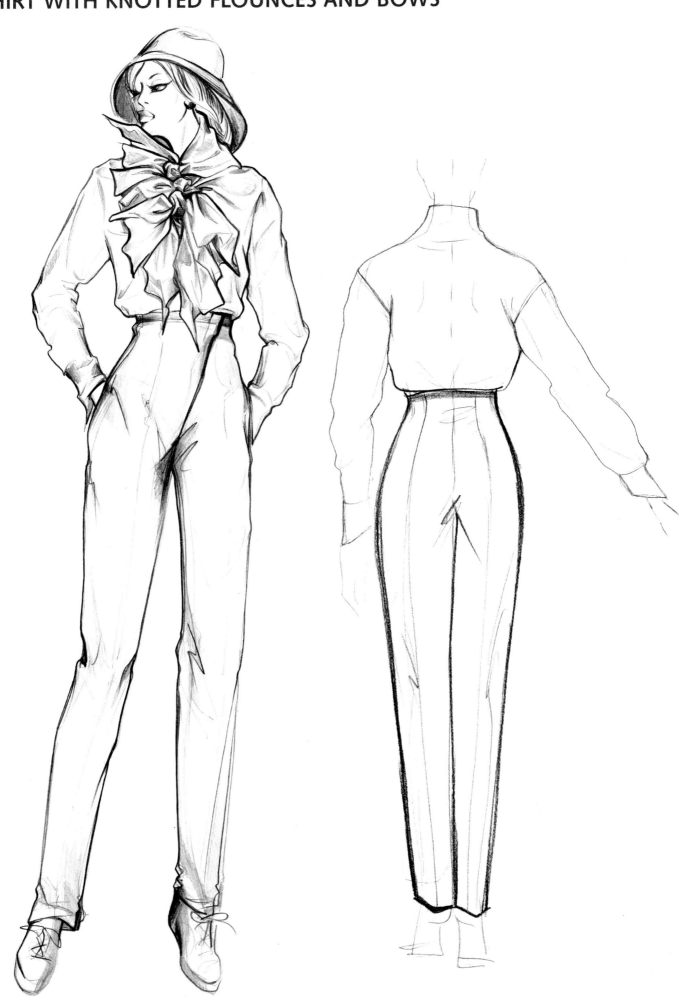

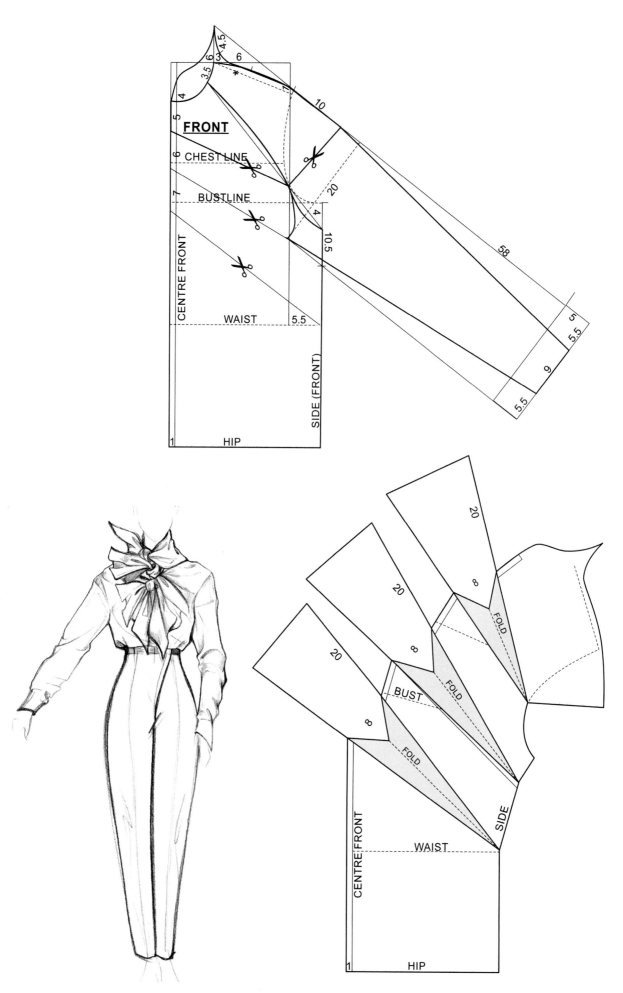

FRONT

CHEST LINE

BUSTLINE

CENTRE FRONT

WAIST

SIDE (FRONT)

HIP

4.5
3
6
6
3.5
4
5
6
7
10
20
4
10.5
5.5
58
5
5.5
9
5.5
1

20
20
20
8
8
8
FOLD
FOLD
FOLD
BUST
SIDE
CENTRE FRONT
WAIST
HIP
1

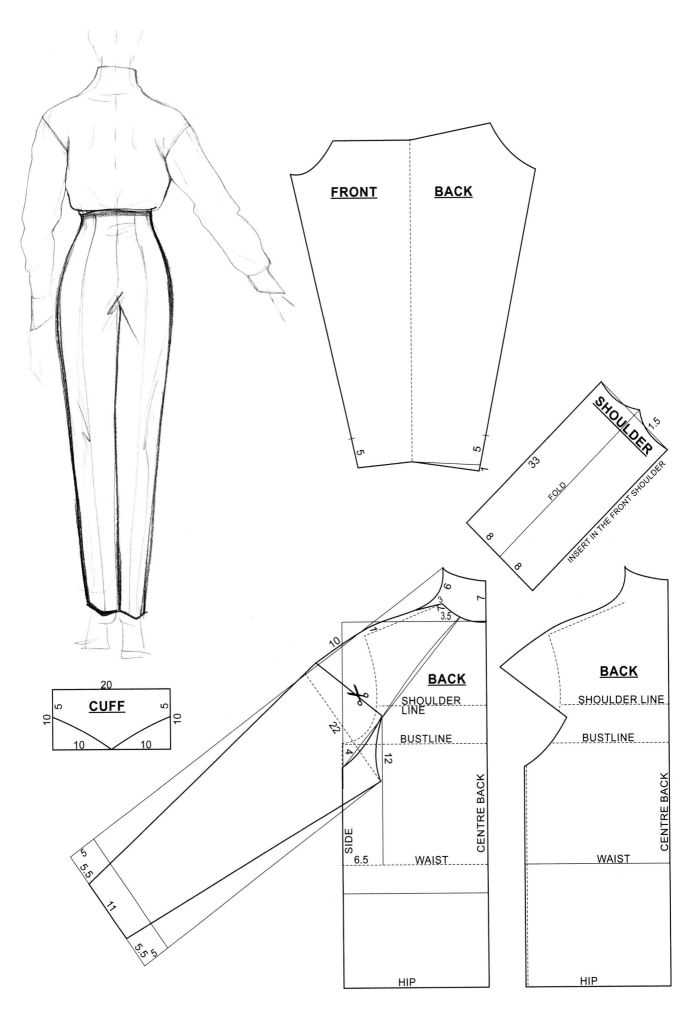

FRONT BACK

5

5

1

SHOULDER

1.5

33

FOLD

8

8

INSERT IN THE FRONT SHOULDER

20

5 5

CUFF

10 10

10 10

5
5.5

11

5.5
5

6

3
3.5

10

7

22

4

12

BACK

SHOULDER LINE

BUSTLINE

SIDE

CENTRE BACK

6.5 WAIST

HIP

BACK

SHOULDER LINE

BUSTLINE

CENTRE BACK

WAIST

HIP

107

DRESS WITH FLOUNCES
ON THE FRONT AND SLEEVE

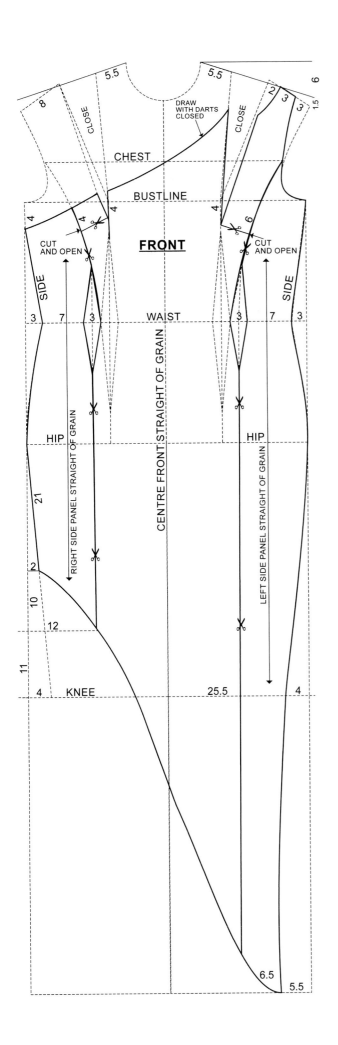

5.5   5.5   6

8   CLOSE   DRAW WITH DARTS CLOSED   CLOSE   2 3 3   1.5

CHEST

BUSTLINE

FRONT

4   4   4   4   6

CUT AND OPEN   CUT AND OPEN

SIDE   SIDE

3   7   3   WAIST   3   7   3

CENTRE FRONT: STRAIGHT OF GRAIN

RIGHT SIDE PANEL STRAIGHT OF GRAIN   LEFT SIDE PANEL STRAIGHT OF GRAIN

HIP   HIP

21

2

10

12

11

4   KNEE   25.5   4

6.5   5.5

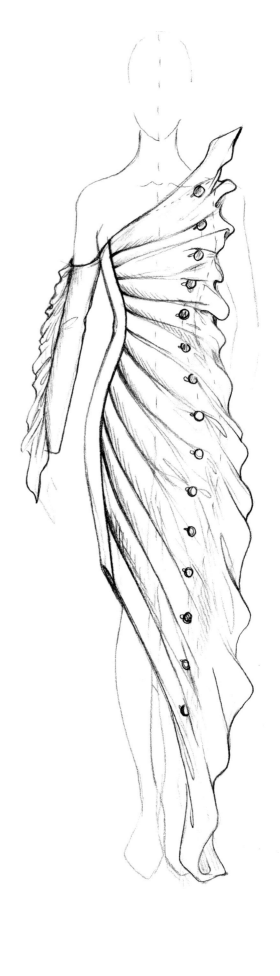

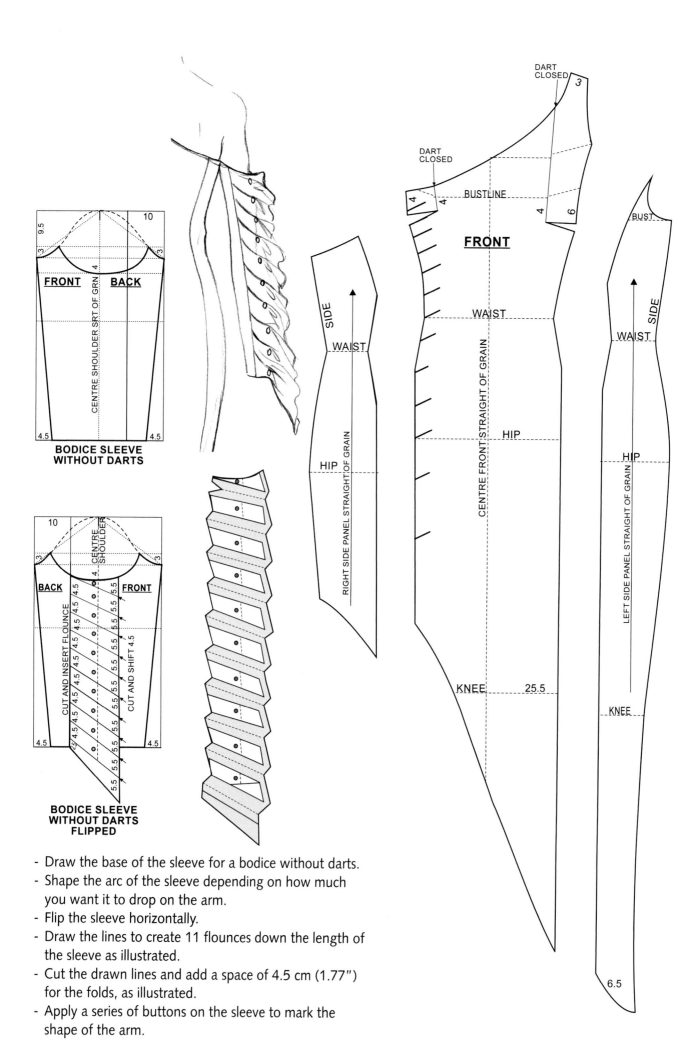

BODICE SLEEVE WITHOUT DARTS

FRONT BACK

9.5 10
3 3
4
CENTRE SHOULDER SRT OF GRN
4.5 4.5

BODICE SLEEVE WITHOUT DARTS FLIPPED

10
3 3
CENTRE SHOULDER
BACK FRONT
4
4.5 / 5.5
4.5 / 5.5
4.5 / 5.5
4.5 / 5.5
4.5 / 5.5
CUT AND INSERT FLOUNCE
CUT AND SHIFT 4.5
4.5 / 5.5
4.5 / 5.5
4.5 4.5
5.5

SIDE
WAIST
HIP
RIGHT SIDE PANEL STRAIGHT OF GRAIN

FRONT

DART CLOSED 3
DART CLOSED
4 4 BUSTLINE 4 6
WAIST
HIP
CENTRE FRONT STRAIGHT OF GRAIN
KNEE 25.5

BUST
SIDE
WAIST
HIP
LEFT SIDE PANEL STRAIGHT OF GRAIN
KNEE
6.5

- Draw the base of the sleeve for a bodice without darts.
- Shape the arc of the sleeve depending on how much you want it to drop on the arm.
- Flip the sleeve horizontally.
- Draw the lines to create 11 flounces down the length of the sleeve as illustrated.
- Cut the drawn lines and add a space of 4.5 cm (1.77") for the folds, as illustrated.
- Apply a series of buttons on the sleeve to mark the shape of the arm.

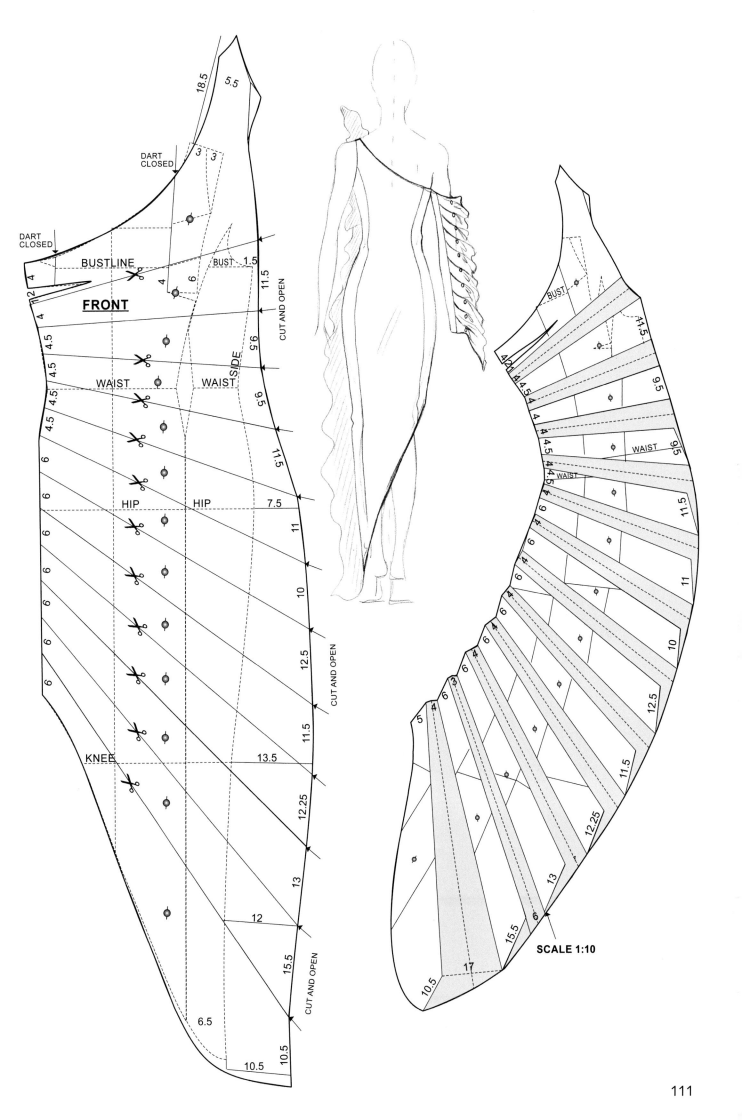

FRONT

DART CLOSED

DART CLOSED

BUSTLINE

WAIST

SIDE

WAIST

HIP

HIP

KNEE

18.5 5.5

3 3

4

4 6

BUST 1.5

11.5

CUT AND OPEN

9.5

9.5

11.5

7.5

11

10

12.5

11.5

13.5

12.25

13

12

15.5

CUT AND OPEN

6.5

10.5 10.5

4

12

4

4.5

4.5

4.5

4.5

6

6

6

6

6

6

CUT AND OPEN

BUST

4.5 4 4 4.5

4.5 4

4 4.5 4

4.5 4

4

6

6

6

6

4

4

4

3

4

5

6

10.5

17

15.5

13

12.25

11.5

10

11

11.5

9.5

9.5

11.5

WAIST

WAIST

6

SCALE 1:10

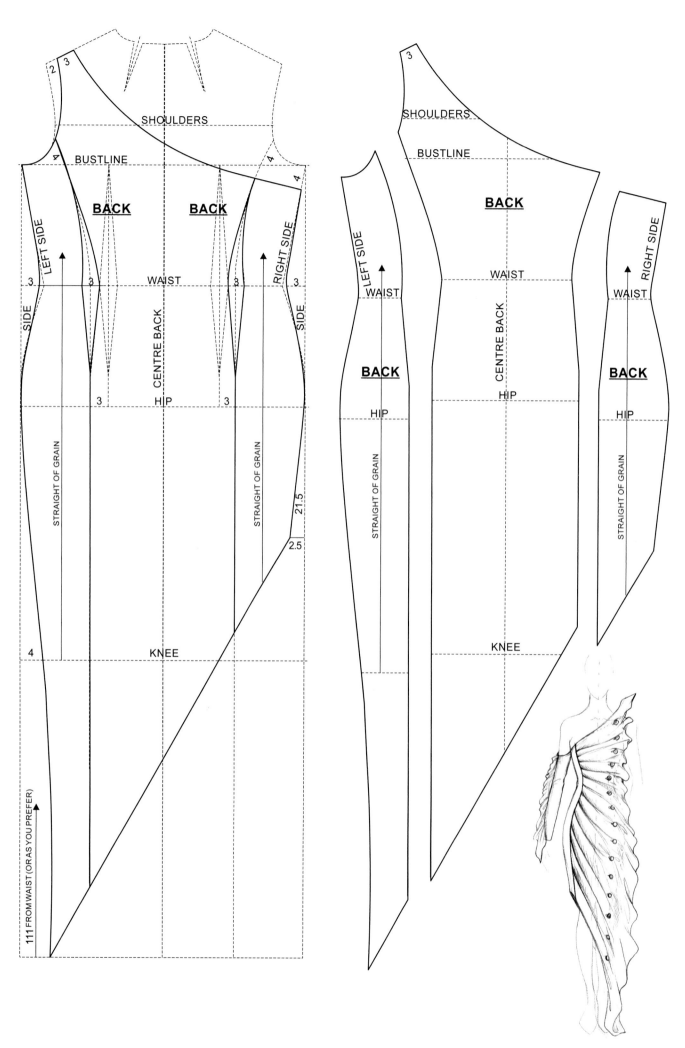

SHOULDERS

BUSTLINE

BACK   **BACK**

LEFT SIDE

RIGHT SIDE

SIDE

SIDE

WAIST

CENTRE BACK

HIP

STRAIGHT OF GRAIN

STRAIGHT OF GRAIN

21.5

2.5

KNEE

111 FROM WAIST (OR AS YOU PREFER)

SHOULDERS

BUSTLINE

BACK

LEFT SIDE

WAIST

BACK

HIP

STRAIGHT OF GRAIN

CENTRE BACK

WAIST

HIP

KNEE

RIGHT SIDE

WAIST

BACK

HIP

STRAIGHT OF GRAIN

STRAIGHT OF GRAIN

4. HAUTE COUTURE DETAILS: COLLARS, NECKLINES AND SLEEVES

This chapter includes the creation of patterns with collars, various necklines, sleeves and other details that can be helpful for patternmakers, tailors and seamstresses as they carry out their profession. Each item of clothing, especially high-fashion, made-to-measure pieces, is unique, but of course there are various ways to classify their value. Just like anything else, the characteristics of the elements are what create the basis for common classifications. And in the fashion industry, women's dresses are often identified in terms of their details, especially their collars, necklines, sleeves, etc. In other words: according to the opening, the height of the collar, the front or back neckline, or based on a special sleeve.

And indeed, while for menswear we generally talk about necklines at the height of the neck and about set-in sleeves, in women's fashion there are many, many types of dresses that can be, for example, open at the back or at the heigh of the bust, etc. This gives rise to the importance of the collar and the neckline, or a special sleeve, in determining the value of the garment, its refinement and elegance, and influence the choice or confirmation of a trend.

A-LINE DRESS WITH A UNIQUE BOAT NECKLINE

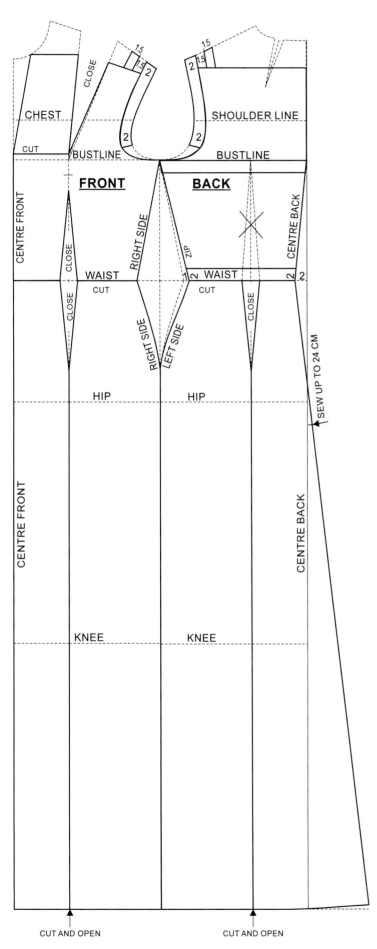

FRONT   **BACK**

CHEST

CUT

BUSTLINE   BUSTLINE

CLOSE

1.5
1.5
2

2   1.5
2

SHOULDER LINE

CENTRE FRONT

RIGHT SIDE

ZIP

CLOSE

CLOSE

WAIST   WAIST

CUT   CUT

CENTRE BACK

CLOSE

RIGHT SIDE

LEFT SIDE

HIP   HIP

CENTRE FRONT

CENTRE BACK

SEW UP TO 24 CM

KNEE   KNEE

CUT AND OPEN   CUT AND OPEN

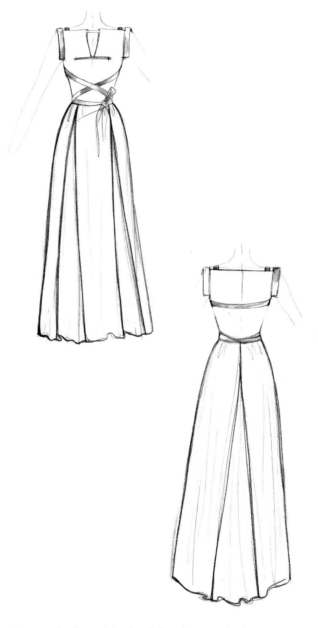

- Create the base block of the dress with the appropriate measurements and ease.
- Draw all the elements necessary to transform the pattern, as illustrated.
- Take up the front bodice, and create a mirror image of it to create the full front.
- Close the bust and waist darts, merging them into the centre front at the height of the bust line.
  Draw the outline of the ribbons, the other transformation lines and of the indications illustrated on the pattern.
- Take up the back of the bodice and carry out the transformations as illustrated.
- Take up the wings on the shoulder and the straps and combine the front and back pieces.

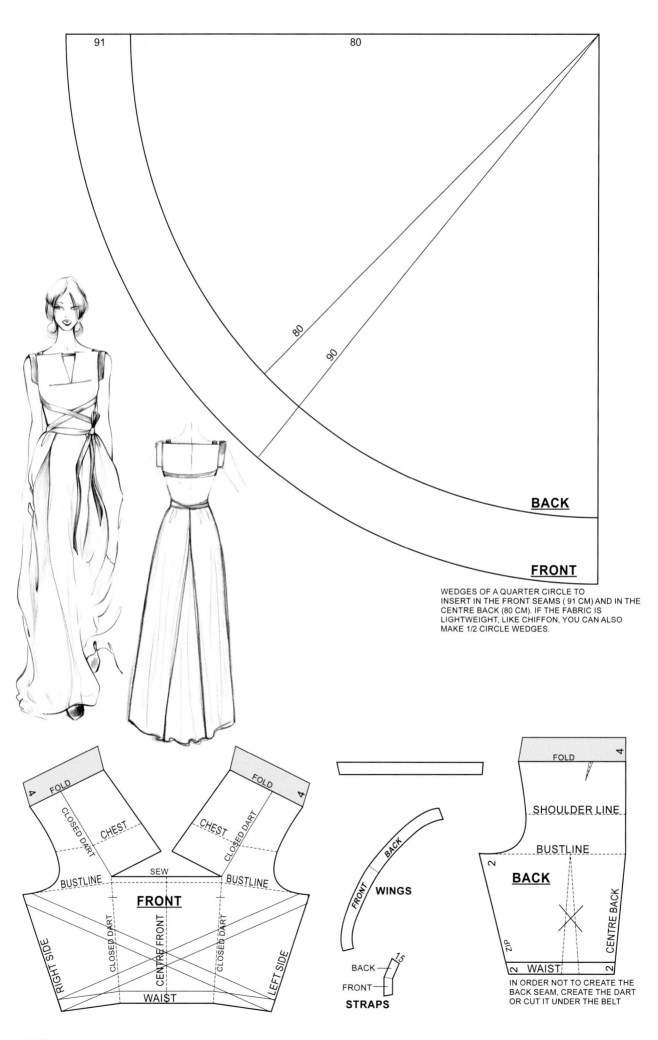

91

80

80

90

2

BACK

FRONT

WEDGES OF A QUARTER CIRCLE TO
INSERT IN THE FRONT SEAMS (91 CM) AND IN THE
CENTRE BACK (80 CM). IF THE FABRIC IS
LIGHTWEIGHT, LIKE CHIFFON, YOU CAN ALSO
MAKE 1/2 CIRCLE WEDGES.

BELT - 350

4 FOLD

FOLD 4

CLOSED DART

CHEST

CHEST

CLOSED DART

BUSTLINE

SEW

BUSTLINE

FRONT

RIGHT SIDE

CLOSED DART

CENTRE FRONT

CLOSED DART

LEFT SIDE

WAIST

BACK

FRONT

WINGS

15

BACK

FRONT

STRAPS

FOLD 4

SHOULDER LINE

BUSTLINE

2

BACK

ZIP

2 WAIST 2

CENTRE BACK

IN ORDER NOT TO CREATE THE
BACK SEAM, CREATE THE DART
OR CUT IT UNDER THE BELT

- Take up the lower front and back of the dress
  and transform as illustrated in the figures.
- Create the wedges to insert in the seams on the
  front and centre back, creating two 1/4 circle
  graphics that are equal in length to the slits.
  If using a lightweight fabric like chiffon, you can
  also make 1/4 circle wedges, in the same length.

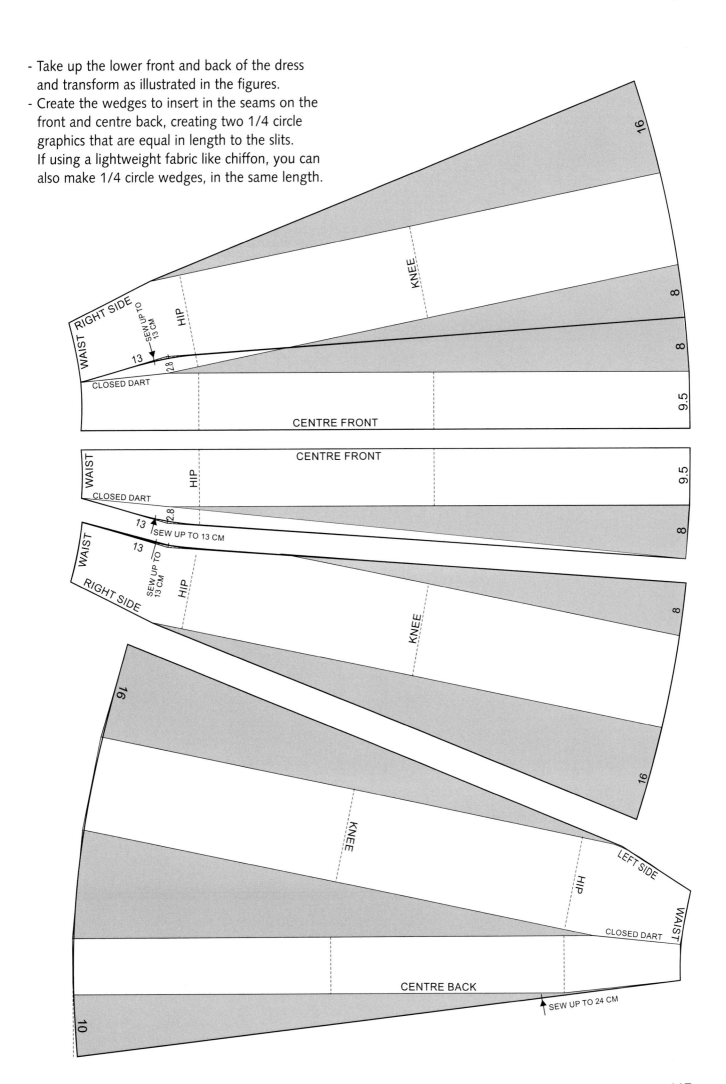

ASYMMETRIC DRESS WITH PANELS AT THE SIDES
A WIDE, WRAP NECKLINE THAT ALSO CREATES THE SLEEVES

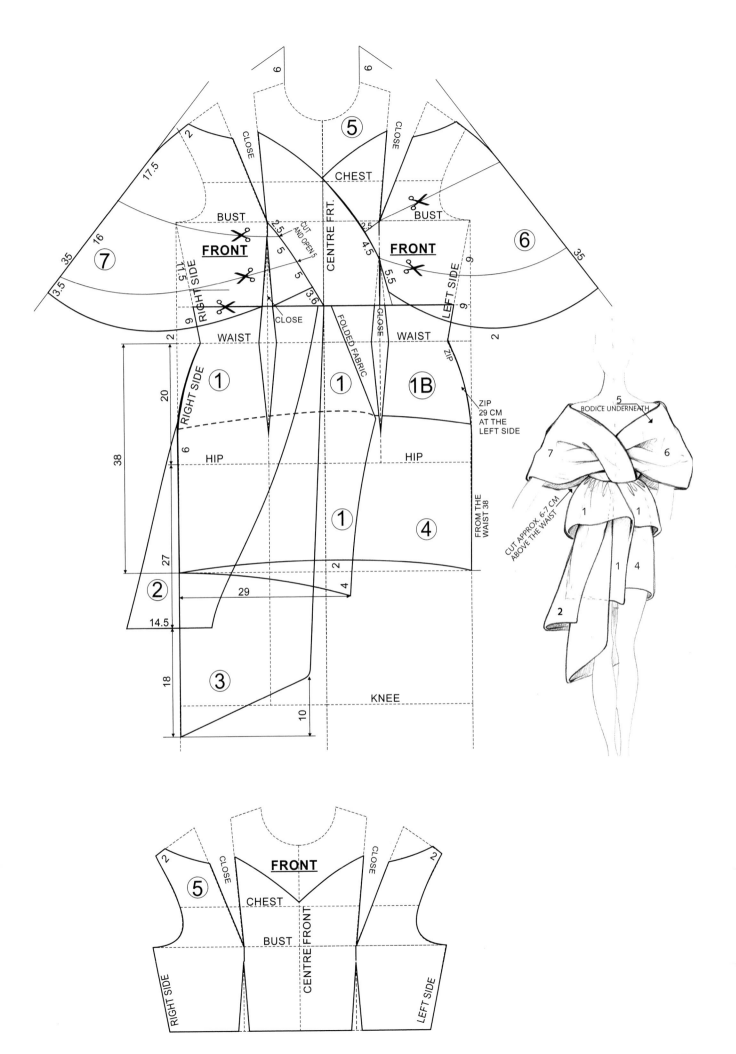

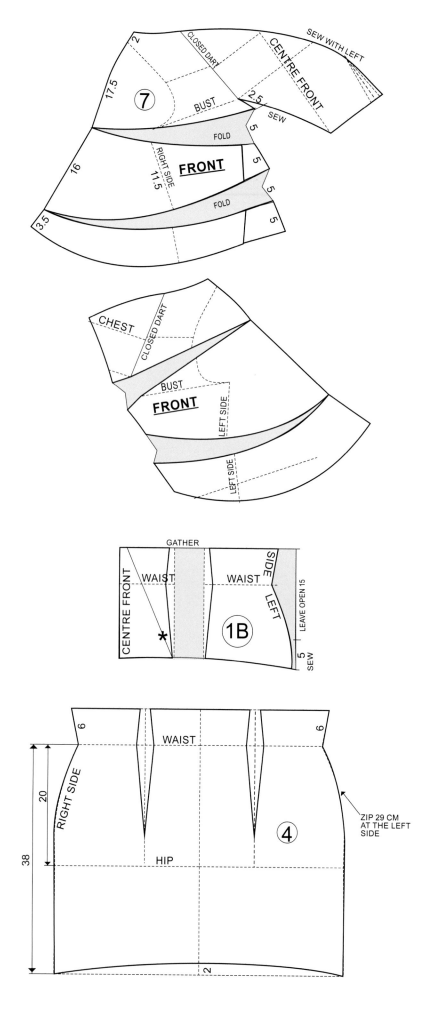

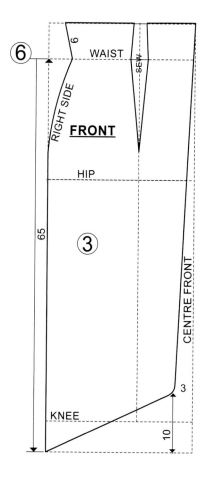

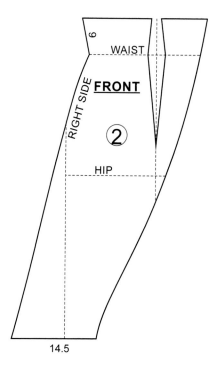

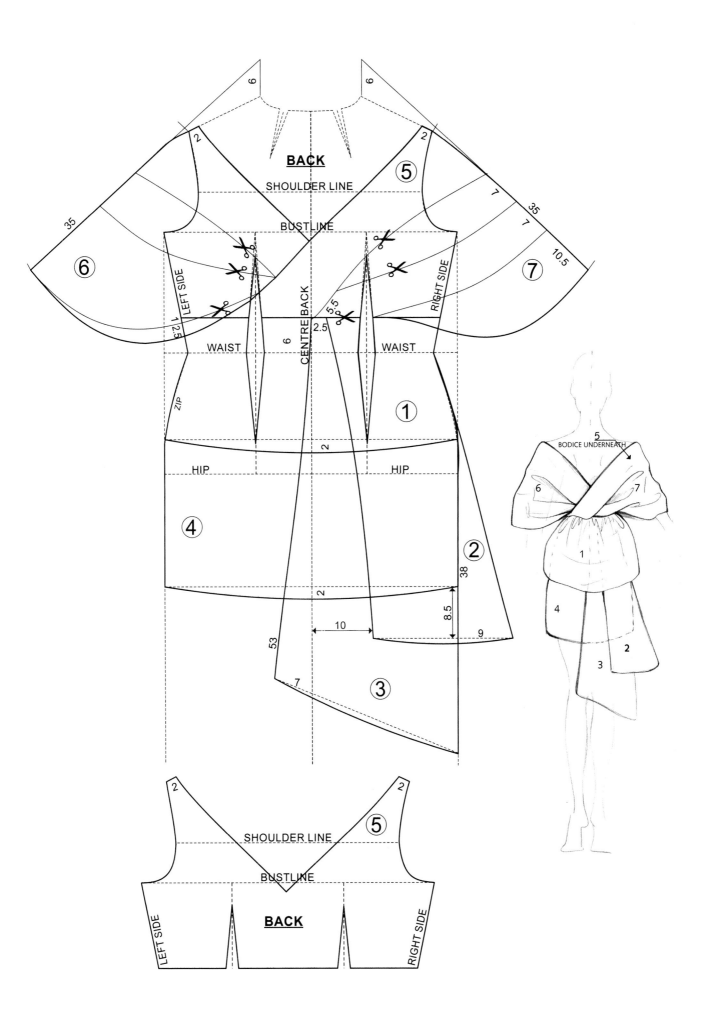

BACK

SHOULDER LINE

BUSTLINE

6

LEFT SIDE

CENTRE BACK

5.5

RIGHT SIDE

2

35

35

7

7

10.5

①

②

③

④

⑤

⑥

⑦

WAIST

WAIST

6

2.5

12.5

ZIP

HIP

HIP

2

2

38

8.5

10

53

7

9

BODICE UNDERNEATH

5

6

7

1

4

2

3

BACK

SHOULDER LINE

BUSTLINE

⑤

2

2

LEFT SIDE

RIGHT SIDE

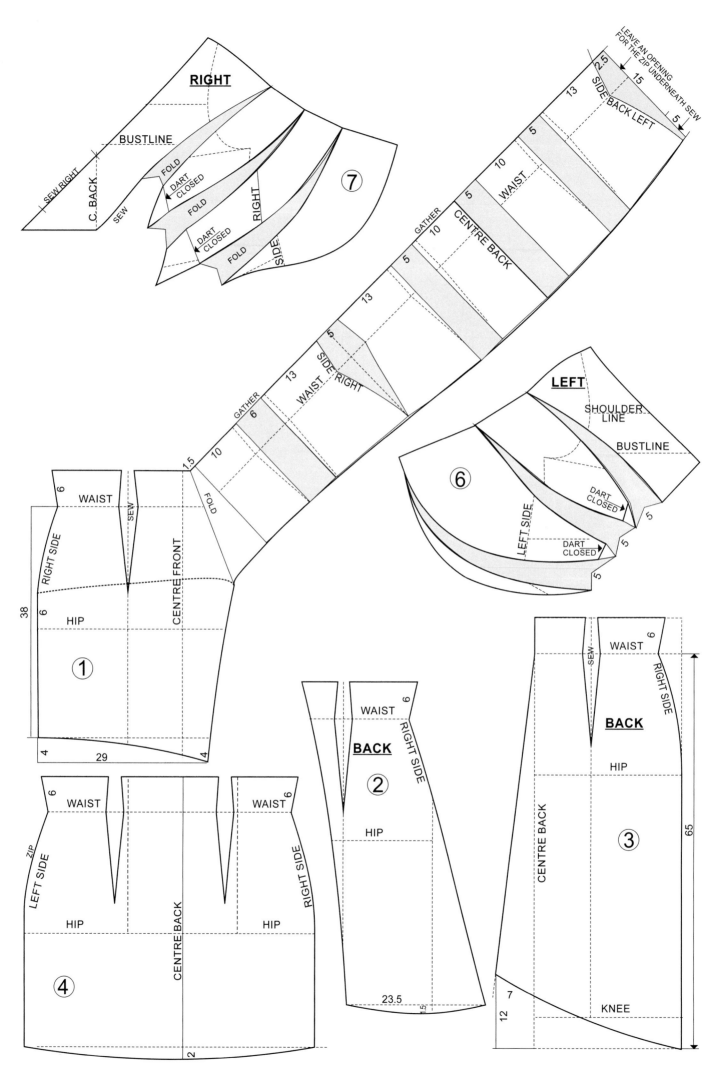

RIGHT

BUSTLINE

SEW RIGHT

C. BACK

SEW

FOLD

DART CLOSED

FOLD

DART CLOSED

FOLD

RIGHT

SIDE

⑦

LEAVE AN OPENING FOR THE ZIP UNDERNEATH SEW

2.5

15

1.5

13

SIDE BACK LEFT

10

5

WAIST

GATHER

10

5

CENTRE BACK

13

5

SIDE

WAIST RIGHT

13

GATHER

6

10

1.5

FOLD

LEFT

SHOULDER LINE

BUSTLINE

⑥

LEFT SIDE

DART CLOSED

DART CLOSED

5

5

5

6

WAIST

SEW

CENTRE FRONT

6

RIGHT SIDE

38

6

HIP

①

4

29

4

WAIST

SEW

BACK

②

RIGHT SIDE

HIP

23.5

1.5

ZIP

LEFT SIDE

6

WAIST

WAIST

6

HIP

CENTRE BACK

HIP

RIGHT SIDE

④

2

6

WAIST

SEW

BACK

RIGHT SIDE

HIP

CENTRE BACK

③

65

7

12

KNEE

122

ARROW-HEM DRESS WITH A HOOD
LONG BELL SLEEVES

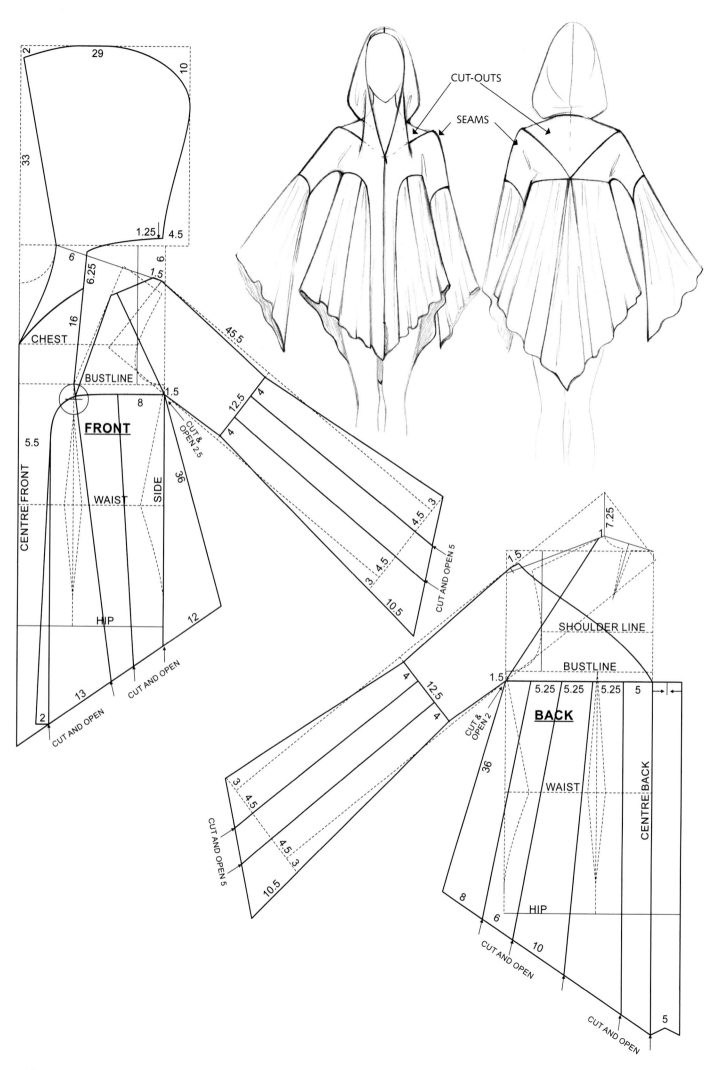

2   29   10

33

                                    1.25 ↓ 4.5

        6
              6.25   1.5 6
        16   45.5

CHEST
                                    12.5   4
BUSTLINE
                    8   1.5   4
            FRONT   CUT &
                              OPEN 2.5

CENTRE FRONT   5.5   SIDE   36
                                                    3
                                              4.5
WAIST   4.5
                                    3
HIP   CUT AND OPEN 5   12
                                              10.5
        13   CUT AND OPEN

2   CUT AND OPEN

CUT-OUTS

SEAMS

                                    7.25
                              1
        1.5

                    SHOULDER LINE

                    BUSTLINE
        3   1.5   5.25 5.25 5.25 5
        4.5   CUT &   BACK
              4.5   OPEN 2
        3   36   CENTRE BACK
CUT AND OPEN 5   12.5
              4   WAIST
        10.5
                    8   6   HIP
                              10
                    CUT AND OPEN
                                                    5
                                    CUT AND OPEN

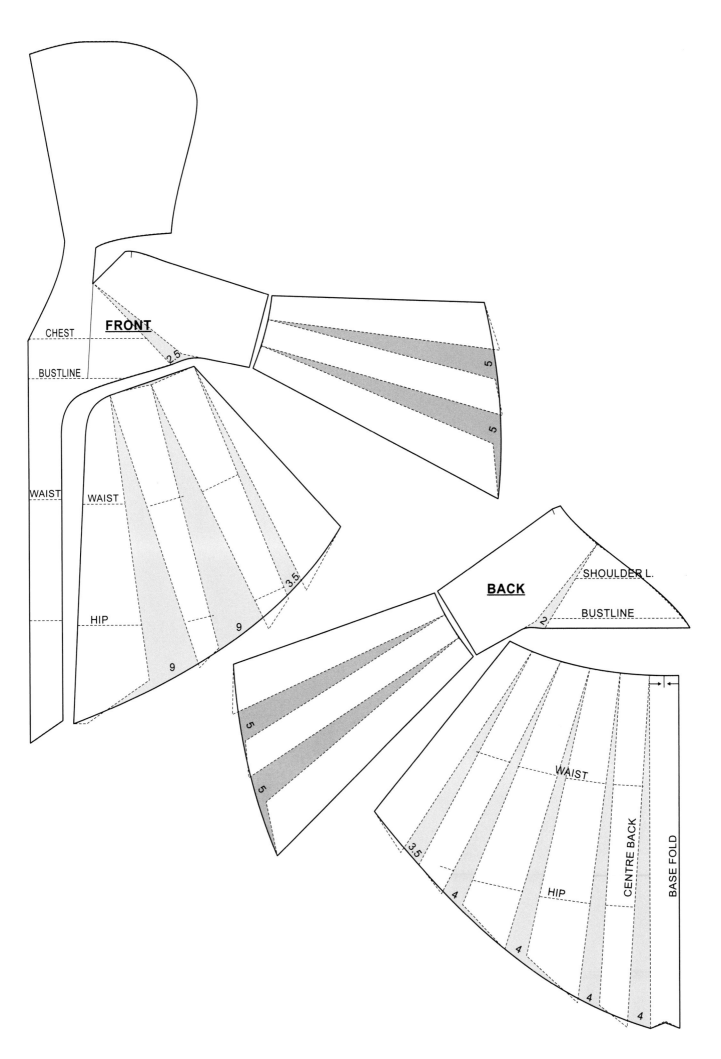

FRONT

CHEST

BUSTLINE

2.5

WAIST

WAIST

HIP

9

9

9

3.5

5

5

BACK

SHOULDER L.

BUSTLINE

2

5

5

WAIST

HIP

CENTRE BACK

BASE FOLD

3.5

4

4

4

4

BALLGOWN-STYLE DRESS WITH PETAL INSERTS

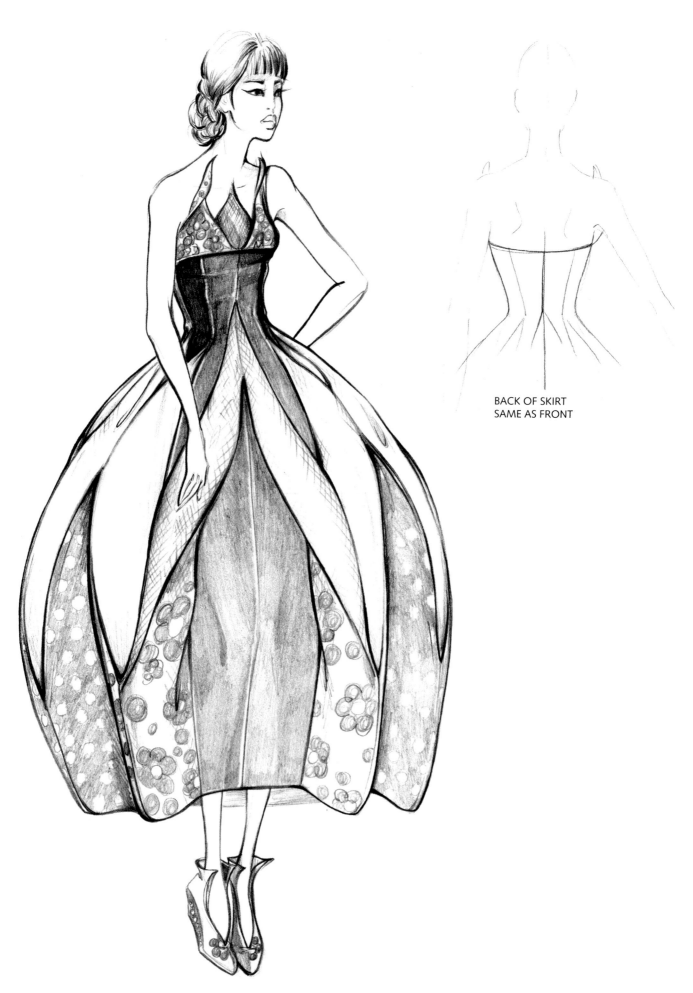

BACK OF SKIRT
SAME AS FRONT

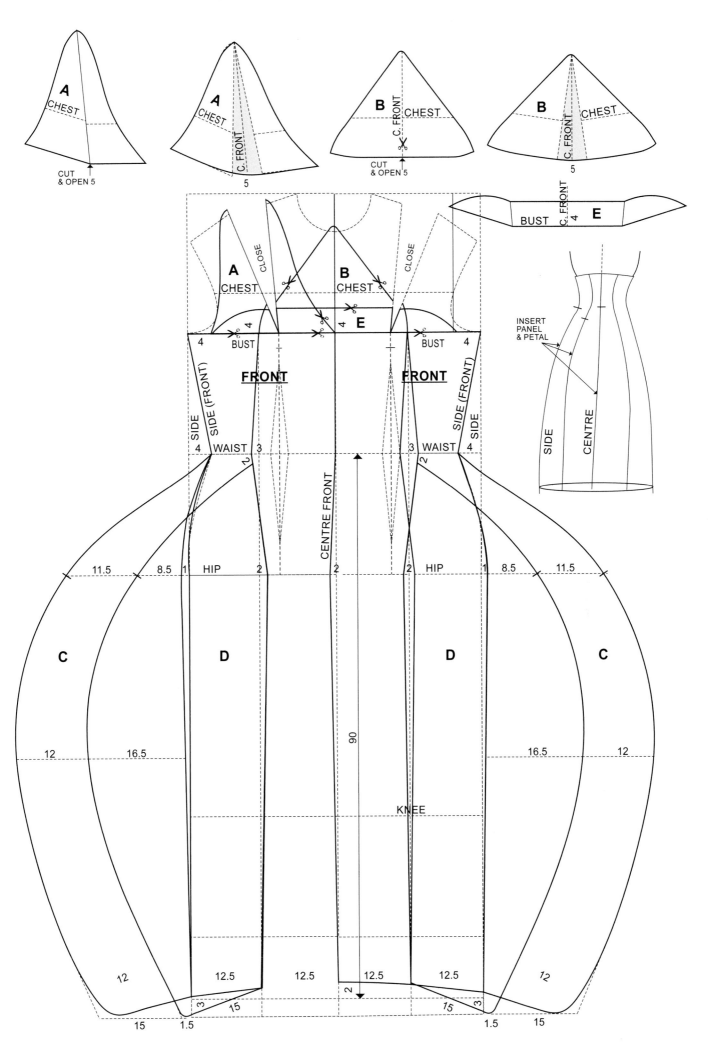

127

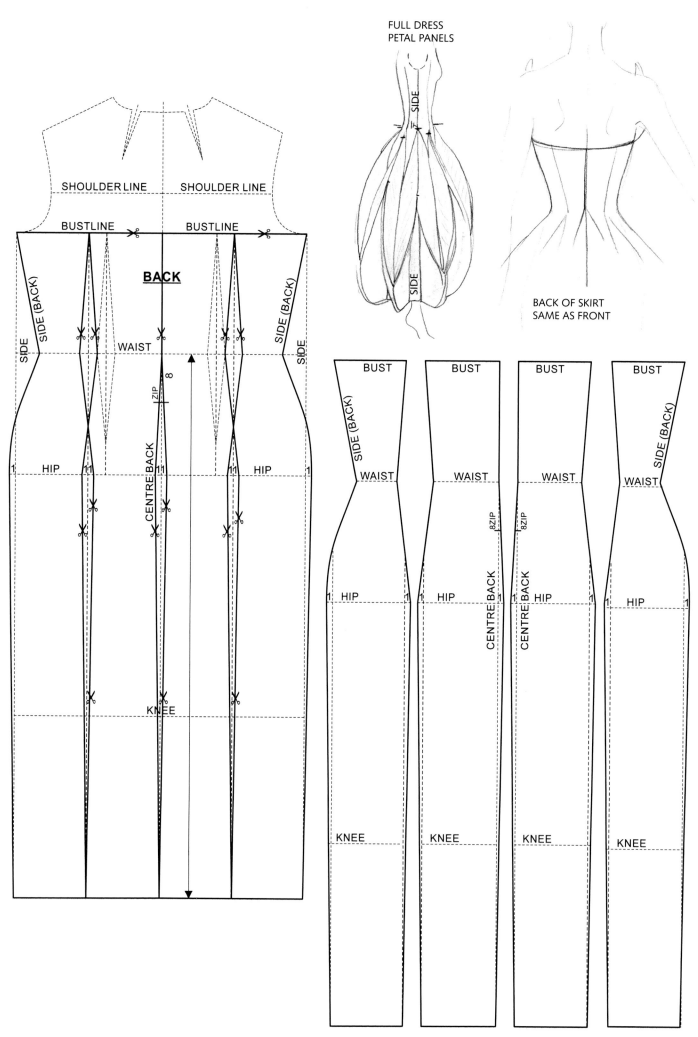

FULL DRESS
PETAL PANELS

SIDE

SIDE

BACK OF SKIRT
SAME AS FRONT

SHOULDER LINE   SHOULDER LINE

BUSTLINE   BUSTLINE

BACK

SIDE (BACK)
SIDE (BACK)
SIDE
SIDE

WAIST

CENTRE BACK

ZIP

8

1   HIP   11   11   11   HIP   1

KNEE

BUST   BUST   BUST   BUST

SIDE (BACK)   SIDE (BACK)

WAIST   WAIST   WAIST   WAIST

8ZIP   8ZIP

CENTRE BACK   CENTRE BACK

1   HIP   1   1   HIP   1   1   HIP   1

KNEE   KNEE   KNEE   KNEE

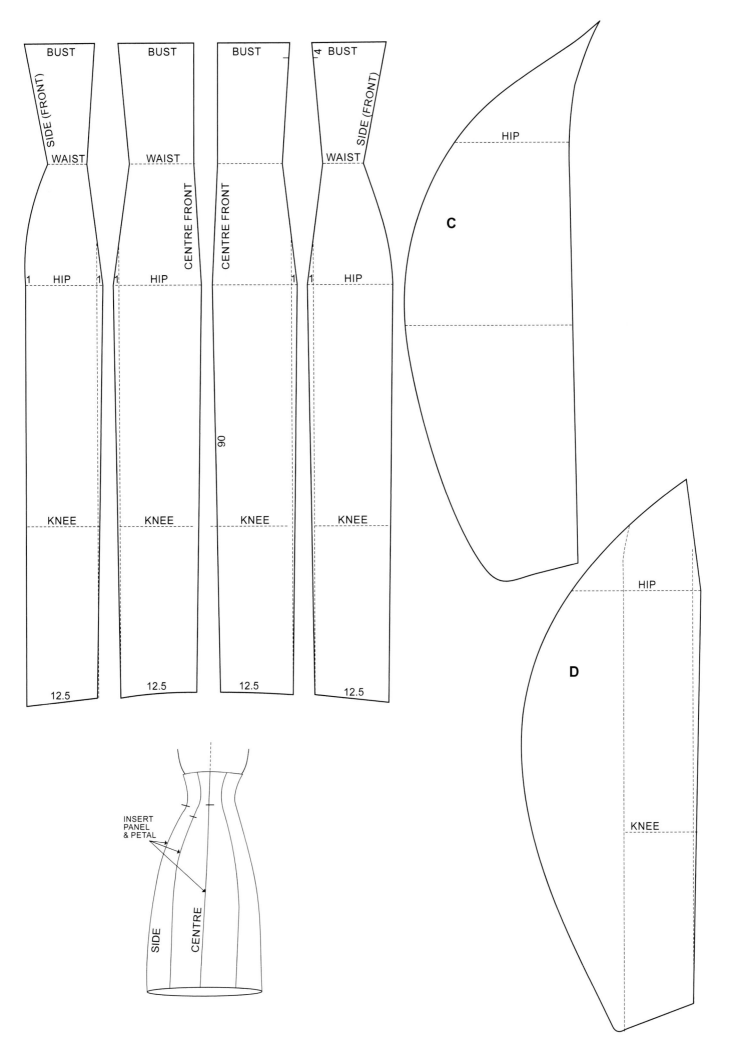

BUST

SIDE (FRONT)

WAIST

1 HIP 1

KNEE

12.5

BUST

WAIST

CENTRE FRONT

HIP

KNEE

12.5

BUST

CENTRE FRONT

90

KNEE

12.5

1 HIP

BUST

SIDE (FRONT)

WAIST

1 HIP

KNEE

12.5

HIP

C

HIP

D

KNEE

INSERT
PANEL
& PETAL

SIDE

CENTRE

129

MERMAID DRESS WITH TRANSPARENCIES

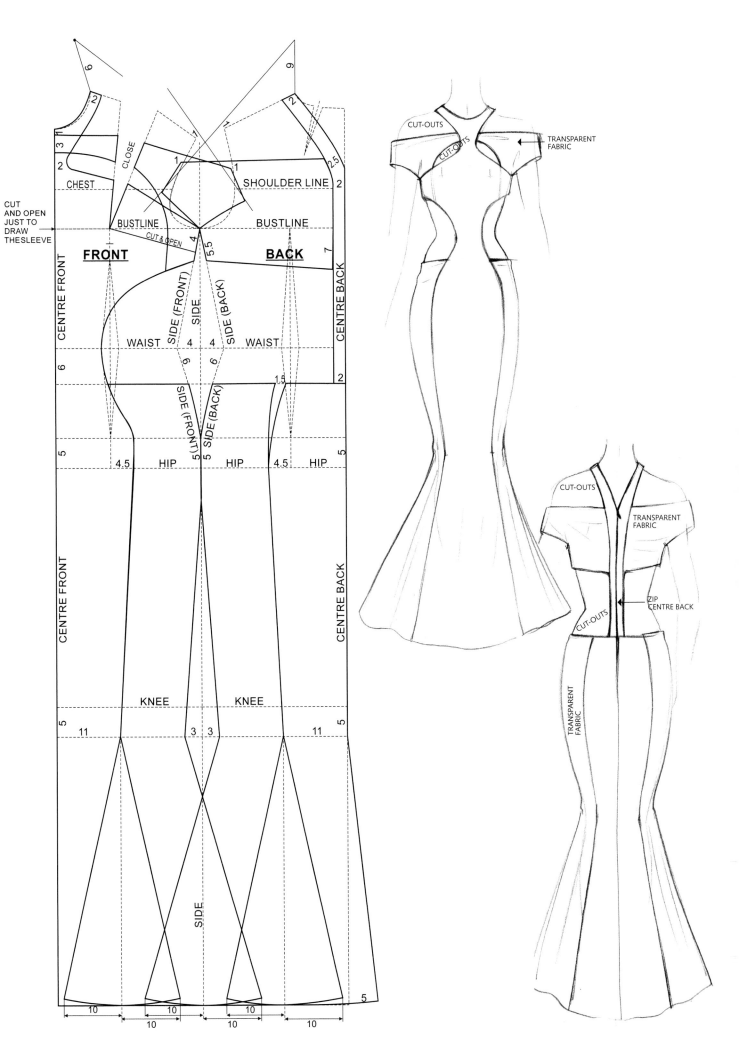

CUT
AND OPEN
JUST TO
DRAW
THE SLEEVE

CLOSE

CHEST

BUSTLINE

CUT & OPEN

FRONT

CENTRE FRONT

WAIST

SIDE (FRONT)

SIDE

SIDE (BACK)

WAIST

BACK

CENTRE BACK

SHOULDER LINE

BUSTLINE

CENTRE FRONT

SIDE (FRONT)

SIDE (BACK)

HIP

HIP

HIP

KNEE

KNEE

CENTRE BACK

SIDE

CUT-OUTS

CUT-OUTS

TRANSPARENT
FABRIC

CUT-OUTS

TRANSPARENT
FABRIC

ZIP
CENTRE BACK

CUT-OUTS

TRANSPARENT
FABRIC

131

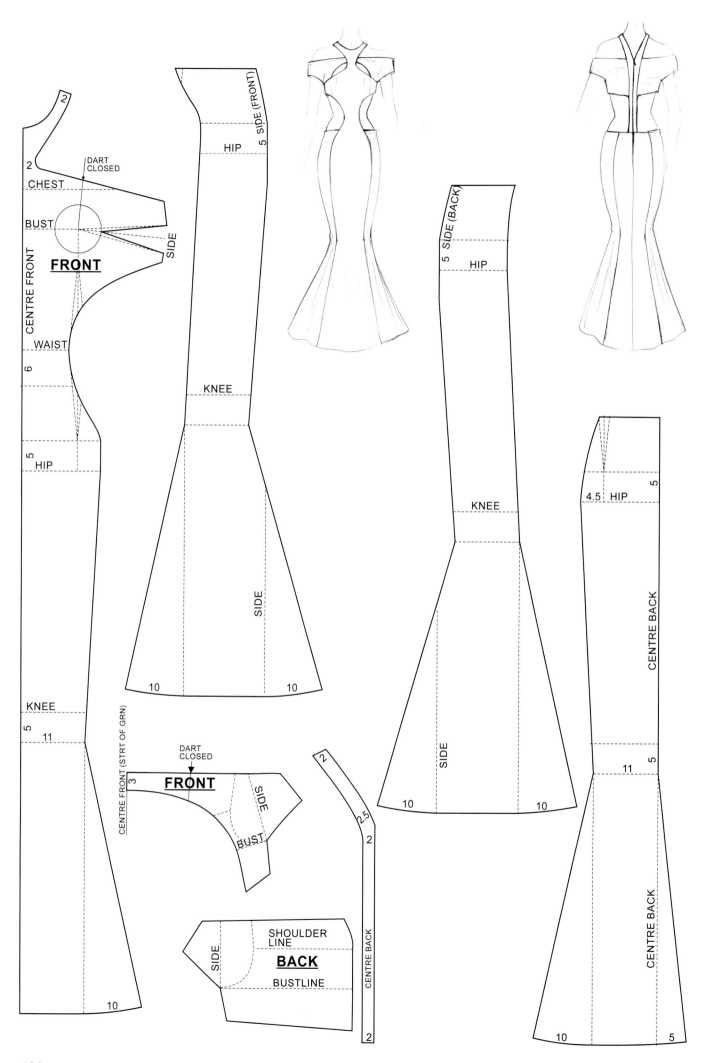

FRONT

CENTRE FRONT

2

CHEST

BUST

DART CLOSED

SIDE

WAIST

6

5 HIP

KNEE

5

11

10

SIDE (FRONT)

HIP

5

KNEE

SIDE

10   10

CENTRE FRONT (STRT OF GRN)

FRONT

3

DART CLOSED

SIDE

BUST

2

2.5

2

CENTRE BACK

2

SIDE

SHOULDER LINE

BACK

BUSTLINE

5 SIDE (BACK)

HIP

KNEE

SIDE

10   10

4.5 HIP 5

CENTRE BACK

11 5

CENTRE BACK

10   5

1950'S VINTAGE STYLE DRESS
SWEETHEART NECKLINE AND HEART MOTIF

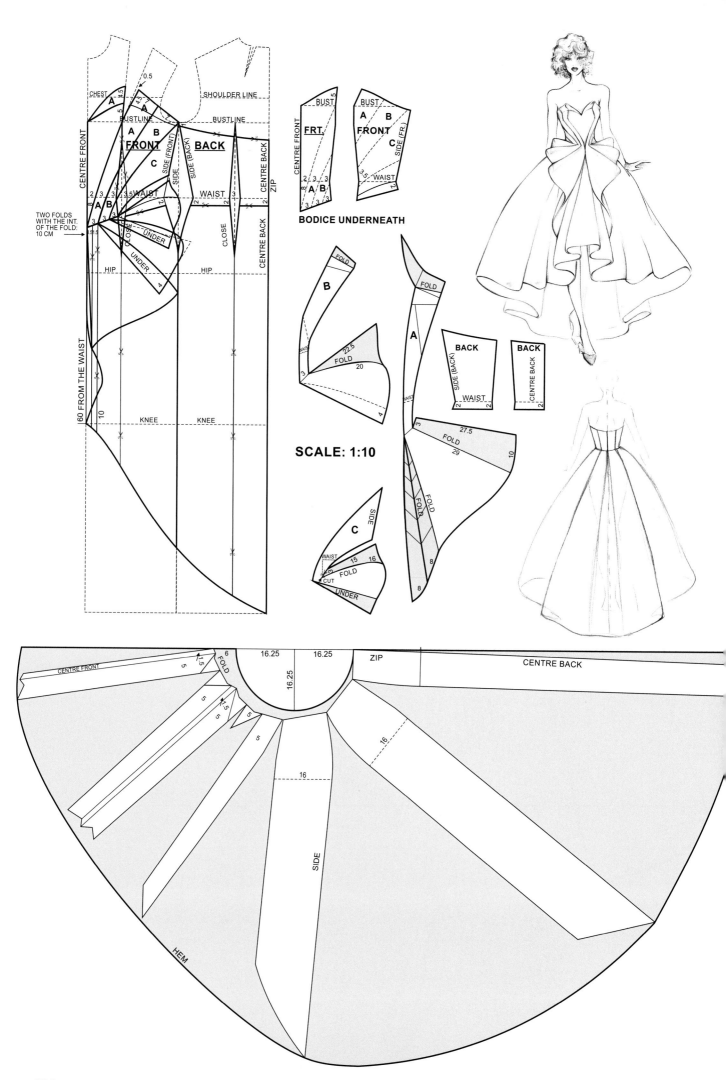

CHEST

0.5

SHOULDER LINE

A
A

BUSTLINE
BUSTLINE

A B
FRONT   BACK
C

CENTRE FRONT
SIDE (FRONT)
SIDE
SIDE (BACK)
CENTRE BACK
ZIP

WAIST
WAIST
WAIST

2 3 3.5
A B
2 3 2 3

TWO FOLDS
WITH THE INT.
OF THE FOLD:
10 CM

CLOSE
UNDER
CLOSE
UNDER

HIP
HIP
4

60 FROM THE WAIST
10

KNEE
KNEE

BUST
FRT

BUST
FRONT

CENTRE FRONT
SIDE (FR.)

A B
C

2 3 3
8
2 3 3

3.5
WAIST
2

BODICE UNDERNEATH

FOLD
B
FOLD
A

WAIST
22.5
FOLD
20
3

BACK
SIDE (BACK)
WAIST
2   2

BACK
CENTRE BACK
2

3
27.5
FOLD
29
10

WAIST

SCALE: 1:10

C
SIDE
WAIST
15 16
FOLD
CUT
UNDER

FOLD
8
8

CENTRE FRONT
6
5
1.5
FOLD

16.25   16.25
16.25

ZIP
CENTRE BACK

5
5
5
1.5
5

16

16

SIDE

16

HEM

ONE-SHOULDER KIMONO JACKET
WITH A LEG OF MUTTON SLEEVE WRAP SKIRT

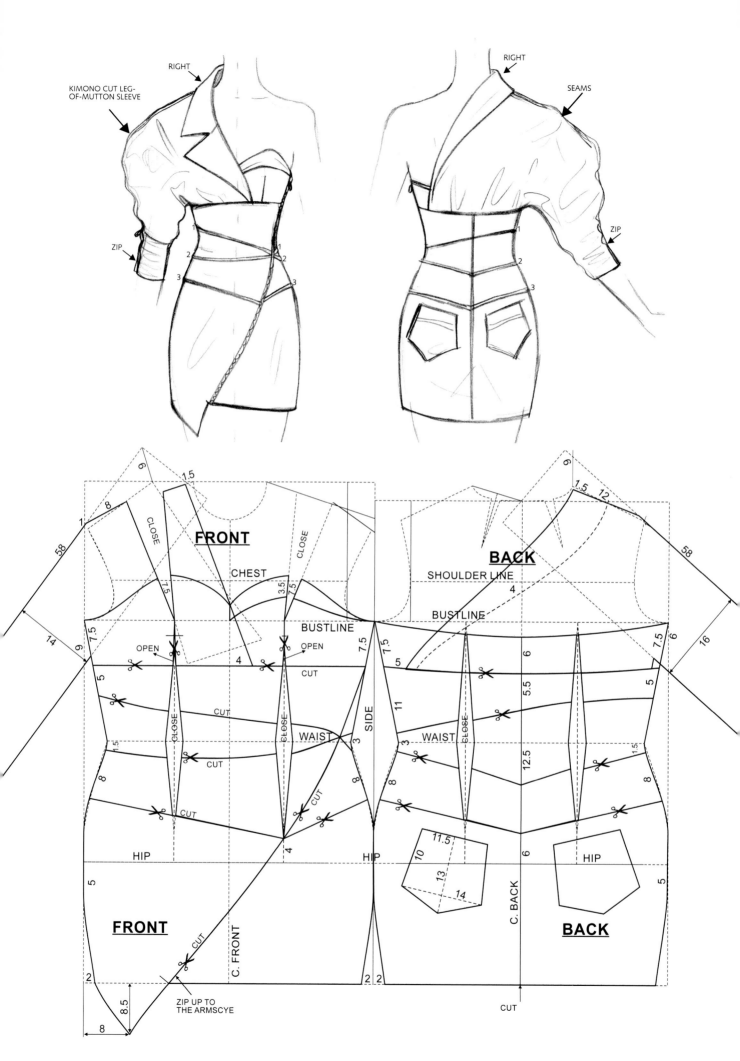

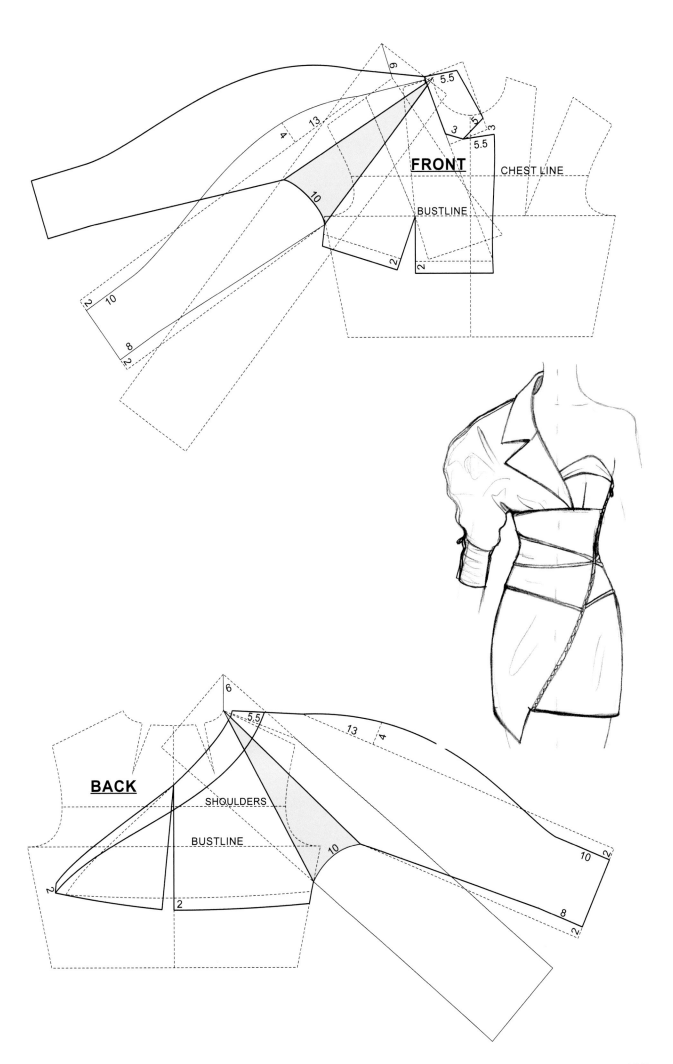

FRONT

CHEST LINE

BUSTLINE

6

5.5

4

13

3

5

3

5.5

10

2

2

2

10

8

2

BACK

SHOULDERS

BUSTLINE

6

5.5

13

4

10

10

2

2

8

2

2

2

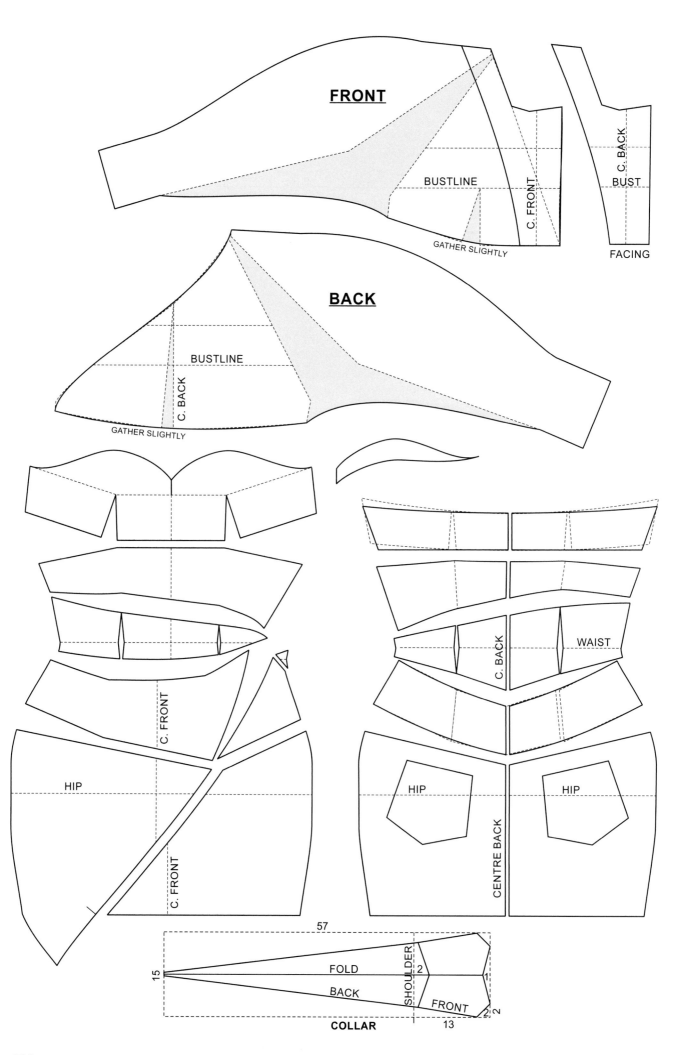

FRONT

BUSTLINE

C. FRONT

C. BACK

BUST

GATHER SLIGHTLY

FACING

BACK

BUSTLINE

C. BACK

GATHER SLIGHTLY

C. FRONT

C. FRONT

HIP

C. BACK

WAIST

HIP

HIP

CENTRE BACK

57

15

FOLD

SHOULDER

2

1

BACK

FRONT

2

COLLAR

13

138

DRESS WITH PANEL PUFF SLEEVES

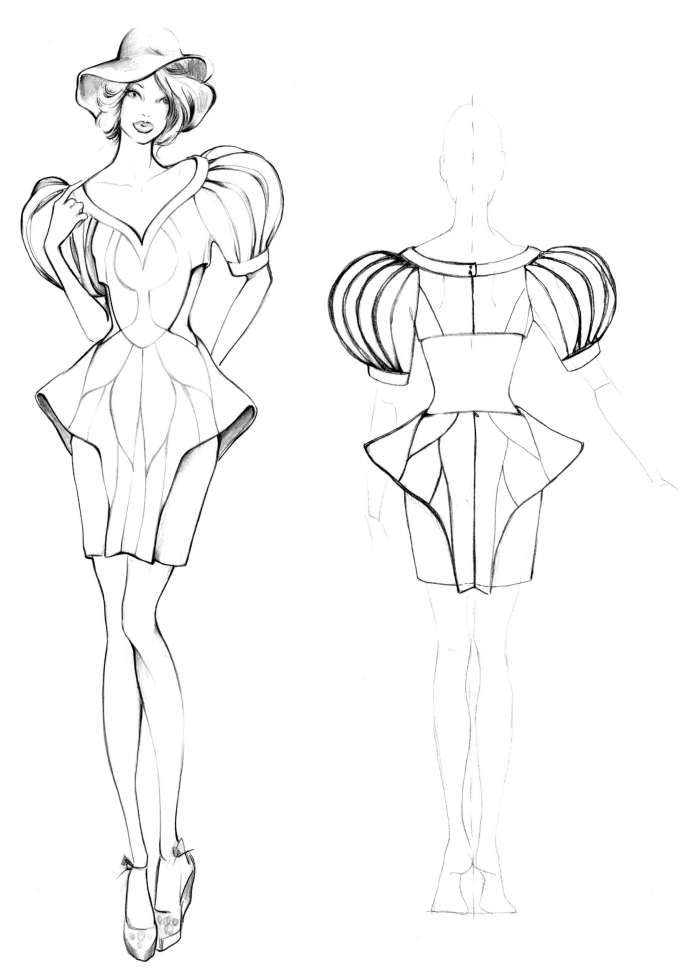

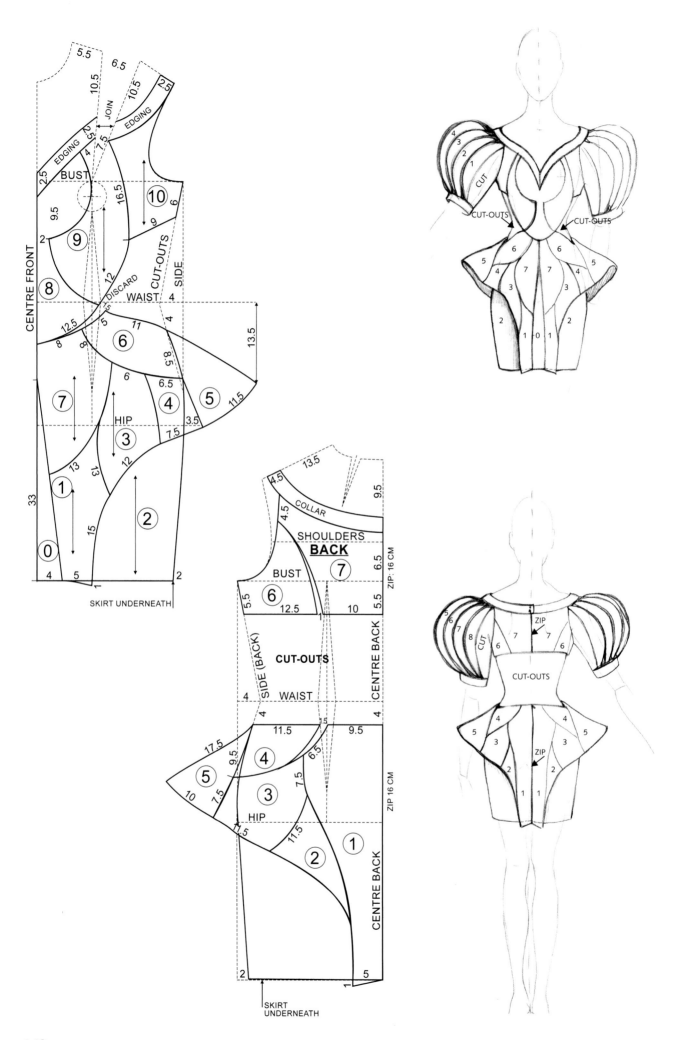

CENTRE FRONT

5.5 6.5
10.5 10.5
2.5 JOIN 2.5
EDGING 7.5 EDGING
2.5 4
2.5 BUST
9.5 16.5 (10) 6
2 (9) 9
(8) CUT-OUTS
DISCARD SIDE
WAIST 4
12.5 5 11 4 13.5
8 8 (6)
8.5
6 6.5
(7) 4 (5)
HIP (4) 11.5
(3) 3.5
7.5
13 13 12
(1)
33 15 (2)

(0)
4 5 1 2

SKIRT UNDERNEATH

13.5
4.5 9.5
COLLAR
4.5
SHOULDERS
BACK
BUST (7) 6.5
5.5 (6)
12.5 10 5.5

SIDE (BACK) CUT-OUTS CENTRE BACK

WAIST 4
4 11.5 1.5 9.5
17.5 9.5 (4) 6.5
(5) 7.5 7.5
10 7.5 (3)
HIP
11.5
11.5 (1)
(2)

CENTRE BACK

ZIP: 16 CM
ZIP 16 CM

2 5
1

SKIRT
UNDERNEATH

140

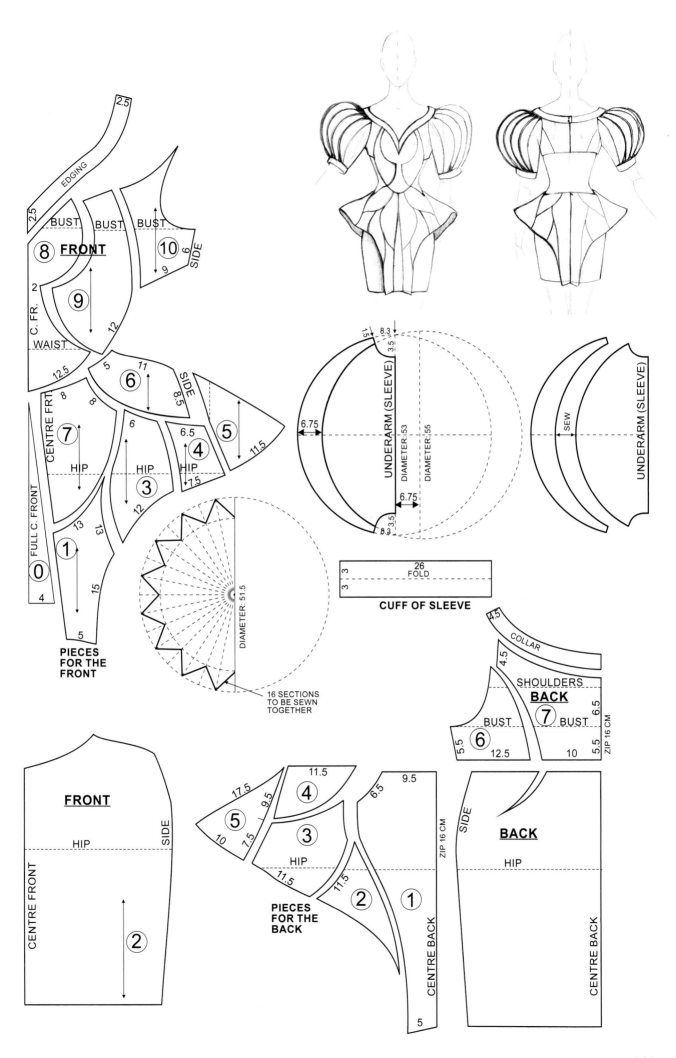

8 **FRONT**

EDGING
2.5
2.5
BUST
BUST
BUST
10
6
SIDE
9
9
2
C. FR.
9
12
WAIST
12.5
5
11
SIDE
CENTRE FRT
8.5
6
8
8
6
6.5
SIDE
5
4
11.5
HIP
HIP
HIP
7
3
7.5
FULL C. FRONT
12
13
13
1
0
15
4
5

**PIECES
FOR THE
FRONT**

DIAMETER: 51.5

16 SECTIONS
TO BE SEWN
TOGETHER

UNDERARM (SLEEVE)
1.5
8.3
3.5
6.75
DIAMETER: 53
DIAMETER: 55
6.75
8.3 3.5

UNDERARM (SLEEVE)
SEW

3
26
FOLD
3
3

CUFF OF SLEEVE

4.5
COLLAR
4.5
SHOULDERS
BACK
7
6.5
BUST
BUST
5.5
6
5.5
12.5
10
ZIP 16 CM

FRONT

HIP
SIDE
CENTRE FRONT
2

17.5
9.5
11.5
4
5
9.5
3
10
7.5
HIP
11.5
2
11.5
6.5
9.5
1
CENTRE BACK
5
ZIP 16 CM

**PIECES
FOR THE
BACK**

SIDE
BACK
HIP
CENTRE BACK

141

BUBBLE DRESS WITH AN OVERSIZE STAND-UP COLLAR

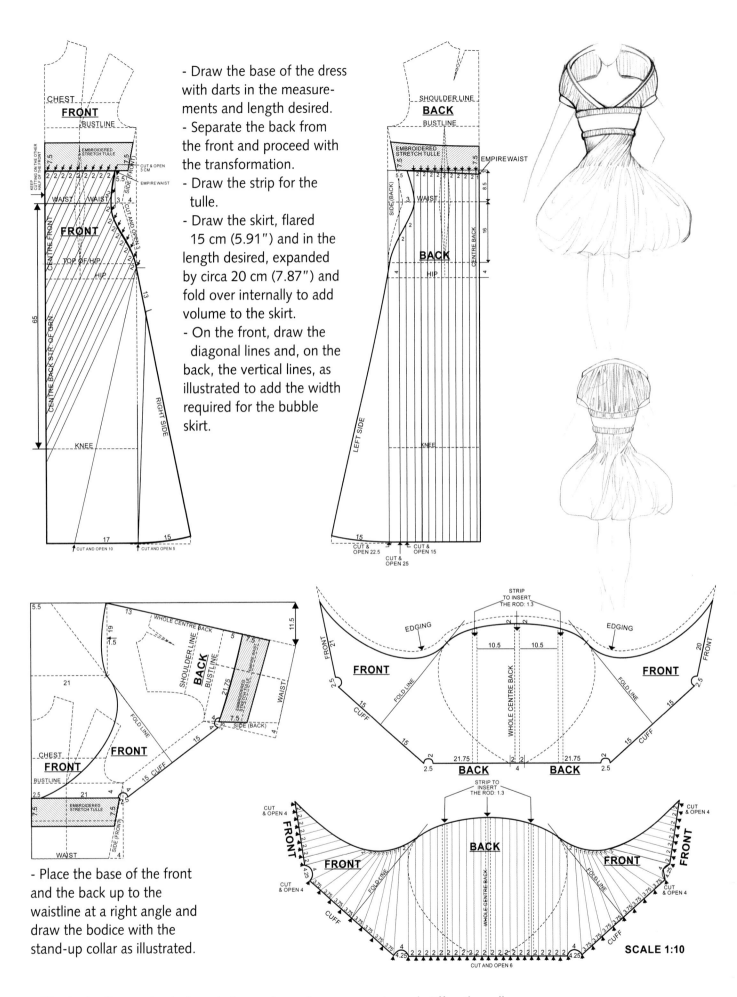

- Draw the base of the dress with darts in the measurements and length desired.
- Separate the back from the front and proceed with the transformation.
- Draw the strip for the tulle.
- Draw the skirt, flared 15 cm (5.91") and in the length desired, expanded by circa 20 cm (7.87") and fold over internally to add volume to the skirt.
- On the front, draw the diagonal lines and, on the back, the vertical lines, as illustrated to add the width required for the bubble skirt.

- Place the base of the front and the back up to the waistline at a right angle and draw the bodice with the stand-up collar as illustrated.

- Flip the bodice you've just made to create a mirror image and draw the vertical lines to cut, open and add width to the fabric, which will be needed to cover the crin and stiffen the collar.
- Cut 3 strips to insert 3 rods to support the stand-up collar.

143

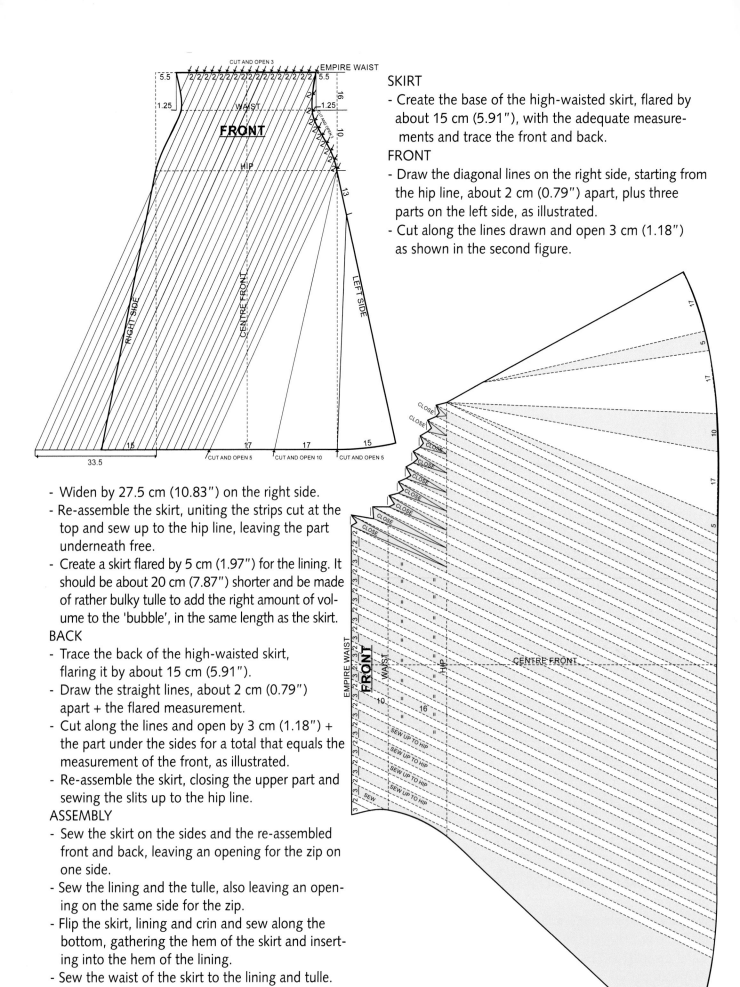

SKIRT
- Create the base of the high-waisted skirt, flared by about 15 cm (5.91"), with the adequate measurements and trace the front and back.

FRONT
- Draw the diagonal lines on the right side, starting from the hip line, about 2 cm (0.79") apart, plus three parts on the left side, as illustrated.
- Cut along the lines drawn and open 3 cm (1.18") as shown in the second figure.

- Widen by 27.5 cm (10.83") on the right side.
- Re-assemble the skirt, uniting the strips cut at the top and sew up to the hip line, leaving the part underneath free.
- Create a skirt flared by 5 cm (1.97") for the lining. It should be about 20 cm (7.87") shorter and be made of rather bulky tulle to add the right amount of volume to the 'bubble', in the same length as the skirt.

BACK
- Trace the back of the high-waisted skirt, flaring it by about 15 cm (5.91").
- Draw the straight lines, about 2 cm (0.79") apart + the flared measurement.
- Cut along the lines and open by 3 cm (1.18") + the part under the sides for a total that equals the measurement of the front, as illustrated.
- Re-assemble the skirt, closing the upper part and sewing the slits up to the hip line.

ASSEMBLY
- Sew the skirt on the sides and the re-assembled front and back, leaving an opening for the zip on one side.
- Sew the lining and the tulle, also leaving an opening on the same side for the zip.
- Flip the skirt, lining and crin and sew along the bottom, gathering the hem of the skirt and inserting into the hem of the lining.
- Sew the waist of the skirt to the lining and tulle. Sew the zip and finish it by joining it to the stretch tulle at the waist, then test it.
- Combine the entire lower half to the upper part of the dress.

SCALE 1:10

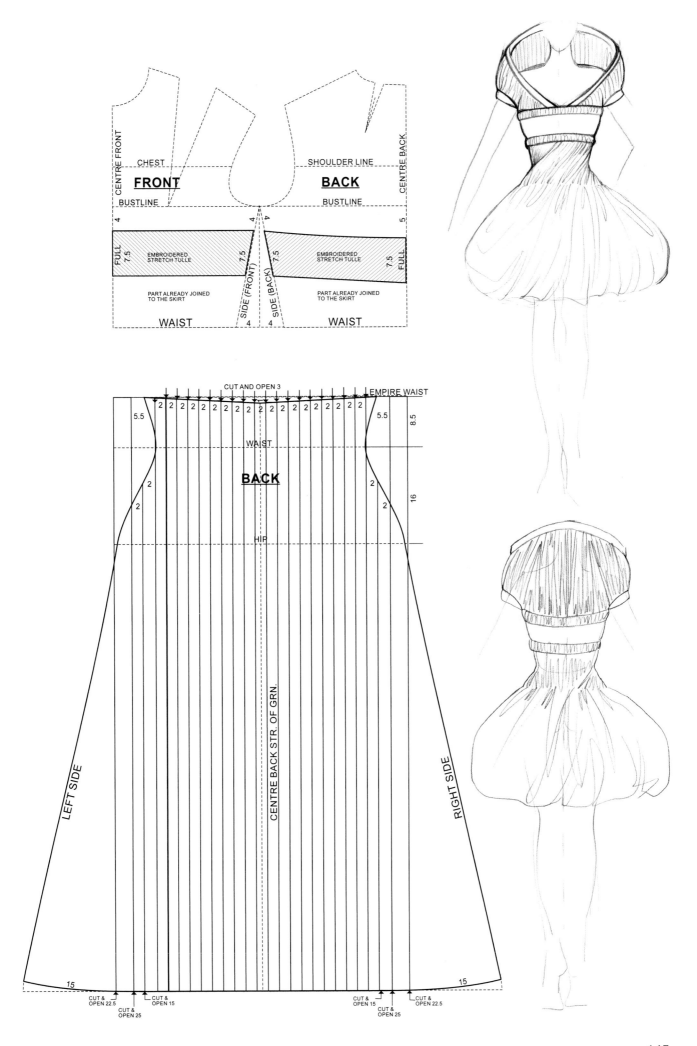

CENTRE FRONT

CHEST

FRONT

BUSTLINE

4

FULL 7.5

EMBROIDERED
STRETCH TULLE

7.5

PART ALREADY JOINED
TO THE SKIRT

WAIST

SIDE (FRONT)

4

SHOULDER LINE

BACK

BUSTLINE

CENTRE BACK

5

SIDE (BACK)

4

7.5

EMBROIDERED
STRETCH TULLE

7.5

FULL

PART ALREADY JOINED
TO THE SKIRT

WAIST

CUT AND OPEN 3

EMPIRE WAIST

5.5

2 2 2 2 2 2 2 2 2 2 2 2 2 2 2 2

5.5

8.5

WAIST

BACK

2

2

2

2

HIP

16

LEFT SIDE

CENTRE BACK STR. OF GRN.

RIGHT SIDE

15

CUT &
OPEN 22.5

CUT &
OPEN 15

CUT &
OPEN 25

CUT &
OPEN 15

CUT &
OPEN 25

CUT &
OPEN 22.5

15

145

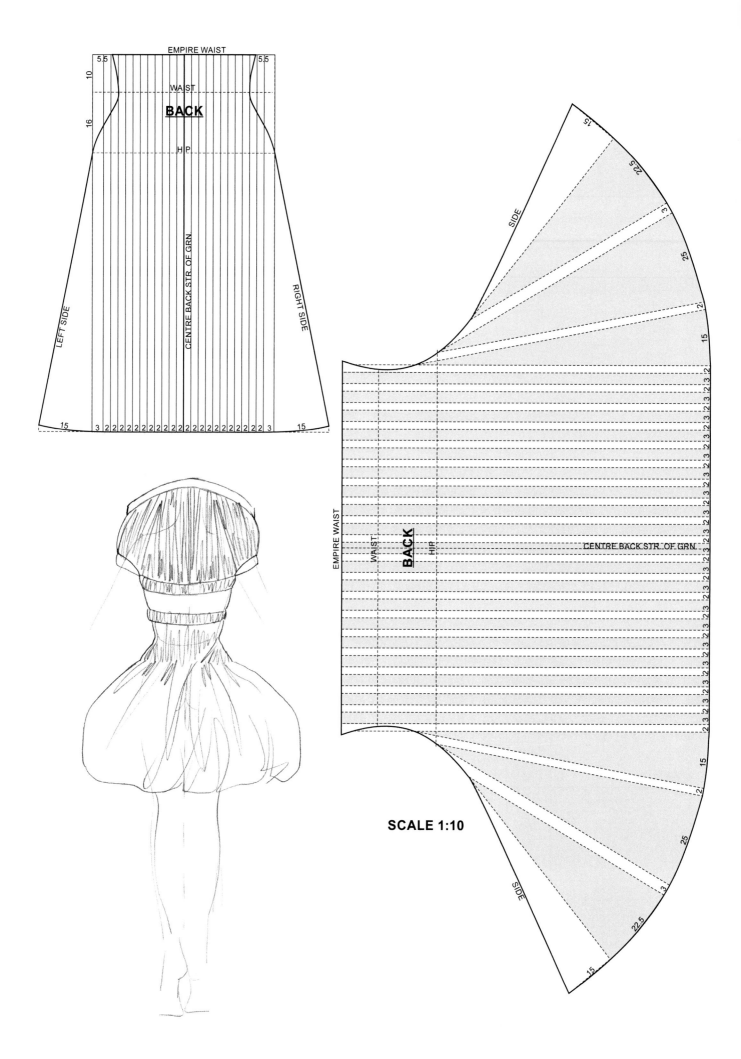

EMPIRE WAIST

5.5   5.5
10

WAIST

BACK

16

HIP

LEFT SIDE

RIGHT SIDE

CENTRE BACK STR. OF GRN

15   3 2 2 2 2 2 2 2 2 2 2 2 2 2 2 2 2 2 2 2 2 2 2 2 3   15

15
22.5
3
SIDE
25
2

EMPIRE WAIST

WAIST
BACK
HIP
CENTRE BACK STR. OF GRN

2 3 2 3 2 3 2 3 2 3 2 3 2 3 2 3 2 3 2 3 2 3 2 3 2 3 2 3 2 3 2 3 2 3 2 3 2 3

15
2
25
3
SIDE
22.5
15

SCALE 1:10

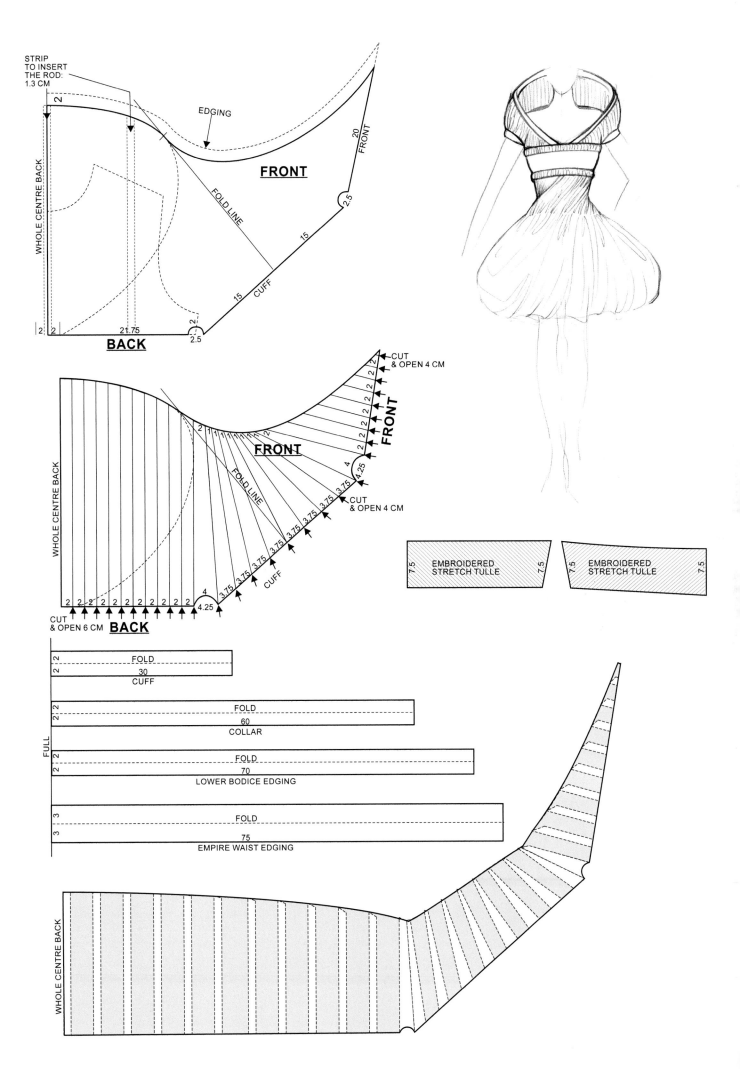

STRIP TO INSERT THE ROD: 1.3 CM

2

WHOLE CENTRE BACK

EDGING

FOLD LINE

20 FRONT

FRONT

2.5

15

15 CUFF

2.5

BACK

2 2

21.75

2
2.5

CUT & OPEN 4 CM

2 2 2 2 2

2 2 2 2

FRONT

2 1 1 1 2

WHOLE CENTRE BACK

FOLD LINE

4
4.25
3.75

CUT & OPEN 4 CM

3.75 3.75 3.75 3.75 3.75 3.75 3.75 3.75 3.75

CUFF

2 2 2 2 2 2 2 2 2 2 2

4
4.25

CUT & OPEN 6 CM **BACK**

FRONT

EMBROIDERED STRETCH TULLE 7.5

7.5 EMBROIDERED STRETCH TULLE 7.5

2 2
FOLD
30
CUFF

2 2
FOLD
60
COLLAR

FULL

2 2
FOLD
70
LOWER BODICE EDGING

3 3
FOLD
75
EMPIRE WAIST EDGING

WHOLE CENTRE BACK

SUIT-DRESS WITH KIMONO SLEEVES
THAT TURN INTO GLOVES; DOUBLE SKIRT

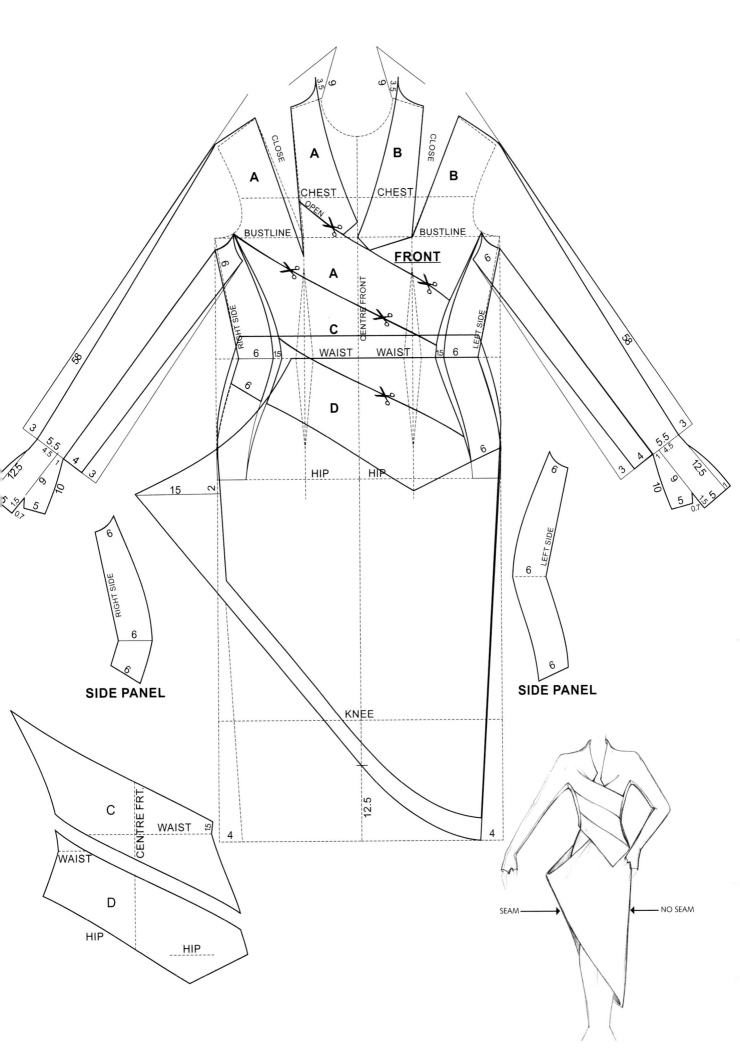

CLOSE

A

B

CLOSE

A

B

3.5
9
9
3.5

CHEST

CHEST

OPEN

BUSTLINE

BUSTLINE

FRONT

A

9

6

RIGHT SIDE

CENTRE FRONT

LEFT SIDE

A

C

6   15

WAIST

WAIST

15   6

6

D

6

58

58

3

5.5

4.5   1

4

3

3

4

1   4.5

5.5

3

12.5

9

12.5

5

9

5

1.5

10

10

0.7

0.7   1.5

0.7

5

HIP

HIP

15   2

6

6

RIGHT SIDE

6

6

SIDE PANEL

6

LEFT SIDE

6

6

SIDE PANEL

KNEE

C

CENTRE FRT.

WAIST

15

12.5

WAIST

4

4

D

HIP

HIP

SEAM

NO SEAM

149

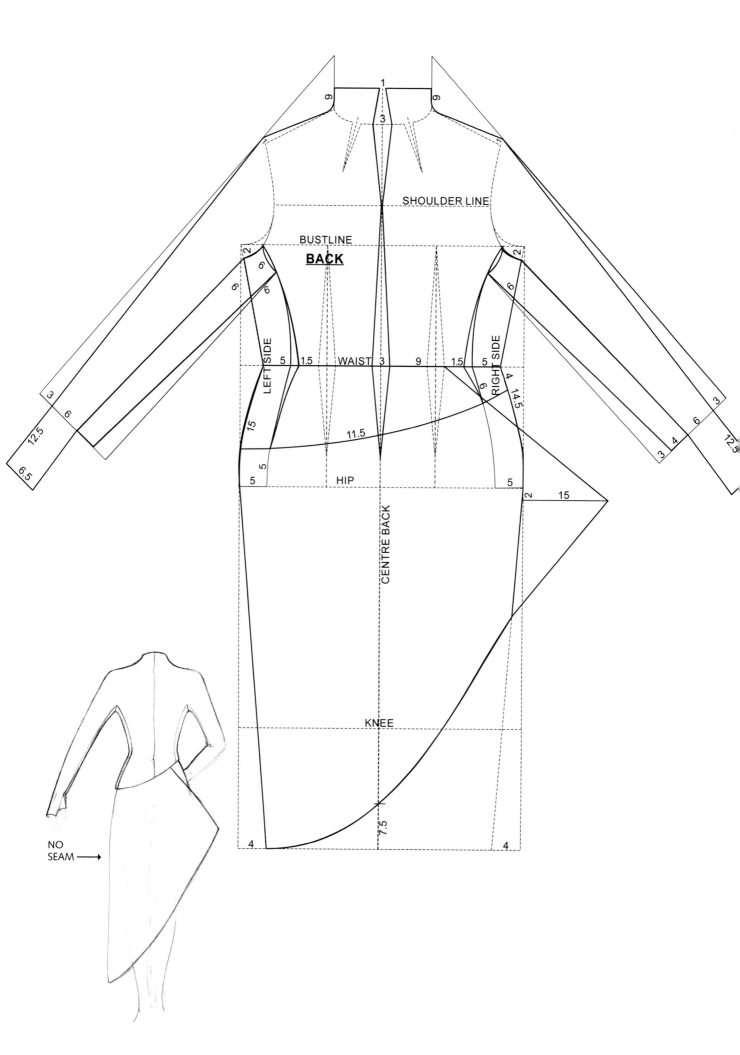

SHOULDER LINE

BUSTLINE
BACK

LEFT SIDE

RIGHT SIDE

WAIST

HIP

CENTRE BACK

KNEE

NO
SEAM →

1

3

9

9

2

6

9

6

2

6

9

6

5

1.5

3

9

1.5

5

4

14.5

6

15

11.5

5

5

5

5

2

15

3

6

12.5

6.5

3

6

12.5

3

4

3

4

7.5

4

4

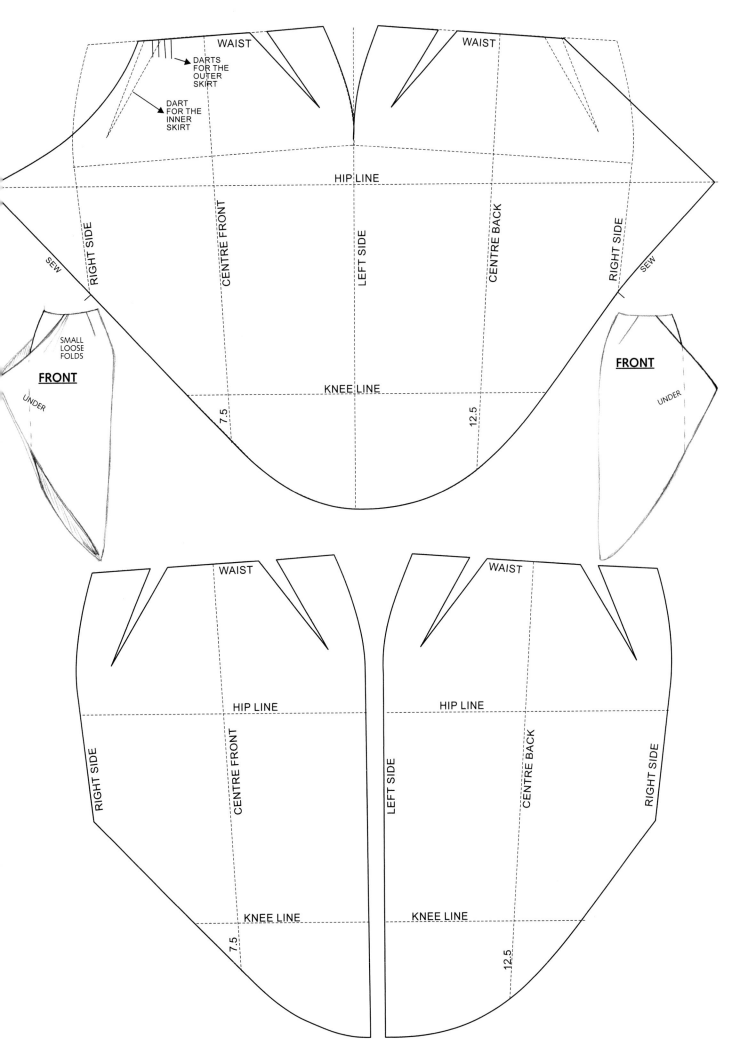

WAIST

DARTS
FOR THE
OUTER
SKIRT

DART
FOR THE
INNER
SKIRT

WAIST

HIP LINE

RIGHT SIDE

CENTRE FRONT

LEFT SIDE

CENTRE BACK

RIGHT SIDE

SEW

SEW

SMALL
LOOSE
FOLDS

FRONT

UNDER

FRONT

UNDER

KNEE LINE

7.5

12.5

WAIST

WAIST

HIP LINE

HIP LINE

RIGHT SIDE

CENTRE FRONT

LEFT SIDE

CENTRE BACK

RIGHT SIDE

KNEE LINE

KNEE LINE

7.5

12.5

151

SINGLE-SLEEVE ROSETTE MOTIF DRESS
WITH WHIRLS AND A DOUBLE ASYMMETRICAL COLLAR

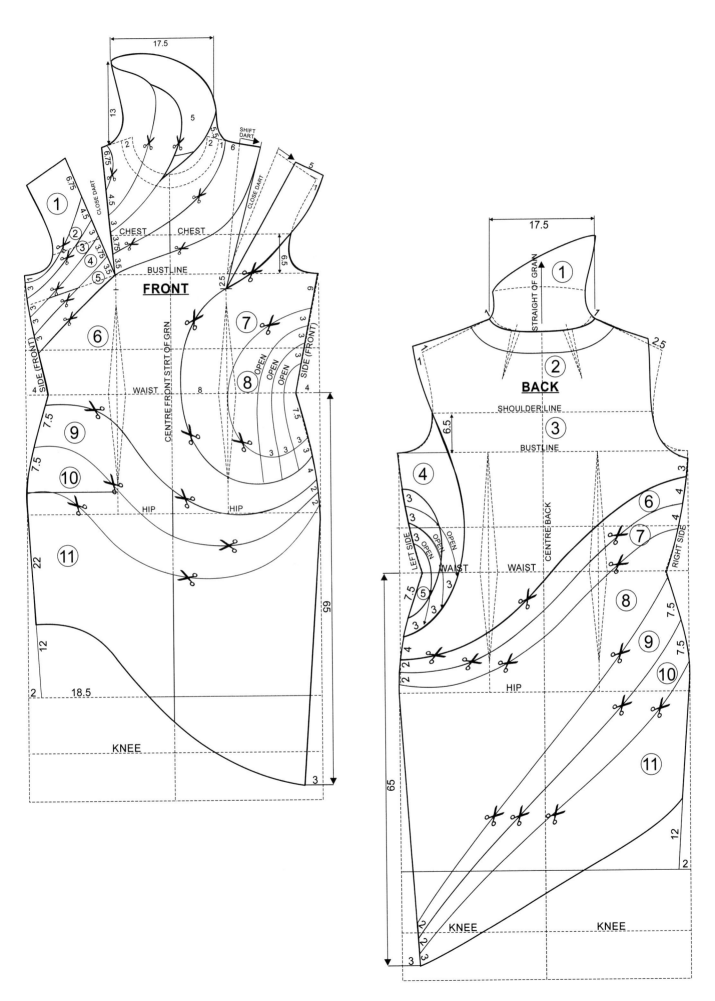

FRONT

BACK

153

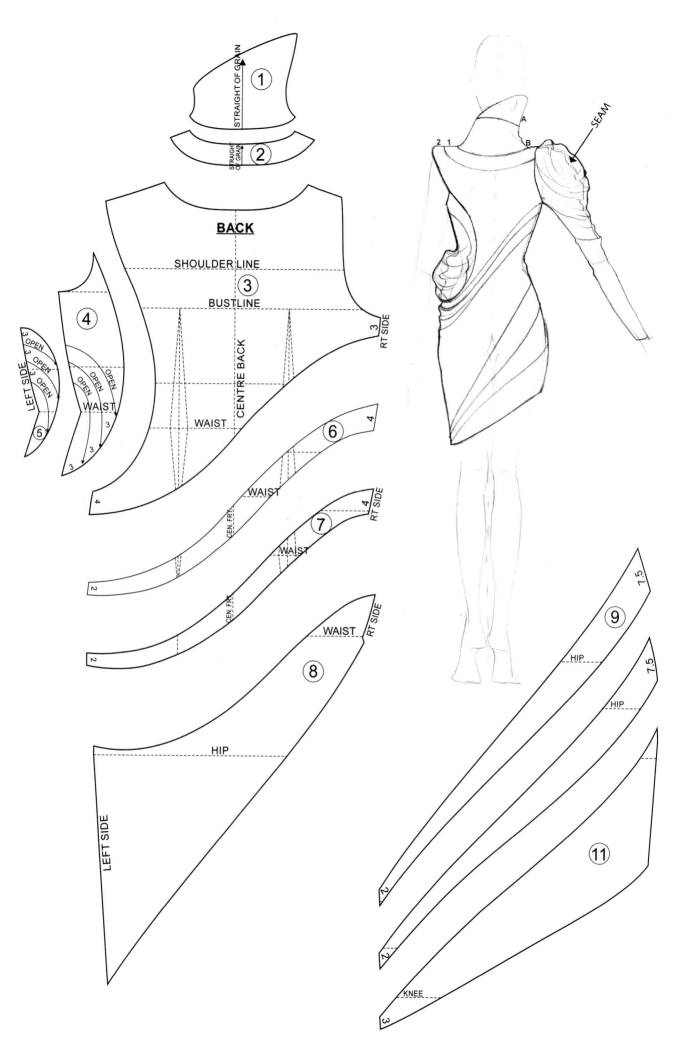

STRAIGHT OF GRAIN

① ②

STRAIGHT OF GRAIN

BACK

SHOULDER LINE

③

BUSTLINE

④

CENTRE BACK

RT SIDE

3

3 OPEN
3 OPEN
3 OPEN
OPEN
OPEN
OPEN

LEFT SIDE

WAIST

⑤

WAIST

3
3
3

WAIST

4

⑥

CEN. FRT.

2

RT SIDE

4

⑦

WAIST

CEN. FRT.

2

RT SIDE

WAIST

⑧

HIP

LEFT SIDE

SEAM

2 1
A
B

7.5

⑨

HIP

7.5

HIP

2

⑪

2

KNEE

3

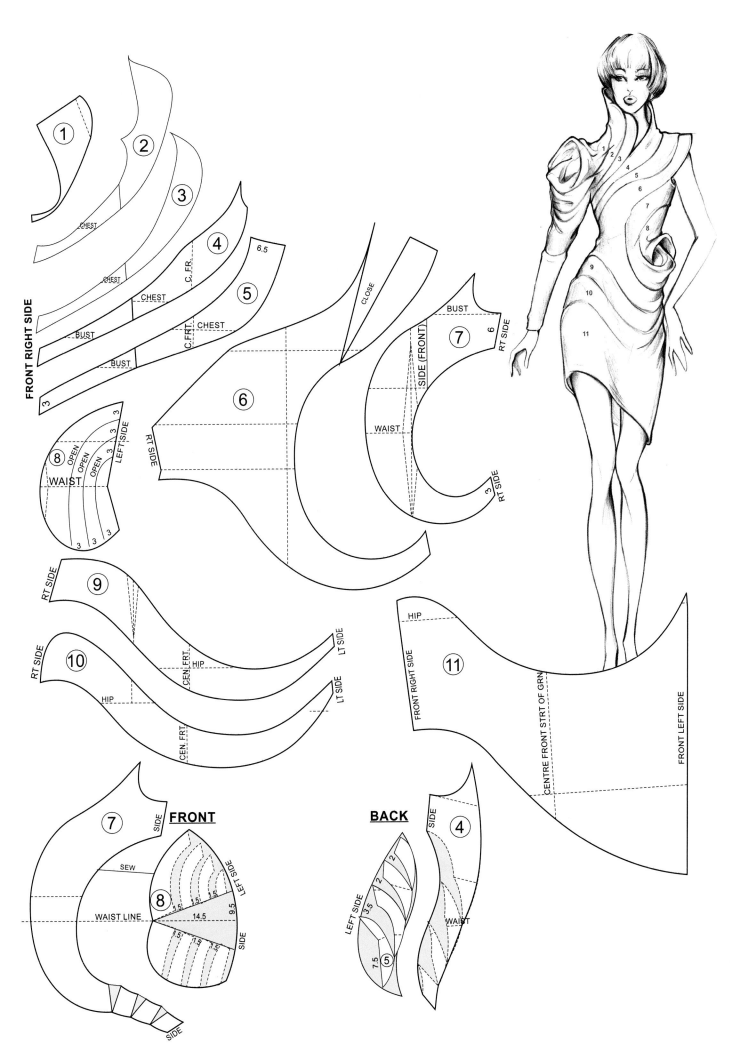

FRONT RIGHT SIDE

① ② ③ ④ ⑤ 6.5

CHEST
CHEST
CHEST C. FR.
C.FRT. CHEST
CHEST
BUST
BUST
BUST
3

⑥ RT SIDE

CLOSE

⑦ SIDE (FRONT)
BUST 6
RT SIDE
WAIST
RT SIDE 3

⑧ WAIST
OPEN OPEN OPEN
LEFT SIDE
3 3 3
3 3 3
3 3 3

⑨ RT SIDE

⑩ RT SIDE HIP
CEN. FRT. HIP LT SIDE
CEN. FRT. LT SIDE

⑪ FRONT RIGHT SIDE
HIP
CENTRE FRONT STRT OF GRN
FRONT LEFT SIDE

⑦ SIDE **FRONT**
SEW
⑧ WAIST LINE
LEFT SIDE
1.5 1.5 1.5
14.5 9.5
1.5 1.5 1.5
SIDE
SIDE

BACK ④ SIDE
2 2
3.5 2
LEFT SIDE
7.5 ⑤ WAIST

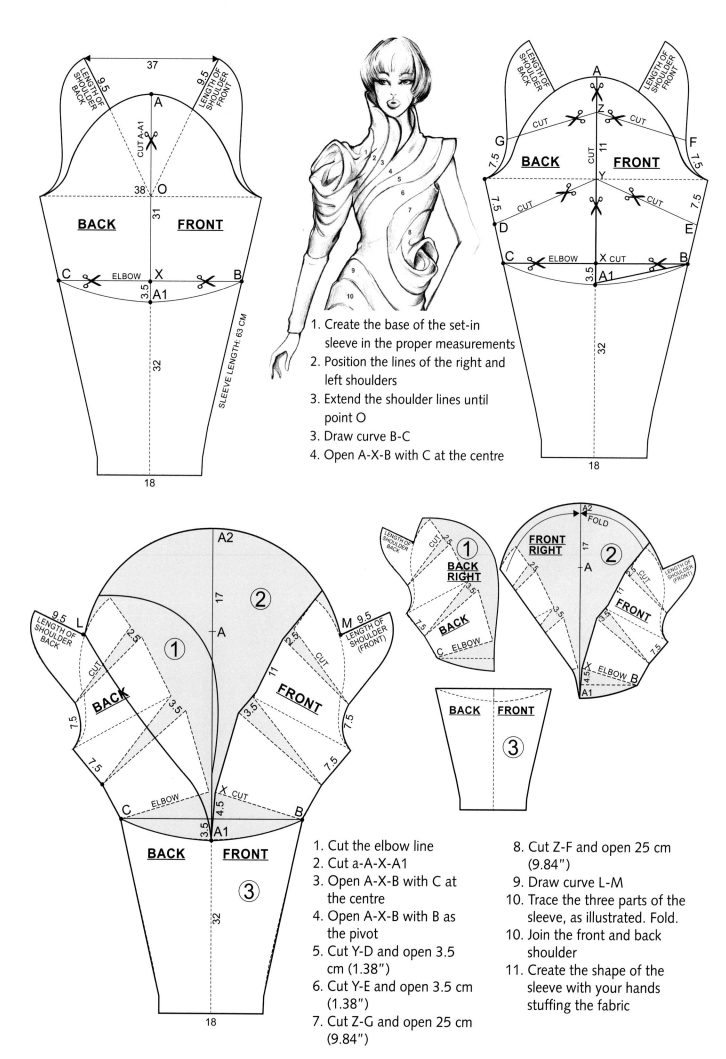

First diagram (top left):

37

9.5 LENGTH OF SHOULDER BACK

9.5 LENGTH OF SHOULDER FRONT

A

CUT A-A1

38   O

31

BACK   **FRONT**

C   ELBOW   X   B

3.5   A1

32

SLEEVE LENGTH: 63 CM

18

Instructions (center top):

1. Create the base of the set-in sleeve in the proper measurements
2. Position the lines of the right and left shoulders
3. Extend the shoulder lines until point O
3. Draw curve B-C
4. Open A-X-B with C at the centre

Second diagram (top right):

LENGTH OF SHOULDER BACK

LENGTH OF SHOULDER FRONT

A

Z

CUT   CUT

G   11   F

7.5   CUT   7.5

BACK   **FRONT**

Y

7.5   CUT   CUT   7.5

D   E

C   ELBOW   X CUT   B

3.5   A1

32

18

Bottom left large diagram:

A2

9.5 L   LENGTH OF SHOULDER BACK

17

A

M 9.5   LENGTH OF SHOULDER (FRONT)

2.5   ①   2.5

CUT   11   CUT

3.5   3.5

BACK   **FRONT**

7.5   ②   7.5

7.5   7.5

C   ELBOW   X CUT   B

3.5   4.5

A1

BACK   **FRONT**

③

32

18

Bottom center small diagrams:

LENGTH OF SHOULDER BACK

CUT   2.5

①

BACK RIGHT

3.5

7.5   **BACK**

C   ELBOW

A2   FOLD

17

FRONT RIGHT

2.5   A   ②

2.5 CUT

3.5   3.5

FRONT

7.5

4.5 X   ELBOW   B

A1

BACK   **FRONT**

③

Instructions (bottom):

1. Cut the elbow line
2. Cut a-A-X-A1
3. Open A-X-B with C at the centre
4. Open A-X-B with B as the pivot
5. Cut Y-D and open 3.5 cm (1.38")
6. Cut Y-E and open 3.5 cm (1.38")
7. Cut Z-G and open 25 cm (9.84")
8. Cut Z-F and open 25 cm (9.84")
9. Draw curve L-M
10. Trace the three parts of the sleeve, as illustrated. Fold.
10. Join the front and back shoulder
11. Create the shape of the sleeve with your hands stuffing the fabric

HOOD-MOTIF TUNIC AND TROUSERS

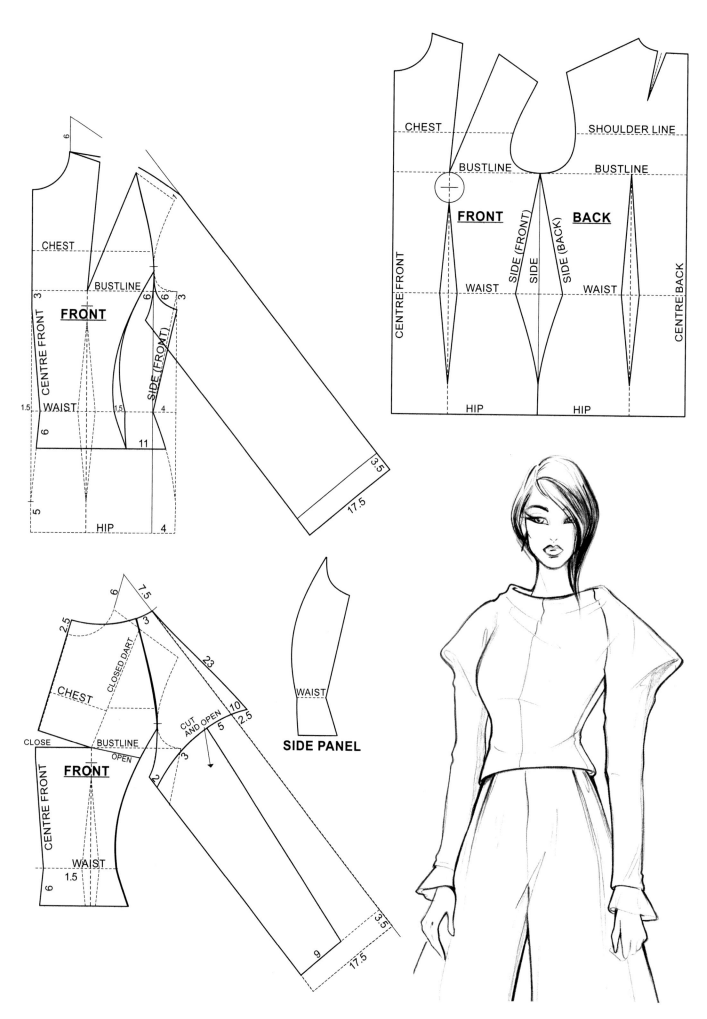

CHEST

BUSTLINE

FRONT

CENTRE FRONT

WAIST

HIP

6

3

1.5

6

1.5

4

11

5

4

3.5

17.5

6

6

3

SIDE (FRONT)

CHEST

SHOULDER LINE

BUSTLINE

BUSTLINE

FRONT

BACK

CENTRE FRONT

WAIST

SIDE (FRONT)

SIDE

SIDE (BACK)

WAIST

CENTRE BACK

HIP

HIP

6

7.5

2.5

3

CLOSED DART

CHEST

CLOSE

BUSTLINE

OPEN

FRONT

CENTRE FRONT

WAIST

1.5

6

23

CUT
AND OPEN

10

2.5

5

3

2

3.5

9

17.5

WAIST

SIDE PANEL

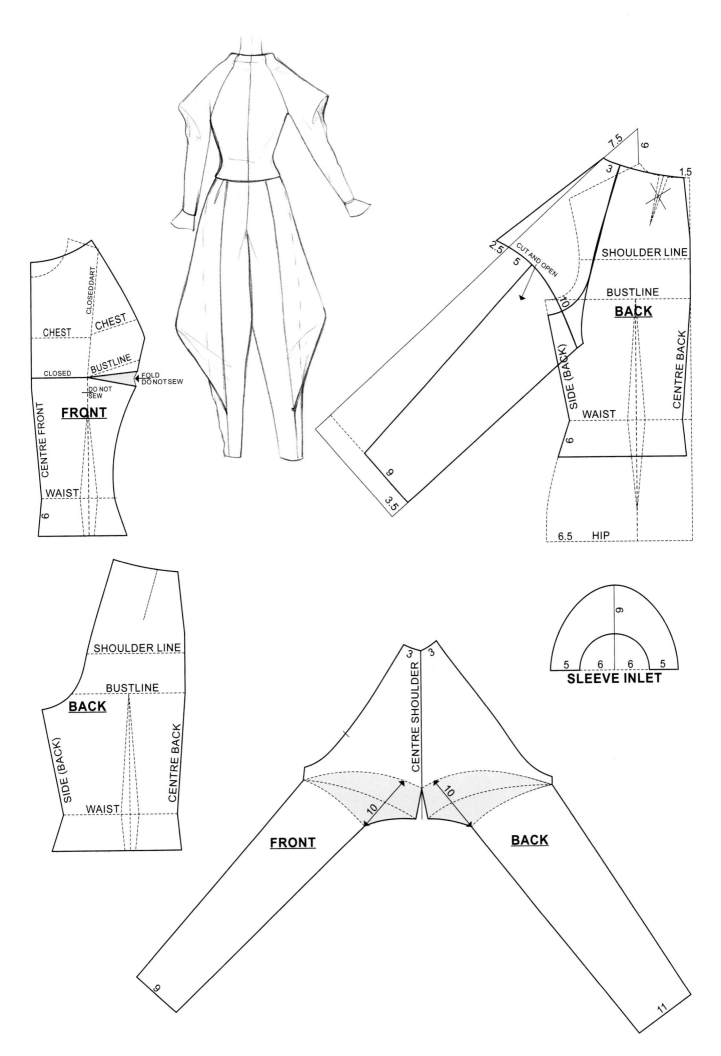

FRONT

CLOSED DART
CHEST
CHEST
BUSTLINE
CLOSED
FOLD DO NOT SEW
DO NOT SEW
CENTRE FRONT
WAIST
6

7.5   6
3   1.5
SHOULDER LINE
BUSTLINE
BACK
2.5   CUT AND OPEN   5
SIDE (BACK)
WAIST
CENTRE BACK
6
9   3.5
6.5   HIP

SHOULDER LINE
BUSTLINE
BACK
SIDE (BACK)
CENTRE BACK
WAIST

FRONT   BACK
CENTRE SHOULDER
3   3
10   10
9   11

SLEEVE INLET
5   6   6   5
9

159

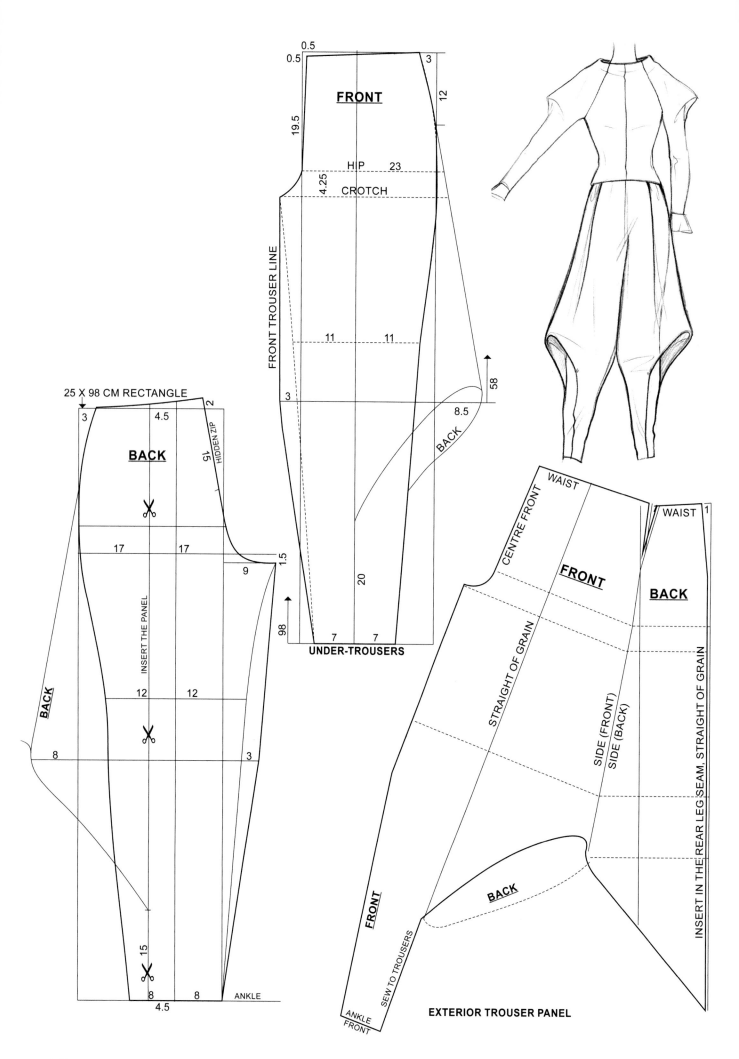

FRONT

0.5
0.5
3
12
19.5
FRONT TROUSER LINE
HIP 23
4.25
CROTCH
11 11
3
58
8.5
BACK
20
98
7 7
UNDER-TROUSERS

25 X 98 CM RECTANGLE
3
4.5
2
15
HIDDEN ZIP
BACK
17 17
1.5
9
BACK
INSERT THE PANEL
12 12
8 3
15
8 8 ANKLE
4.5

WAIST
CENTRE FRONT
WAIST 1
FRONT
BACK
STRAIGHT OF GRAIN
SIDE (FRONT)
SIDE (BACK)
INSERT IN THE REAR LEG SEAM, STRAIGHT OF GRAIN
FRONT
BACK
SEW TO TROUSERS
ANKLE FRONT
EXTERIOR TROUSER PANEL

DRESS WITH A WIDE ASYMMETRICAL NECKLINE

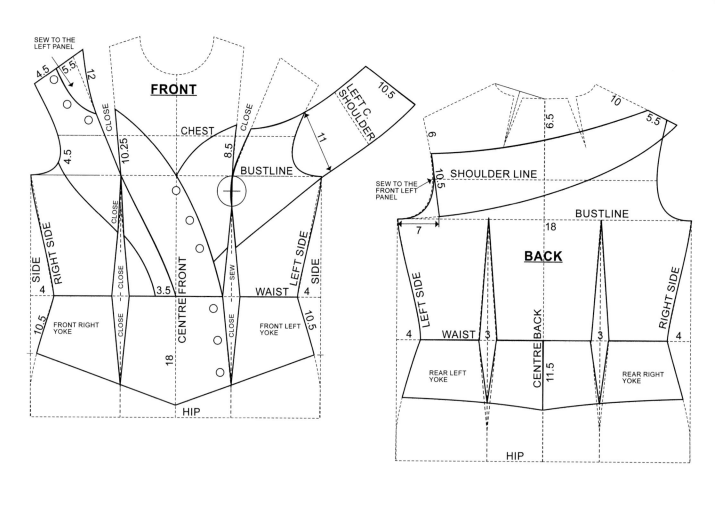

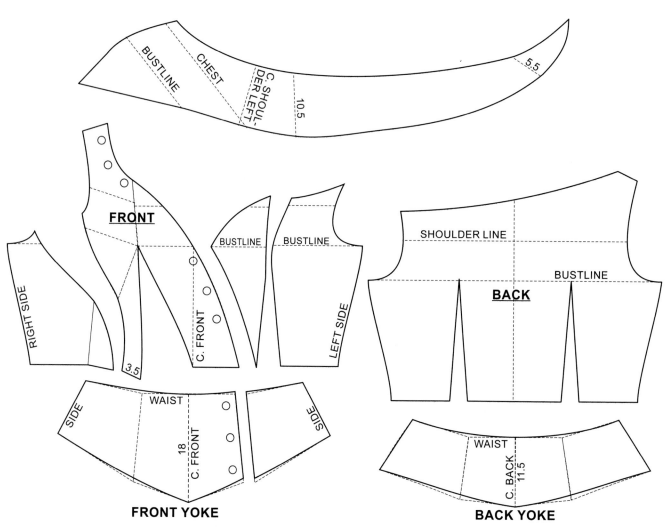

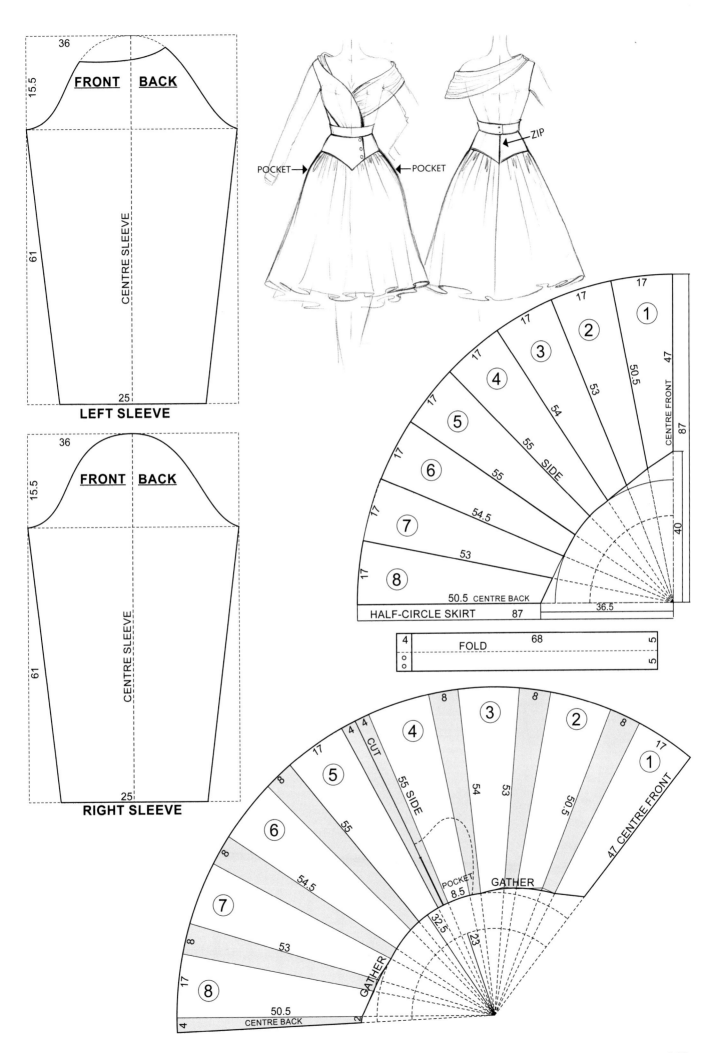

LEFT SLEEVE

36

15.5

61

CENTRE SLEEVE

FRONT   BACK

25

RIGHT SLEEVE

36

15.5

61

CENTRE SLEEVE

FRONT   BACK

25

POCKET ←   ← POCKET

← ZIP

HALF-CIRCLE SKIRT

17
17
17
17
17
17
17
17

① 17
②
③
④
⑤
⑥
⑦
⑧

50.5
53
54
55
55
54.5
53
50.5

CENTRE FRONT   47
87
40
36.5
SIDE
CENTRE BACK

FOLD   68
4   5
○   5
○

① 17
②
③
④
⑤
⑥
⑦
⑧

8
8
8
8
8
8
8

4
4
CUT

17

50.5
53
54
55
55
54.5
53
50.5

47 CENTRE FRONT
SIDE
CENTRE BACK
GATHER
GATHER
POCKET 8.5
32.5
23
4   2

163

DRESS WITH A CAPE COLLAR

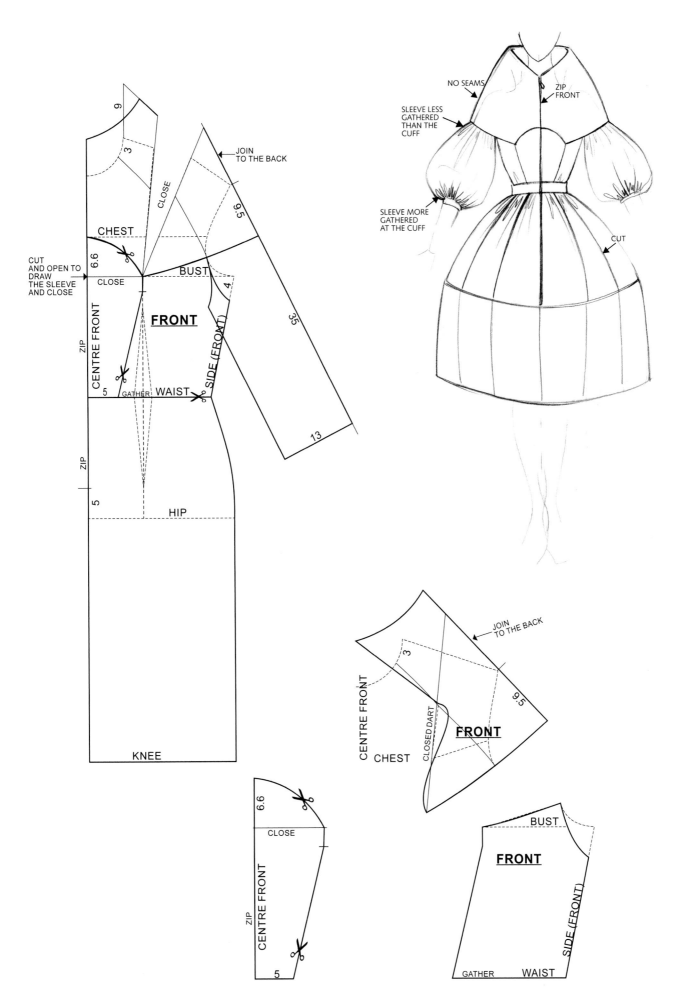

CUT
AND OPEN TO
DRAW
THE SLEEVE
AND CLOSE

9

3

CLOSE

JOIN
TO THE BACK

9.5

CHEST

6.6

CLOSE

BUST

4

35

FRONT

CENTRE FRONT

ZIP

SIDE (FRONT)

5

GATHER

WAIST

13

ZIP

5

HIP

ZIP

KNEE

NO SEAMS

ZIP
FRONT

SLEEVE LESS
GATHERED
THAN THE
CUFF

SLEEVE MORE
GATHERED
AT THE CUFF

CUT

JOIN
TO THE BACK

3

9.5

CENTRE FRONT

CHEST

CLOSED DART

FRONT

6.6

CLOSE

ZIP

CENTRE FRONT

5

BUST

FRONT

SIDE (FRONT)

GATHER

WAIST

BACK

JOIN WITH FRONT

SHOULDERS

BUST

SIDE (BACK)

CENTRE BACK

WAIST GATHER

HIP

KNEE

3.6

9

8

8.5

35

15

4

5

SEAMS CENTRE BACK

JOIN WITH FRONT

BACK

SHOULDERS

BUST

8.5

BACK

SIDE (BACK)

BUST

WAIST GATHER

CENTRE BACK

5

CENTRE BACK

BACK

SHOULDERS

BUST

CENTRE FRONT

CLOSED DART

3

8.5

9.5

FRONT

CHEST

BUST SIDE

GATHER

35

GATHER

35

GATHER

15

SLEEVE BACK

13

SLEEVE FRONT

4

22

FOLD

CUFF

4

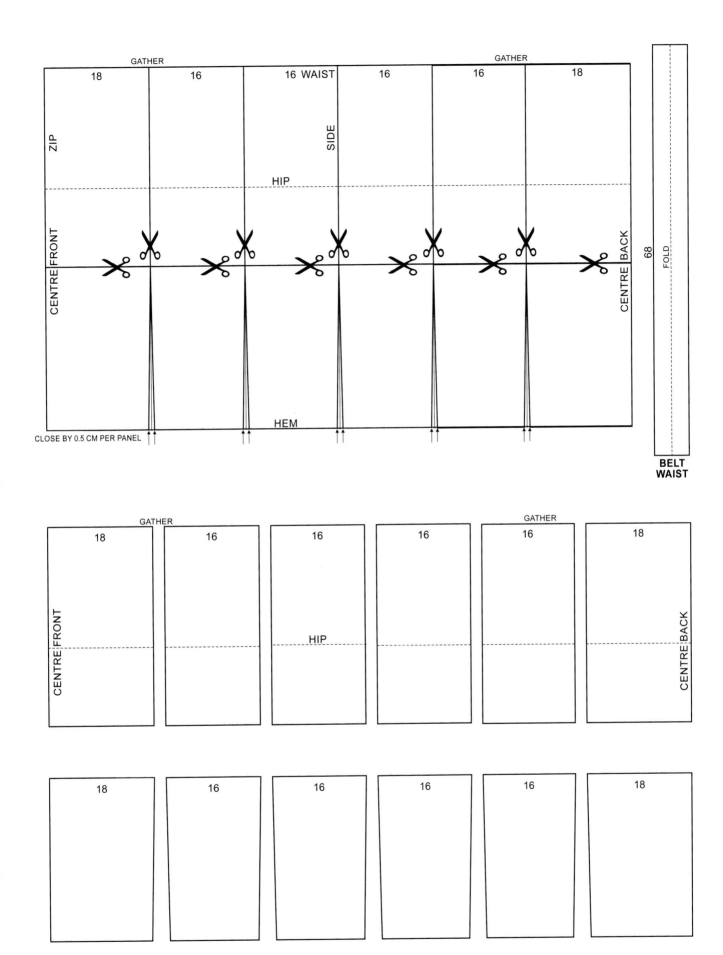

GATHER   GATHER

| 18 | 16 | 16 WAIST | 16 | 16 | 18 |

ZIP   SIDE

HIP

CENTRE FRONT   CENTRE BACK

HEM

CLOSE BY 0.5 CM PER PANEL

68

FOLD

BELT WAIST

GATHER   GATHER

| 18 | 16 | 16 | 16 | 16 | 18 |

CENTRE FRONT HIP CENTRE BACK

| 18 | 16 | 16 | 16 | 16 | 18 |

NB:

Aт each seam, put rods, including on the hem and the horizontal seam.

The gathered fabric at the waist should be well distributed, depending on the circumference.

167

DRESS WITH OFF-SHOULDER SLEEVES

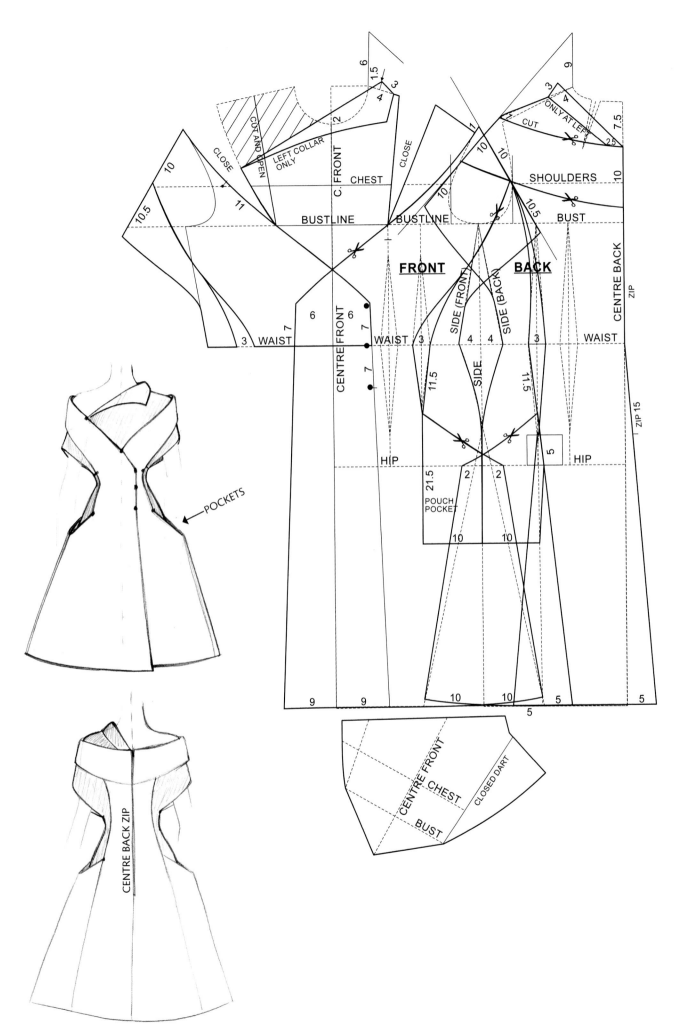

POCKETS

CENTRE BACK ZIP

FRONT   **BACK**

6   1.5   3   4   2   6   3   4   7.5   2.5

CUT AND OPEN

LEFT COLLAR ONLY

CLOSE   CLOSE   ONLY AT LEFT   CUT

10   10.5   11   10   10   10   10.5   10

C. FRONT   CHEST   SHOULDERS

BUSTLINE   BUSTLINE   BUST

CENTRE BACK   ZIP

CENTRE FRONT

6   6   7   SIDE (FRONT)   SIDE (BACK)   CENTRE BACK

3   WAIST   7   WAIST   3   4   4   3   WAIST

7   11.5   SIDE   11.5

ZIP 15

HIP   5   HIP

21.5   2   2

POUCH POCKET

10   10

9   9   10   10   5   5

5

CENTRE FRONT   CHEST   BUST   CLOSED DART

169

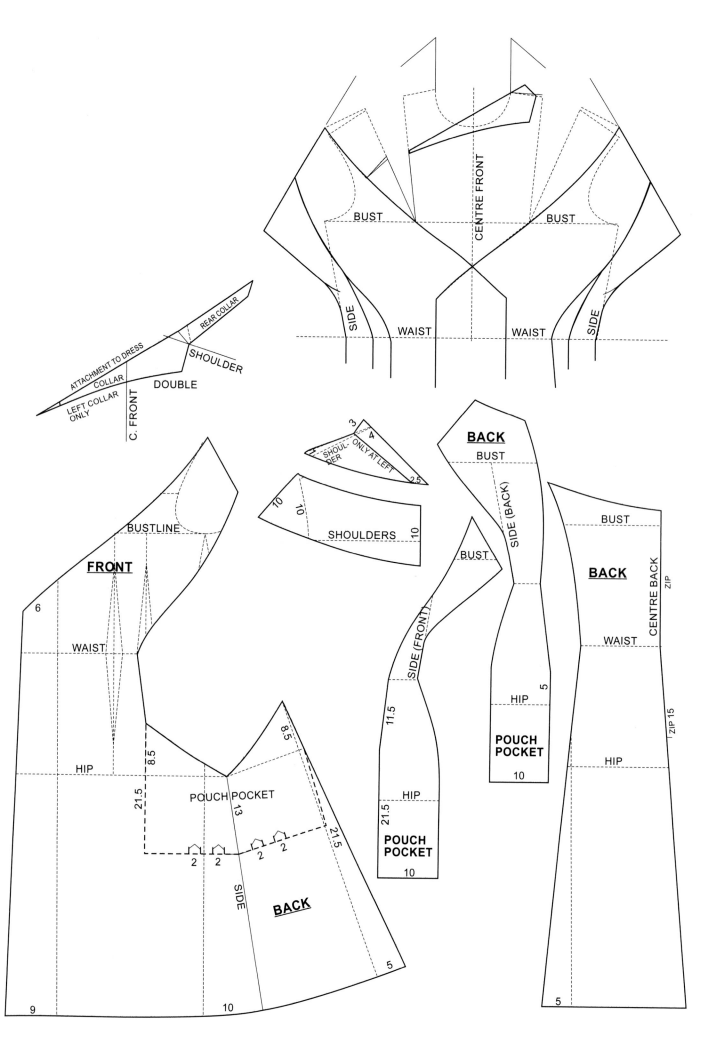

CENTRE FRONT

BUST

BUST

SIDE

WAIST

WAIST

SIDE

REAR COLLAR

ATTACHMENT TO DRESS

COLLAR

SHOULDER

LEFT COLLAR ONLY

C. FRONT

DOUBLE

3 4

SHOUL-DER

ONLY AT LEFT

2.5

10 10

SHOULDERS 10

BACK

BUST

SIDE (BACK)

BUST

BUST

BUST

BACK

CENTRE BACK

ZIP

BUSTLINE

FRONT

6

WAIST

HIP

21.5

8.5

POUCH POCKET

13

8.5

SIDE (FRONT)

11.5

HIP

21.5

POUCH POCKET

10

WAIST

HIP

5

POUCH POCKET

10

WAIST

HIP

ZIP 15

8.5

21.5

2 2 2 2

SIDE

BACK

5

9

10

POUCH POCKET

10

5

DRESS WITH SLEEVES THAT FORM A CAPE IN THE BACK
FRONT PANELS

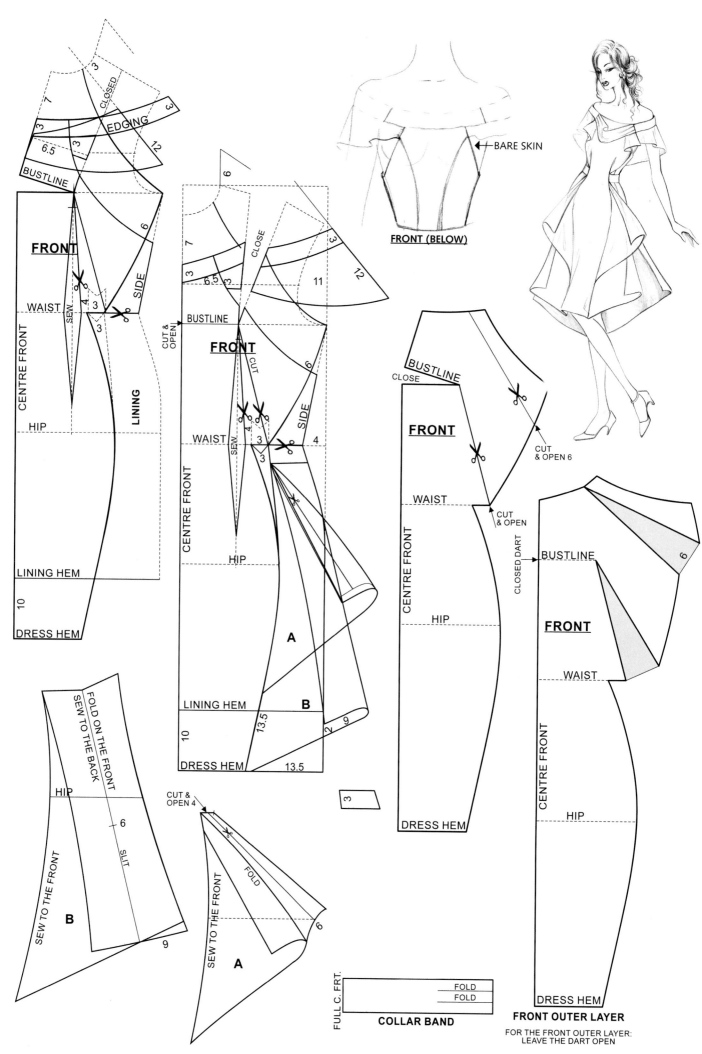

FRONT

CLOSED

EDGING

BUSTLINE

CENTRE FRONT

WAIST

SEW

HIP

LINING

LINING HEM

10

DRESS HEM

SIDE

3 7 3 3 6.5 3 3 12 6

4 3 3

FOLD ON THE FRONT
SEW TO THE BACK

HIP

6

SLIT

SEW TO THE FRONT

B

9

FRONT

CLOSE

CUT

BUSTLINE

CUT & OPEN

CENTRE FRONT

WAIST

SEW

HIP

SIDE

LINING HEM

10 13.5

DRESS HEM 13.5

A

B

13.5 2 9

6 7 3 6.5 3 11 12 3

4 3 3 4

CUT & OPEN 4

FOLD

SEW TO THE FRONT

A

6

3

FRONT (BELOW)

←BARE SKIN

FRONT

BUSTLINE

CLOSE

CENTRE FRONT

WAIST

HIP

DRESS HEM

CUT & OPEN 6

CUT & OPEN

3

FULL C. FRT.

FOLD
FOLD

COLLAR BAND

CLOSED DART

BUSTLINE

FRONT

WAIST

CENTRE FRONT

HIP

DRESS HEM

6

FRONT OUTER LAYER

FOR THE FRONT OUTER LAYER:
LEAVE THE DART OPEN

172

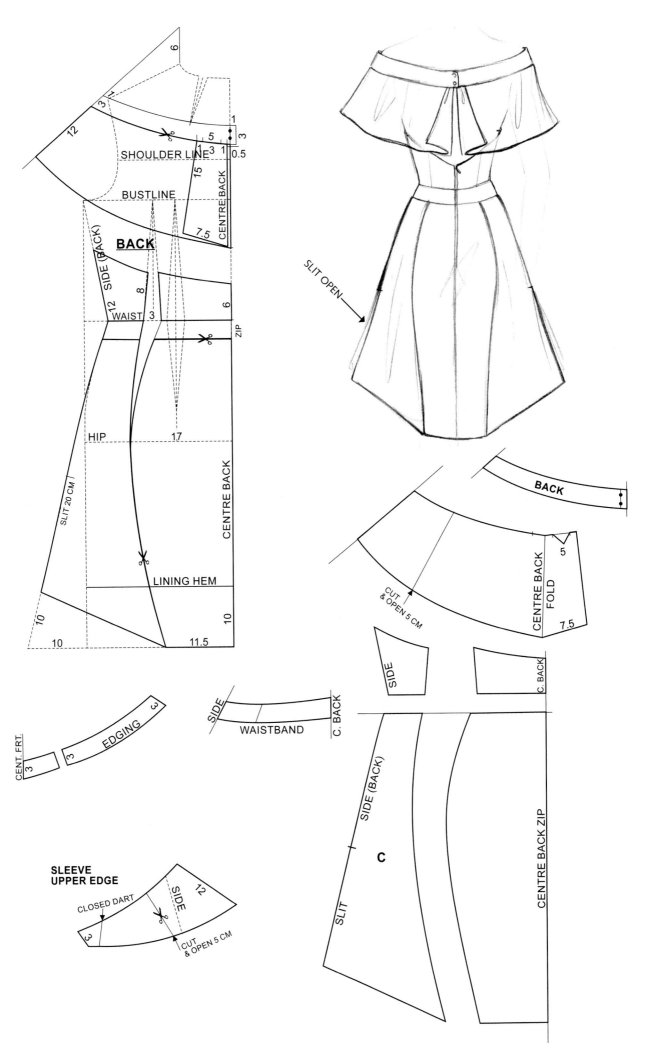

6

SHOULDER LINE

3 1

1

5

1 3 0.5

12

BUSTLINE

15

CENTRE BACK

7.5

BACK

SIDE (BACK)

8

12 WAIST 3

6

ZIP

HIP

17

SLIT 20 CM

CENTRE BACK

LINING HEM

10

10

10

11.5

SLIT OPEN

BACK

CUT & OPEN 5 CM

5

CENTRE BACK FOLD

7.5

CENT. FRT.

3

EDGING

3

3

SIDE

WAISTBAND

C. BACK

SIDE

C. BACK

SIDE (BACK)

SLIT

C

CENTRE BACK ZIP

SLEEVE UPPER EDGE

CLOSED DART

SIDE

12

3

CUT & OPEN 5 CM

173

5. HAUTE COUTURE TROUSERS AND SKIRTS

JUMPSUIT WITH TRANSPARENT SLEEVES AND COLLAR
WITH CRISS-CROSSED STRAPS

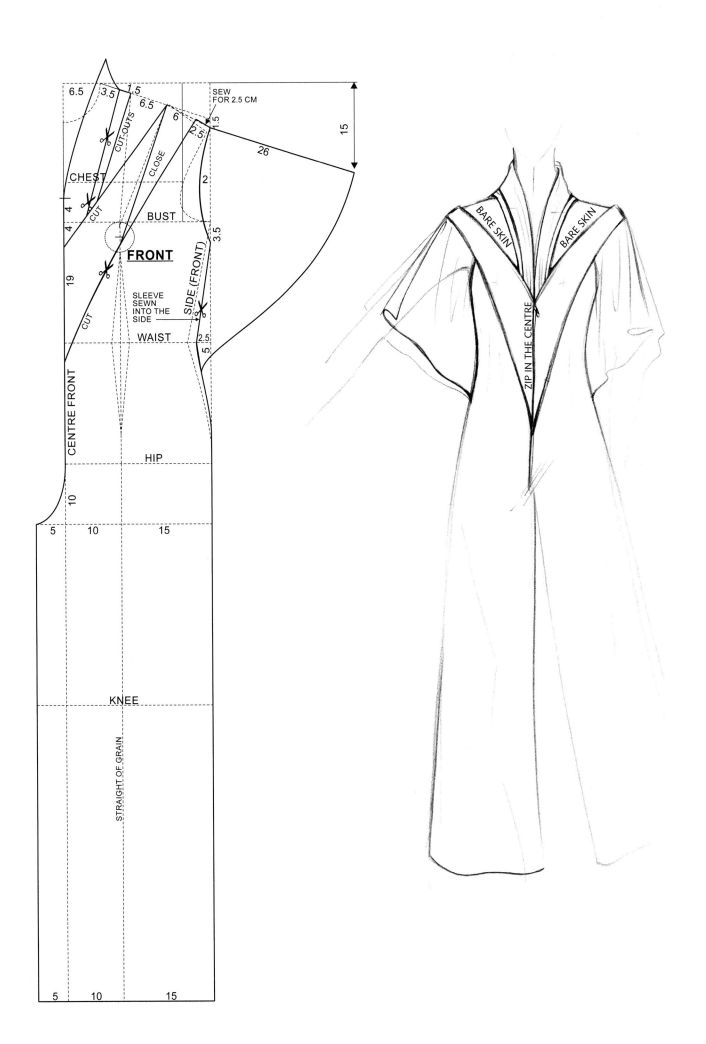

6.5 3.5 1.5 6.5

SEW
FOR 2.5 CM

6

CUT-OUTS

CLOSE

CHEST

2.5 1.5

26

2

BUST

15

4 4

CUT

4

3.5

FRONT

SIDE (FRONT)

19

CUT

SLEEVE
SEWN
INTO THE
SIDE

WAIST

2.5

5

CENTRE FRONT

HIP

10

5 10 15

KNEE

STRAIGHT OF GRAIN

5 10 15

BARE SKIN

BARE SKIN

ZIP IN THE CENTRE

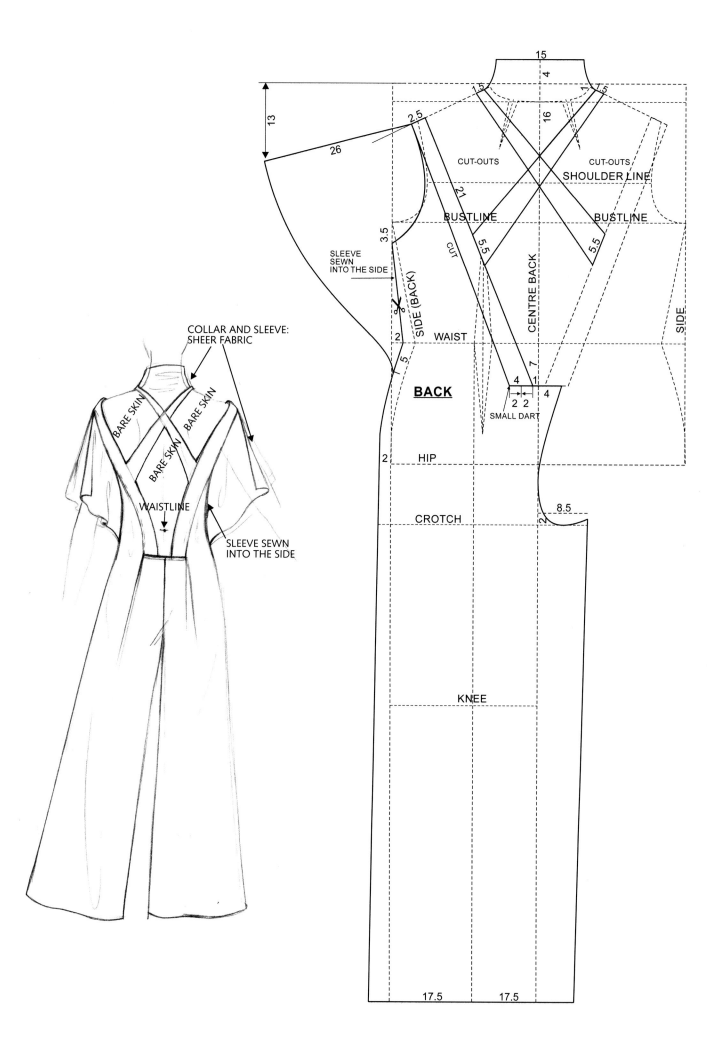

COLLAR AND SLEEVE:
SHEER FABRIC

BARE SKIN
BARE SKIN
BARE SKIN
BARE SKIN

WAISTLINE

SLEEVE SEWN
INTO THE SIDE

15
4
13
26
2.5
1.5
16
1.5
7.5

CUT-OUTS
CUT-OUTS
SHOULDER LINE

BUSTLINE
BUSTLINE
21
3.5
CUT
5.5
5.5
CENTRE BACK
SIDE

SLEEVE
SEWN
INTO THE SIDE

SIDE (BACK)

2
5
WAIST
7
BACK
4
1
4
2 2
SMALL DART

2
HIP
8.5
2
CROTCH

KNEE

17.5
17.5

178

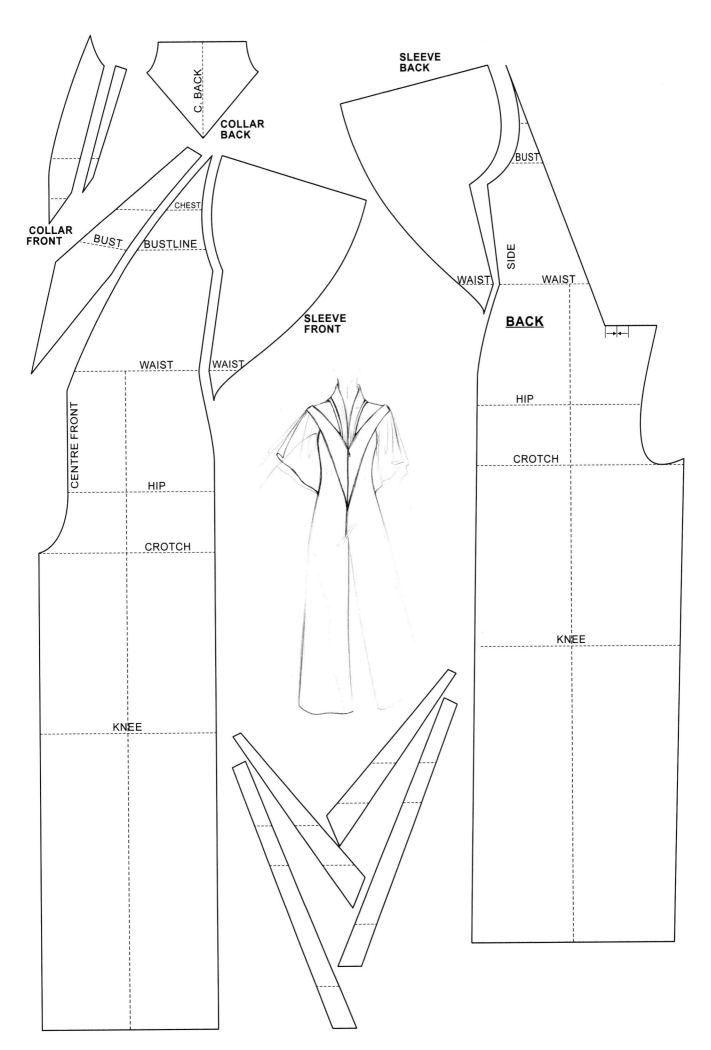

COLLAR
BACK

C. BACK

SLEEVE
BACK

BUST

COLLAR
FRONT

CHEST

BUST

BUSTLINE

SIDE

WAIST

WAIST

BACK

SLEEVE
FRONT

WAIST

WAIST

CENTRE FRONT

HIP

HIP

CROTCH

CROTCH

KNEE

KNEE

ROMPER WITH EMBELLISHED SHOULDERS AND SIDES

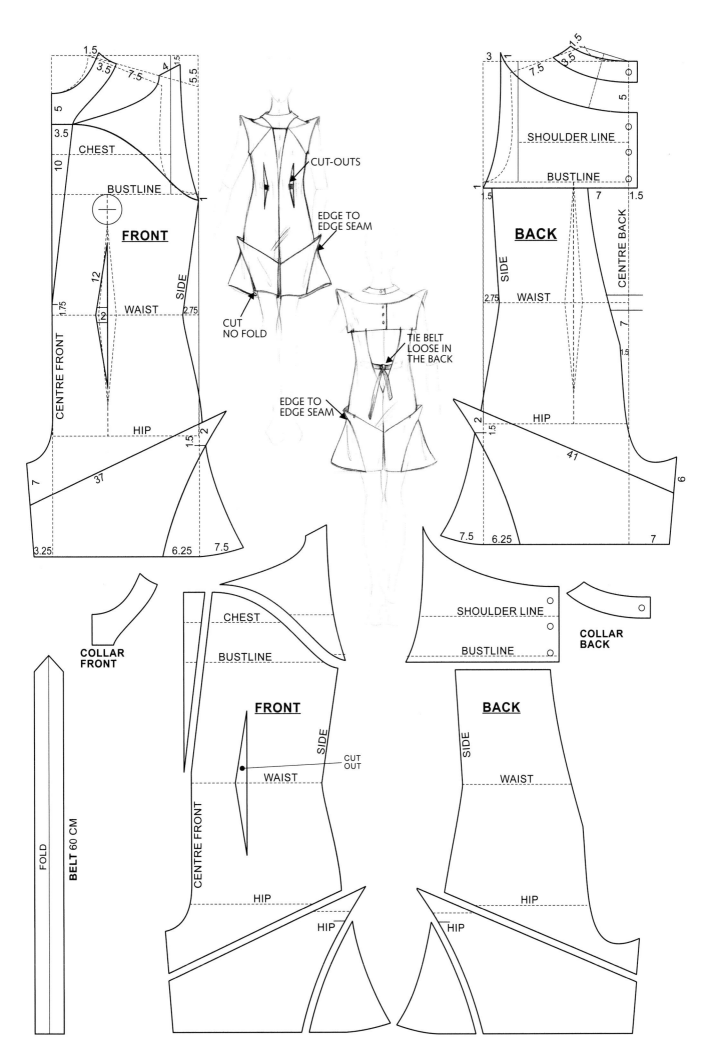

FRONT

CHEST

BUSTLINE

WAIST

HIP

CENTRE FRONT

SIDE

CUT-OUTS

EDGE TO
EDGE SEAM

CUT
NO FOLD

EDGE TO
EDGE SEAM

TIE BELT
LOOSE IN
THE BACK

BACK

SHOULDER LINE

BUSTLINE

SIDE

WAIST

HIP

CENTRE BACK

COLLAR
FRONT

COLLAR
BACK

FOLD

BELT 60 CM

FRONT

CHEST

BUSTLINE

WAIST

CENTRE FRONT

SIDE

CUT
OUT

HIP

HIP

BACK

SHOULDER LINE

BUSTLINE

SIDE

WAIST

HIP

HIP

SPLIT SKIRT AND TUNIC

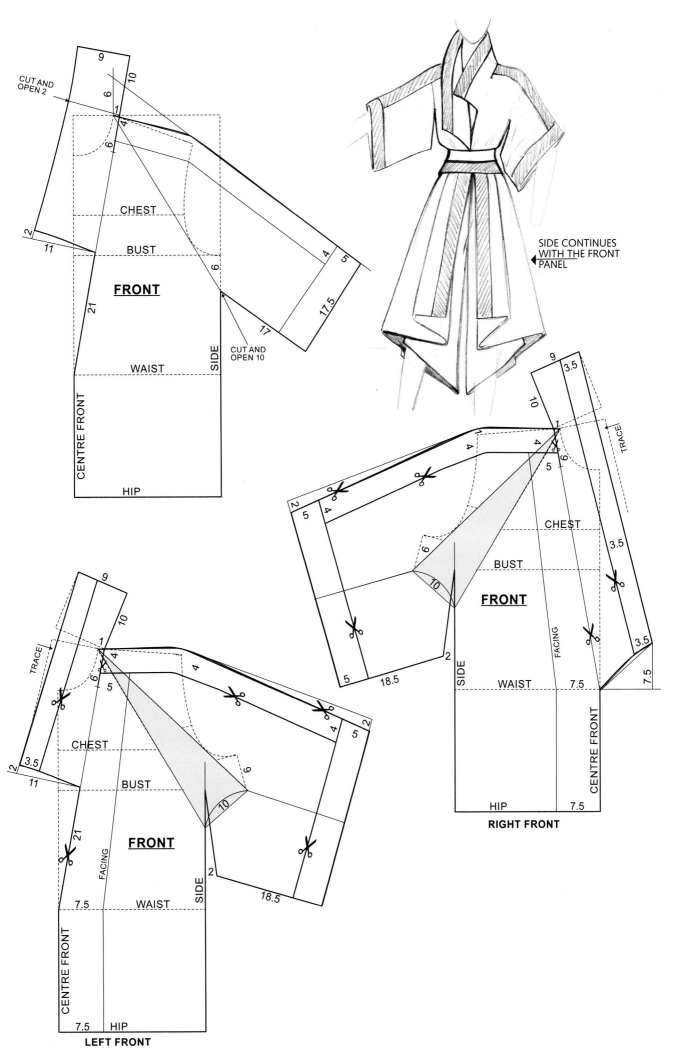

FRONT

CUT AND OPEN 2

CHEST

BUST

WAIST

CENTRE FRONT

HIP

CUT AND OPEN 10

SIDE

SIDE CONTINUES WITH THE FRONT PANEL

FRONT

CHEST

BUST

WAIST

CENTRE FRONT

SIDE

FACING

TRACE

HIP

RIGHT FRONT

FRONT

TRACE

CHEST

BUST

WAIST

CENTRE FRONT

FACING

SIDE

HIP

LEFT FRONT

183

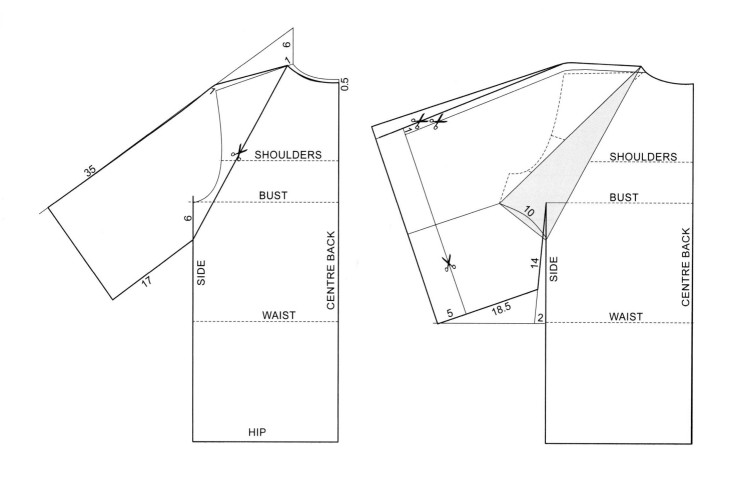

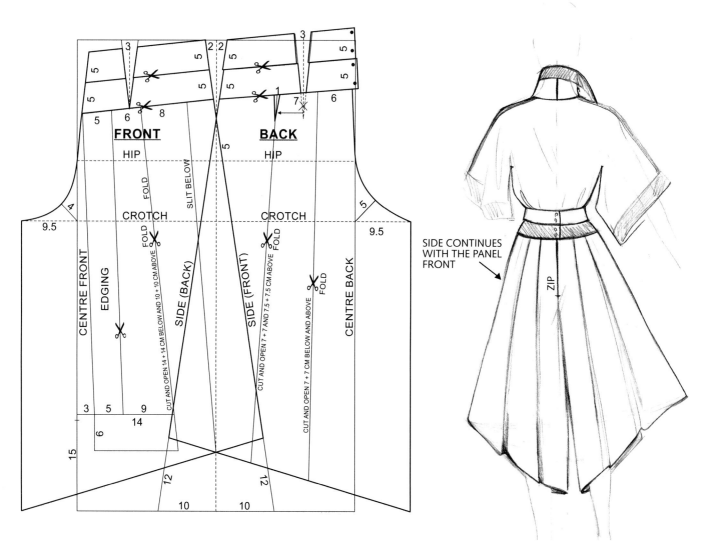

FRONT

BACK

SIDE CONTINUES
WITH THE PANEL
FRONT

184

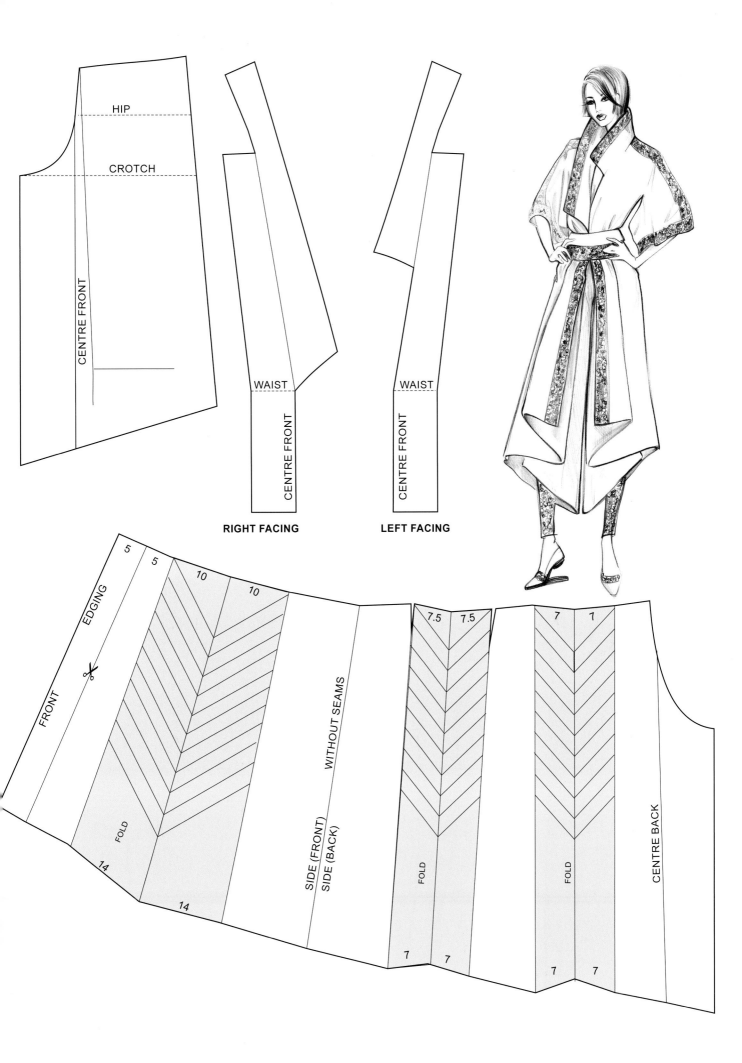

HIP

CROTCH

CENTRE FRONT

WAIST

CENTRE FRONT

RIGHT FACING

WAIST

CENTRE FRONT

LEFT FACING

FRONT

EDGING

5   5   10   10

7.5   7.5   7   7

FOLD

14

14

SIDE (FRONT)

SIDE (BACK)

WITHOUT SEAMS

FOLD

7   7

FOLD

CENTRE BACK

7   7

TUNIC AND CULOTTES
16TH CENTURY INSPIRED

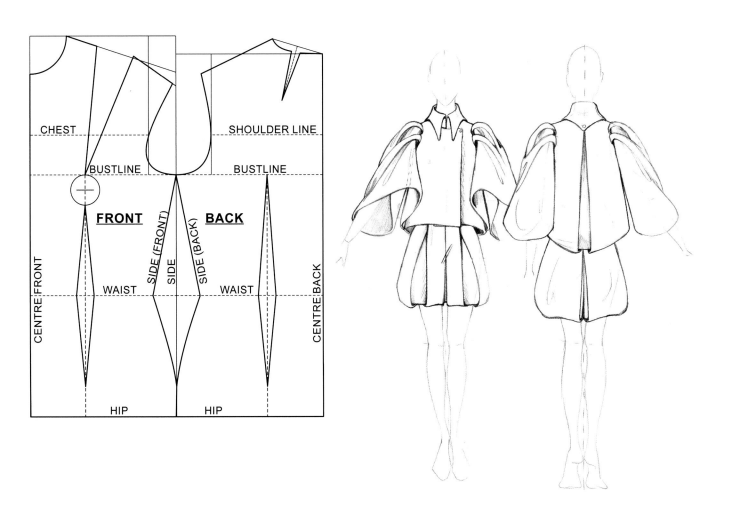

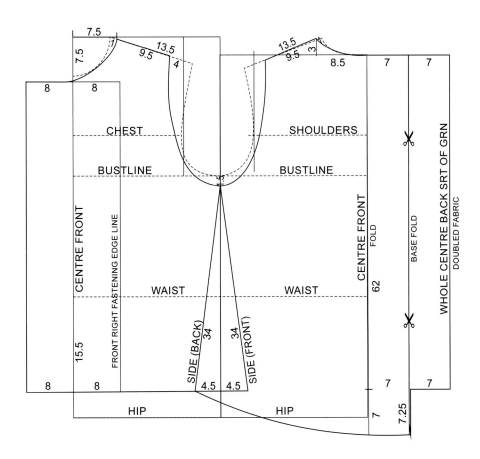

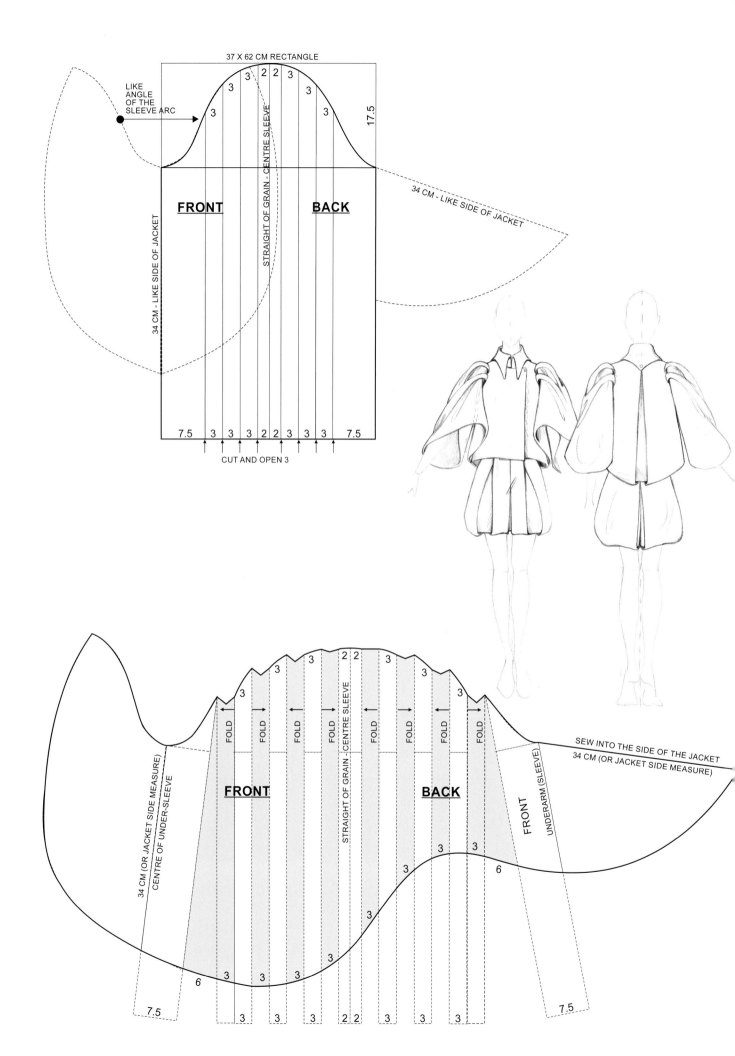

37 X 62 CM RECTANGLE

LIKE ANGLE OF THE SLEEVE ARC

3
3 3 2 2 3
3 3
3

FRONT   **BACK**

34 CM - LIKE SIDE OF JACKET

STRAIGHT OF GRAIN - CENTRE SLEEVE

34 CM - LIKE SIDE OF JACKET

17.5

7.5 3 3 3 2 2 3 3 3 7.5

CUT AND OPEN 3

3
3 3 2 2 3
3 3
3

FOLD FOLD FOLD FOLD FOLD FOLD FOLD FOLD

FRONT   **BACK**

SEW INTO THE SIDE OF THE JACKET
34 CM (OR JACKET SIDE MEASURE)

34 CM (OR JACKET SIDE MEASURE)
CENTRE OF UNDER-SLEEVE

STRAIGHT OF GRAIN - CENTRE SLEEVE

FRONT
UNDERARM (SLEEVE)

3 3
6

3

3

3

6 3 3 3

3 3 3 3 2 2 3 3 3

7.5   7.5

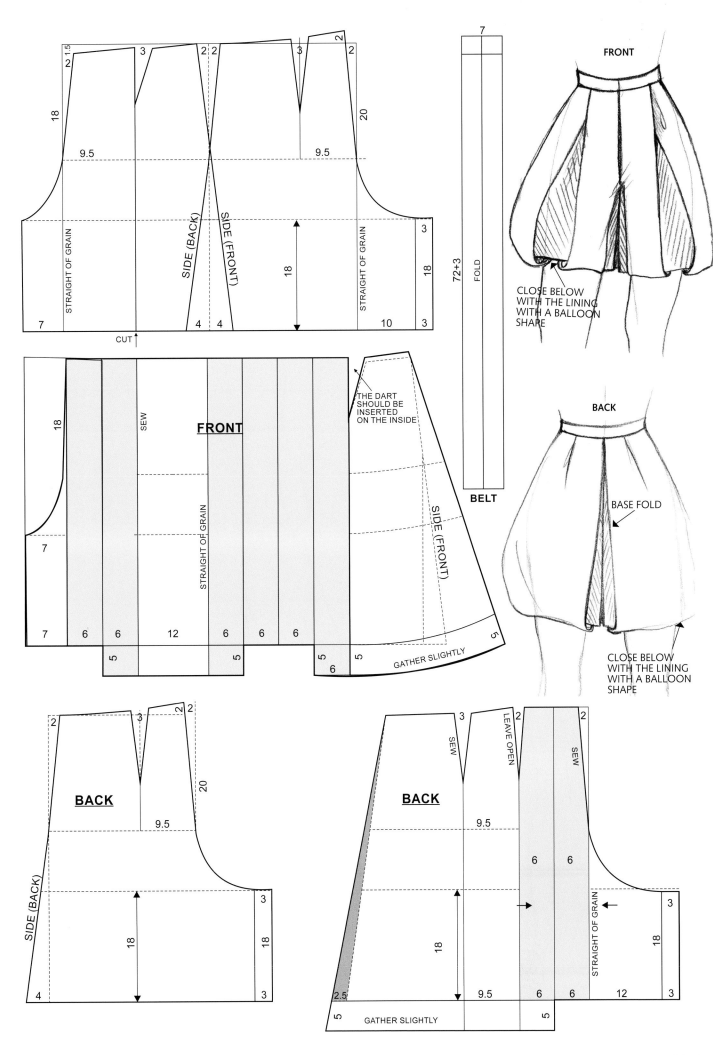

FRONT

CLOSE BELOW
WITH THE LINING
WITH A BALLOON
SHAPE

BACK

BASE FOLD

CLOSE BELOW
WITH THE LINING
WITH A BALLOON
SHAPE

Top-left pattern piece:

2 1.5   3   2 2   3   2 2
18

9.5   9.5

STRAIGHT OF GRAIN   SIDE (BACK) SIDE (FRONT)   STRAIGHT OF GRAIN   20

18   18

7   4 4   10   3
CUT

Belt:

7

FOLD   72+3

BELT

Center pattern (FRONT):

18

SEW   **FRONT**

THE DART
SHOULD BE
INSERTED
ON THE INSIDE

7

STRAIGHT OF GRAIN   SIDE (FRONT)

7   6   6   12   6   6   6   5
5   5   5 5
6
GATHER SLIGHTLY

Bottom-left (BACK):

2   3   2 2

BACK

20

9.5

SIDE (BACK)   18   18

4   3

Bottom-right (BACK):

3   2   LEAVE OPEN 2   SEW 2

BACK

9.5

6   6

18   18

STRAIGHT OF GRAIN

2.5   9.5   6   6   12   3
5
GATHER SLIGHTLY   5

189

SHIRT WITH 'HOODED' SLEEVES
AND KNICKERBOCKERS

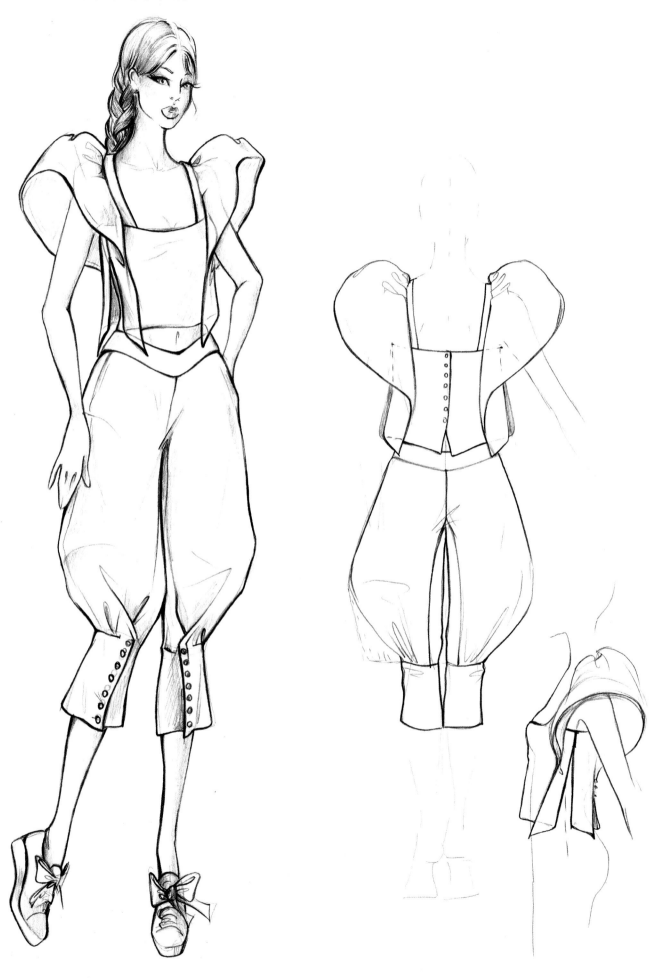

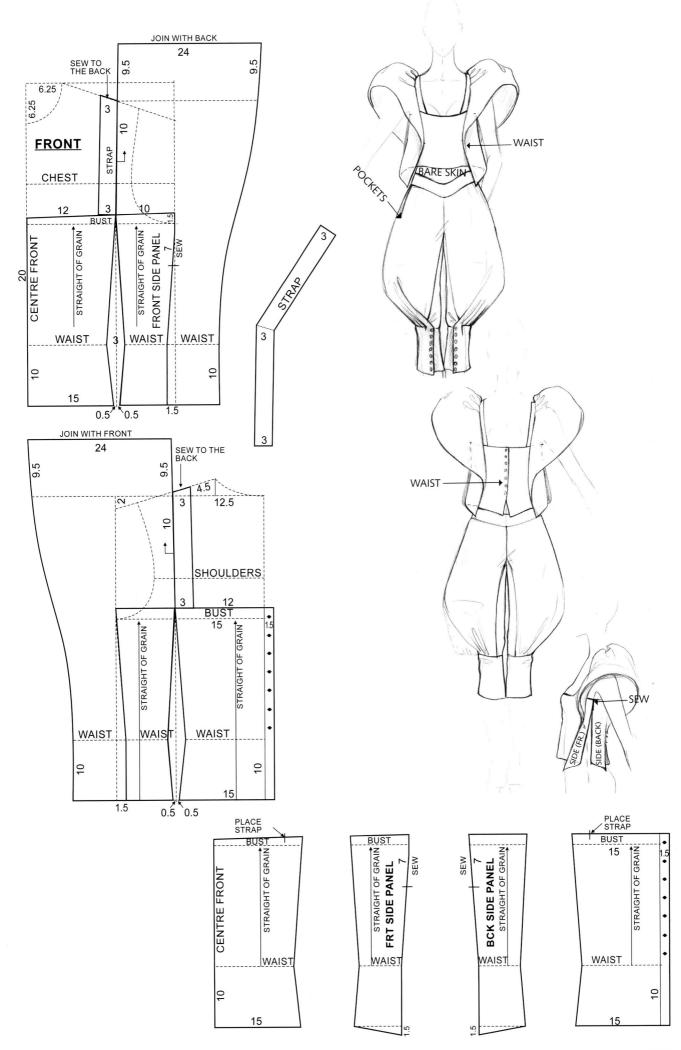

FRONT

JOIN WITH BACK
24

SEW TO THE BACK

9.5 · 9.5

6.25 · 6.25

3

10

STRAP

CHEST

12 · 3 · 10 · 1.5

BUST

20

CENTRE FRONT

STRAIGHT OF GRAIN

STRAIGHT OF GRAIN

FRONT SIDE PANEL

SEW · 7

WAIST · 3 · WAIST · WAIST

10 · 10

15

0.5 · 0.5 · 1.5

STRAP
3
3
3
3

JOIN WITH FRONT
24

SEW TO THE BACK

9.5 · 9.5 · 4.5

2 · 3 · 12.5

10

SHOULDERS

3 · 12

BUST
15 · 1.5

STRAIGHT OF GRAIN

STRAIGHT OF GRAIN

WAIST · WAIST · WAIST

10 · 10

15

1.5 · 0.5 · 0.5

PLACE STRAP
BUST

CENTRE FRONT

STRAIGHT OF GRAIN

WAIST

10

15

BUST

FRT SIDE PANEL

STRAIGHT OF GRAIN

SEW · 7

WAIST

1.5

BUST

BCK SIDE PANEL

SEW · 7

STRAIGHT OF GRAIN

WAIST

1.5

PLACE STRAP
BUST
15 · 1.5

STRAIGHT OF GRAIN

WAIST

10

15

WAIST

POCKETS

BARE SKIN

WAIST

SEW

SIDE (FR.) · SIDE (BACK)

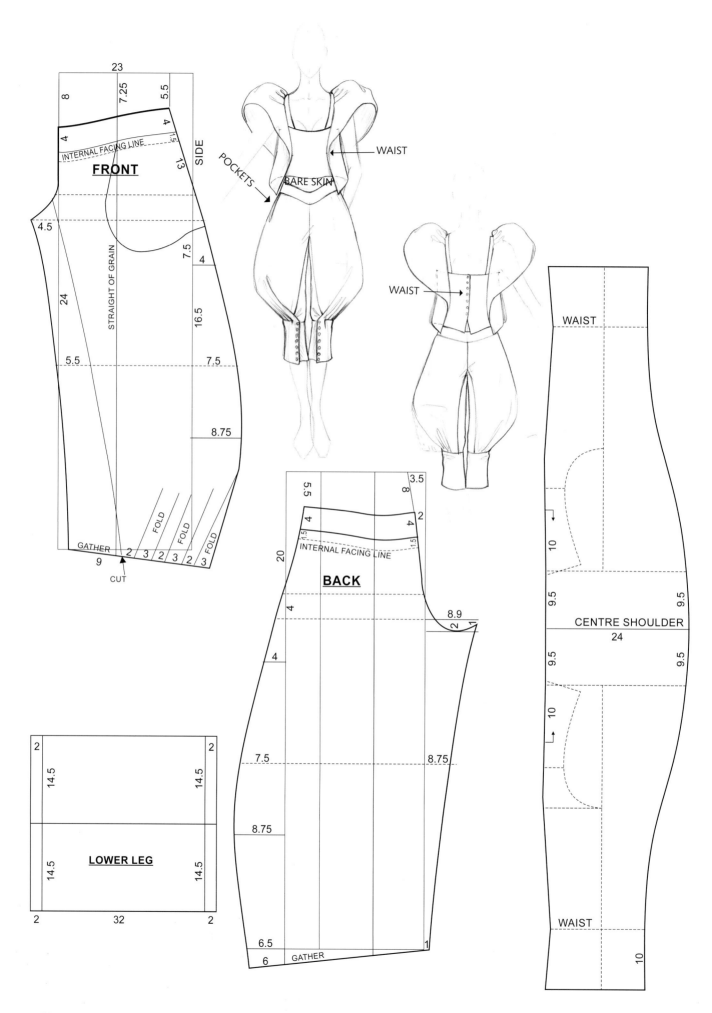

FRONT

23

8   7.25   5.5

4

INTERNAL FACING LINE

1.5

13

SIDE

4.5

7.5

STRAIGHT OF GRAIN

4

24

16.5

5.5   7.5

8.75

FOLD   FOLD   FOLD

GATHER   2   3   2   3   2   3

9

CUT

LOWER LEG

2   2

14.5   14.5

14.5   14.5

2   32   2

BACK

5.5   8   3.5

4   4   2

1.5   INTERNAL FACING LINE   1.5

20   4

4   8.9

2   1

7.5   8.75

8.75

6.5   1

6   GATHER

WAIST   →   POCKETS

BARE SKIN   →   WAIST

WAIST   →   WAIST

WAIST

10

9.5   9.5

CENTRE SHOULDER

24

9.5   9.5

10

WAIST

10

192

CROPPED JACKET WITH MAXI RAGLAN SLEEVES
HIGH DOUBLE COLLAR AND TROUSERS WITH
CRISS-CROSSED PANELS

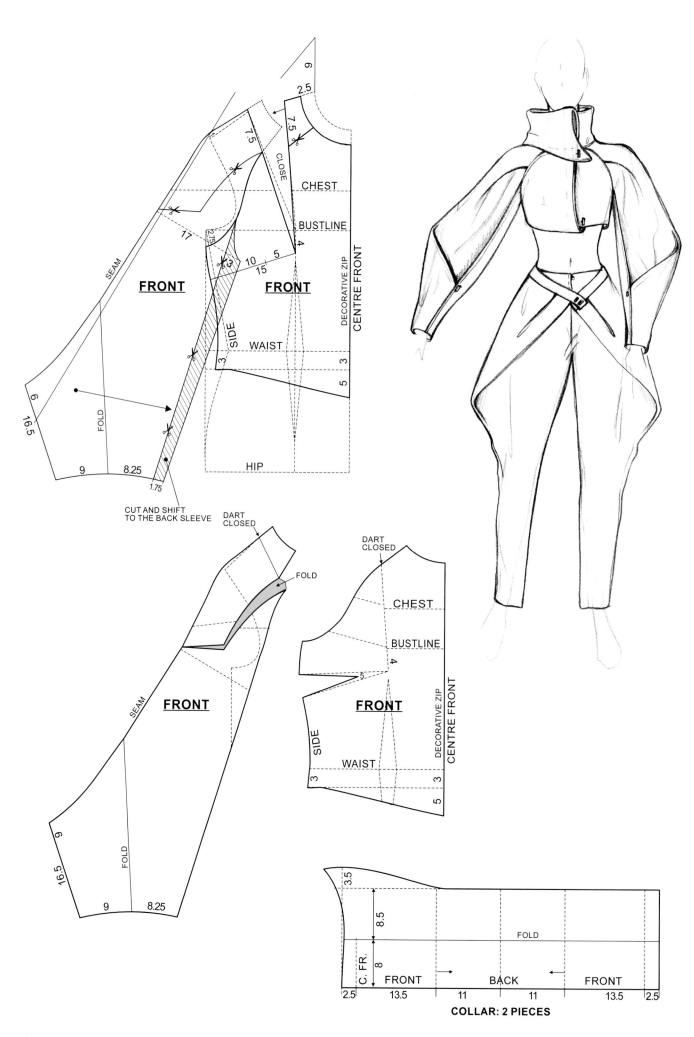

FRONT

FRONT

9

2.5

7.5

7.5

CLOSE

CHEST

BUSTLINE

DECORATIVE ZIP

CENTRE FRONT

SEAM

17

2.75

10

5

15

3

FOLD

6

16.5

9

8.25

1.75

4

SIDE

WAIST

3

3

5

HIP

CUT AND SHIFT
TO THE BACK SLEEVE

DART
CLOSED

FOLD

FRONT

SEAM

FOLD

9

16.5

9

8.25

DART
CLOSED

FRONT

CHEST

BUSTLINE

4

5

SIDE

WAIST

3

3

5

DECORATIVE ZIP

CENTRE FRONT

3.5

8.5

C. FR.

8

FOLD

FRONT

BACK

FRONT

2.5

13.5

11

11

13.5

2.5

COLLAR: 2 PIECES

194

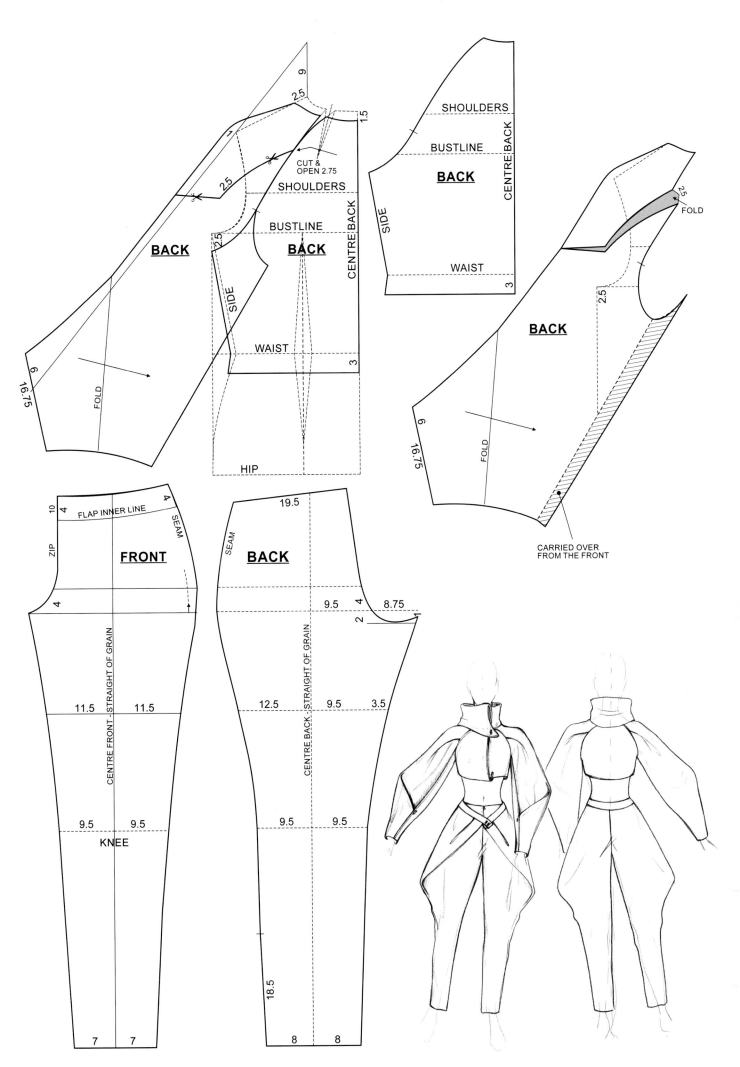

BACK

9

2.5

2.5

2.5

CUT &
OPEN 2.75

SHOULDERS

BUSTLINE

BACK

SIDE

WAIST

CENTRE BACK

3

HIP

1.5

16.75

6

FOLD

SHOULDERS

BUSTLINE

BACK

SIDE

CENTRE BACK

WAIST

3

2.5

FOLD

BACK

2.5

16.75

6

FOLD

CARRIED OVER
FROM THE FRONT

10

4

4

FLAP INNER LINE

SEAM

ZIP

4

FRONT

CENTRE FRONT - STRAIGHT OF GRAIN

11.5

11.5

9.5

9.5

KNEE

7

7

19.5

SEAM

BACK

9.5

4

8.75

2

12.5

9.5

3.5

CENTRE BACK - STRAIGHT OF GRAIN

9.5

9.5

18.5

8

8

195

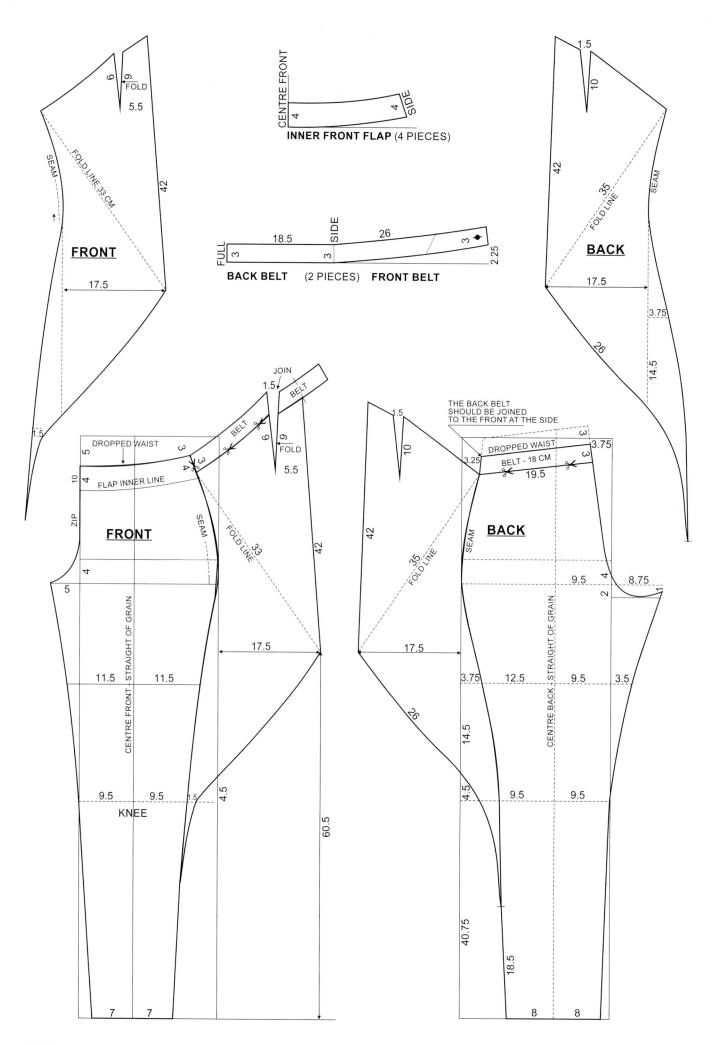

FRONT

BACK

INNER FRONT FLAP (4 PIECES)

CENTRE FRONT

SIDE

4   4

BACK BELT (2 PIECES)   **FRONT BELT**

FULL

SIDE

3   18.5   3   26   3

2.25

6   9
FOLD
5.5

FOLD LINE 33 CM

SEAM

42

17.5

1.5

1.5

10

42

35
FOLD LINE

SEAM

17.5

3.75

26

14.5

JOIN
1.5
BELT

BELT
6   9
FOLD
5.5

DROPPED WAIST

5   3
10   4   3
FLAP INNER LINE

ZIP

4

5

CENTRE FRONT | STRAIGHT OF GRAIN

SEAM

FOLD LINE
33

42

17.5

11.5   11.5

9.5   9.5   1.5
KNEE

4.5

60.5

7   7

THE BACK BELT
SHOULD BE JOINED
TO THE FRONT AT THE SIDE

1.5
10

42

35
FOLD LINE

SEAM

DROPPED WAIST

3.25   3
3.75
BELT - 18 CM   3
19.5

BACK

17.5

9.5   4   8.75
2   1

CENTRE BACK | STRAIGHT OF GRAIN

3.75   12.5   9.5   3.5

14.5

4.5   9.5   9.5

40.75

18.5

8   8

FRONT

TECHNIQUES FOR GIVING SHAPE TO FABRIC

There are various techniques that make it possible to shape a flat piece of fabric to the curves of the body. They can be both functional and decorative at the same time. Darts, gathering and pleats help determine the volume and shape, though each can create a different effect.

Darts pivot around the part of the body that protrudes most. They make fabric fit closely at the bust, hips, shoulders and elbows, adapting to the shape of the wearer's physique.

How far the fabric extends outward, which corresponds to the point or apex of the dart, depends on the width of the fabric, folded at the other end. Where only slight modelling is required, like on elbows and shoulders, small, narrow darts are used. Wider darts

are used to shape more ample areas, such as the bust. Easy to implement and comfortable to wear, gathering is used to create a soft, rounded shape. You can gather fabric along the waist, sleeves, cuffs, yokes and collars. Ruffles are strips of fabric gathered and applied along the seam at the edge of a hem. They are generally purely decorative. However, the technique used to sew a ruffle and gather fabric is the same.

Tucks and ribbing are used mainly above the waistline on bodices, blouses and sleeves. They can also be used to determine the volume of the fabric at the sleeve cap or cuffs. Sewn tucks and folds have the same form-fitting effect as darts, while un-pressed pleats create soft shapes similar to gathered fabric. Both are used to create a straight, vertical line. Folds, darts, tucks and

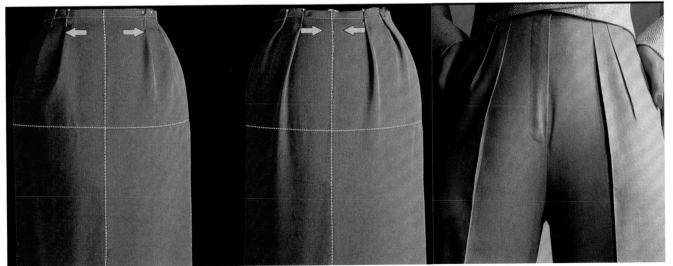

pleats can be decorative (ribbing) and used to shape a garment. They can be vertical, horizontal or diagonal.

How to use each technique

The aforementioned techniques are all rather similar in that they help shape a garment. In some cases they are interchangeable. A shoulder dart, for example, can be replaced with gathering, if you want to make a form-fitting pattern a bit softer and looser.

Sewn folds and darts in part control the volume, then they free it, similar to gathered fabric.

The style and cut of the garment will dictate what technique to use. On a fitted skirt, for example, there will be darts that shape the garment at the waist, while a loose-fitting garment may be gathered at the top and held in place by a waistband to create soft folds. The shape of the finished garment will also be determined by the type of fabric used. Silky, soft fabric, like crêpe de chine, is easily gathered into soft folds that drape perfectly. Stiffer fabric categories, like poplin, are better suited to pleats and structured folds, as they are too rigid to fall softly on the body. Heavy fabric like gabardine is ideal for suits because it can be shaped with folds and seams, the perfect way to resolve problems relating to various physiques and body types.

Creating darts and pleats

For perfect, professional-quality darts, pleats, folds and gathered fabric, you'll need to adhere to a few basic rules.

1) Darts should be sewn evenly, creating a perfect point or apex. They should be pressed before being joined to other parts of the garment.

2) Gathered fabric is used when you need to adapt a longer edge to a shorter one. Depending on the type of fabric you're using, the end result will be soft and flowing or clean and springy.

3) Box pleats are generally created 'inward' a dress, while folds and ribbing are outward. To ensure they are uniform in depth, it is important to mark them clearly and sew them with precision.

4) For flat abdomens, the folds should be sewn in the direction of the hip or side to create a fuller look and hide the protruding hip bones.

5) For protruding abdomens, the folds should be sewn towards the centre, creating a flatter appearance and slimming the figure.

6) For trousers, folds and tucks should follow the shape of the body, keeping the external line of the main fold on the straight of grain.

Shaping and pressing darts

Darts create contours and curves in the fabric. So, precision when shaping and pressing darts is essential, and must be suitable to the dart and fabric used. Here are some tips.

7) Press the dart along the seam from the widest part of the legs up to 1 cm / 0.39" from the apex. If necessary, you can also use a presser plate to create a clean fold on the edge of the dart.

8) On the ironing ham, with the side folded as it will be in the finished garment, place a strip of clean white paper under the edge to ensure the iron doesn't make a mark, then press the longest side up to 1 cm from the apex.

9) Place the apex of the dart on the ironing ham and press lightly to fold it into the fabric. Then iron the dart from the face of the fabric, starting from the widest part of the legs, using a ironing cloth. Reposition the fabric to press the apex and let dry to set the shape.

10) If the darts are wide, trim them leaving a 1.5 cm / 0.59" margin and iron along the seam. Do not cut or press the apex. Open the seam margins with the iron and fold the apex from one side into a box pleat, using a knitting needle to facilitate the task. Iron on the face of the fabric.

11) For double ended darts, you'll need to create a few small slits on the widest part, up to 3 mm / 0.12" from the seam. Follow the same steps as above, folding one half at a time, from the centre towards the point.

12) If adding darts to lightweight fabric, iron along the seam without crushing the margins. Rest the dart on an ironing ham with a piece of paper along the edges, then flatten it, stopping 1.5 cm / 0.59" from the apex. Shift it to shape the apex and then iron on the face of the fabric.

TECHNIQUES FOR GARMENT CONSTRUCTION

THE MAGIC OF BONING RODS

Haute couture or evening gowns can be perfectly tailored and stable, even without straps, thanks to what is called "whalebone" or "boning". Used since the late nineteenth century to stiffen corsets, these thin rods were made of baleen (whalebone) found in the mouths of some whale species. They have been used for both men's and women's wear.

This material was ideal because it is rigid but also flexible, thus able to provide support without breaking. Over time, and especially in less-expensive garments, it has been replaced by metal rods, which have one main drawback: they rust when they come into contact with water. Today, boning can be made of steel coils or strips of plastic. They should be used according to the amount of support required: the former is stiffer, while the latter is more supple.

Most designers use plastic strips covered in fabric or non-woven cloth, or a weave of polyester and polypropylene filaments. If done correctly, garments finished with these rods adhere perfectly to the body. Boning can be applied to any part of the garment that requires extra support. They are usually sewn along vertical seams or, in lined garments, within the lining on an axis determined according to their purpose, so that they remain perfectly invisible. Being able to flex and follow the shape of the body, boning should be placed so that the ends curve towards the body: in this way, cut and assembled tailored garments will perfectly adhere to the wearer, without slipping or falling down.

HOW-TO

WITH PLASTIC BONING

1) Cut the boning covered in fabric 2.5 to 3 cm / 0.98 to 1.18" longer than the placement line. Push it into place so that it peeks out from the covering on both ends. Cut off 1 cm / 0.39" and round the edges on both parts.

2) Fold the ends of the lining that cover the boning and, on the back of the fabric, place the boning on the seam or placement lines so that it curves towards the body.

3) Sew the seam margins of the garment or to the lining, using a sewing machine with a normal presser foot and suitable thread.

WITH POLY BONING

1) Cut the boning to be as long as the placement line. Take two pieces of 1 cm (0.39") wide braided trim and cut them to be 2.5 cm (0.98") long. Fold them in half, then wrap them around the edges of the boning. Sew on all layers.

2) Place the boning as desired, so that it curves towards the body. Sew the edges of the boning to the seam margins of the garment or to the lining, using a sewing machine with a normal presser foot and suitable thread.

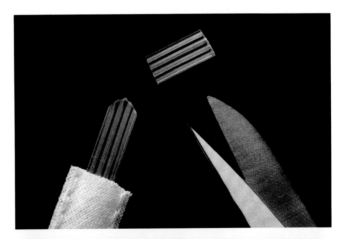

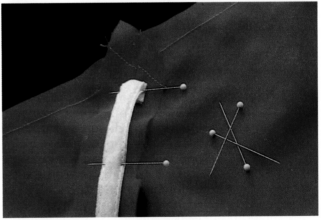

APPLIED DECORATIONS AND INSERTS

Customising garments to make them unique is an absolute must in haute couture. To do so, often all you need to do is place trimmings, lace, contrast stitching or shimmering passementerie in an unexpected location. These details are easy to apply because they don't require changes to the pattern or particularly complicated construction techniques. However, it is necessary for each aspect of their application to be perfectly planned and timed, simulating their position and, if possible, applying them before the garment is assembled.

SEQUINS AND BEADS

The history of sequins has been lost in the mists of time. It seems that Egyptian Pharaoh Tutankhamen (1341-1323 BCE) had garments embellished by small discs of shiny metal, discovered in his tomb in 1922. Over the following centuries, and for the entire Middle Ages, numerous sources document the fact that people used to sew gold and silver coins with holes in the middle to their garments. In addition, showier, more sumptuous decorations began to show up on sacred clothes and vestments, accenting their embroidery. In the early eighteenth century, French jeweller Georges

Friedrich Strass invented rhinestones (called 'strass' in many European languages) with a mixture of chemicals, realistically reproducing precious stones. They were then used to decorate clothes and accessories. The intention was to embellish the black clothing of royalty with faux jewels and eye-catching embroidery: a triumph of rhinestones and sequins illuminated and enriched even simple accessories. Shoes and bags were decorated with rhinestones and real stones; gloves were trimmed with beads and sequins; and exquisite oversize brooches appeared on coat and cape collars. The materials and techniques used to create sequins and paillettes have changed drastically over the centuries. They have gone from metal to a sort of gelatin (which is lightweight but very sensitive to heat), to then be made of plastic and vinyl.

In fashion during the 1970s and 1980s, sequins were a must-have for disco attendees at the time, used by many stylists in their collections or to create costumes for stars like Michael Jackson and David Bowie. Today, all sorts of shiny embellishments are fashionable, appearing cyclically on runways around the globe, adding a bit of sparkle to dresses, skirts, jumpers and accessories for day and evening.

LACE TRIM

Lace inserts bring elegance and sophistication to high fashion garments. Such inserts can be taken from pieces of lace fabric, or they can be purchased already cut out from a haberdashery.

How to apply lace

1. After having positioned the lace on the paper pattern, affix it with lots of pins. Cut around the motif, leaving one or two rows of mesh around it to better define the motif and to ensure the lace doesn't unravel, or use an already-cut lace decoration with the proper margin. If there are any beads, you'll need to remove those that are on the seam line so that you don't break the needle of your sewing machine. Add a bit of glue to the back of all the other beads, to make sure they don't accidentally come off.

2. There are three techniques you can use to apply lace to a garment: a) hand sewn, creating a row of small stitches 5 mm (0.20") from the edges of the piece to be applied, keeping the stitches loose so that the fabric underneath doesn't bunch up and the decoration doesn't get crushed; b) with a sewing machine, creating a narrow zig-zag seam or with a short straight stitch 5 mm (0.20") from the margins, trimming the fabric underneath the applied piece close to the zig-zag to make it transparent; c) apply it with heat-set glue or tape, placing the garment on a padded ironing board with the right side up, ensuring the piece to be applied is in the correct position. Then put some double-adhesive gauze under the piece, cover it with an absorbent cloth or with a paper towel and iron carefully, careful not to ruin the lace or fabric.